Arjuna's 15 Questions

Life Lessons from the Bhagavad Gita

Arjuna's 15 Questions

Life Lessons from the Bhagavad Gita

A guide to help you prepare
for the examination of life

Satish Modh

JAICO PUBLISHING HOUSE

Ahmedabad Bangalore Chennai
Delhi Hyderabad Kolkata Mumbai

Published by Jaico Publishing House
A-2 Jash Chambers, 7-A Sir Phirozshah Mehta Road
Fort, Mumbai - 400 001
jaicopub@jaicobooks.com
www.jaicobooks.com

ARJUNA'S 15 QUESTIONS
ISBN 978-93-48098-38-2

First Jaico Impression: 2025

Page design and layout: R. Ajith Kumar, Delhi

CONTENTS

INTRODUCTION

How do I pass the exam of life?

Very few people would admit being under stress. Some may attend a yoga class or talk about going to a spiritual master to learn about meditation and *pranayama* but will not admit that they are under stress. In Western societies, such people are advised to see a counsellor.

Most of the time, these anxieties and panic attacks are ignored unless they hinder the achievement of the organization's goals and objectives. People who are going through such situations move about in life with smiling faces but suffer great harm later on. In a competitive environment, there is hardly any bonhomie or friendship (like the one between Krishna and Arjuna), where one may confide in another, discuss such issues or seek help. There is a pressing need to build a strong friendship or mentorship with someone in life—someone with whom one can share a conversation about these mental-health issues.

The Bhagavad Gita is a conversation between Arjuna, the leader of the Pandava army, who is going through an anxiety attack, and Krishna, who is his friend, philosopher and guide. I have attempted to arrange this conversation in a question-and-answer format to make it more valuable for all of us to deal with our own anxieties and panic attacks. Arjuna asks Krishna many questions (15 in all) on the battlefield to overcome his panic. Krishna engages him in an all-encompassing conversation and calms him down. The dialogue concludes when Arjuna tells Krishna that he has overcome his anxiety and is ready to fight.

The Bhagavad Gita is a conversation between two family men who are among the greatest leaders of that era. They are not saints, gurus or ascetics. Every one of us, with family and organizational responsibilities, has the same questions in our minds as Arjuna. In my earlier work, *Discover the Arjuna in You*, I tried to trace the overarching psychological, emotional and spiritual journey of Arjuna in the 18 chapters of the Gita. In this book, my focus is on the content of each question and its answer in detail.

I understand that many wise people may take exception to a retelling of the Gita in this format. They are wise people, and they are already on the path of self-realization. Many of us, however, struggle to cope with the day-to-day challenges of life. Like Arjuna, we are confused about which path to take for self-realization: *karma yoga*, *jnana yoga*, *bhakti yoga* or *dhyana yoga*. This format helped me understand the teachings of the Gita, and I am confident that this format will help young and old alike to understand the message of the Gita in a simplified way.

In my days as a student, many of us would use 'digests' that presented key points and heavily summarised the body of knowledge in a given subject, providing information that was just enough to pass the examination. I believe that this *Arjuna's 15 Questions* will help many students of life to pass this exam. Many people who have learnt the Gita in the traditional way may also get a new perspective on it if they look at this book with an open and unbiased mind. That is what Krishna himself desired.

The first chapter of the Gita introduces the two opposing armies and their principal warriors. The stage is set for war. In Arjuna's mind, however, there is a different war going on, which is finally resolved by Krishna. The journey Arjuna takes to resolve this mental war presents us—the keen students of life—with basic lessons on the purpose of actions, the cause of actions and the action itself. This book provides answers to basic questions in our mind, such as 'Why should I act?' 'What if I fail?' 'How do I remain calm in a crisis?' 'Is the path shown to me by my predecessors appropriate?' 'Do people understand the larger goal I am trying to achieve?' 'Why should I take all this trouble when I can simply relax and enjoy my life?'

These are questions we also ask while appearing in this examination of life. I hope you will find the answers to your questions in this book.

Satish Modh

Wherever there is Yogeshwar Krishna and Arjuna,
there will be Prosperity, Victory,
Happiness, and Morality (Gita 18:78)

PROLOGUE
The battlefield

Why do we work?

Why do we work, and what do we get out of it? 'Why should I work on something?' Or more broadly, 'Why should I work at all?' We ask ourselves these questions many times, at least when we are under tremendous pressure or stress. We would be lying to ourselves if we believe that this phase has never come to pass in our lives.

What do we expect from 'work'? Why do we need jobs? Why do we decide to be entrepreneurs? Why do we work for the betterment of society? These are some basic questions, and here are some standard answers:

For money

Admit it. If we want to exist in this society in any reasonable capacity, we need to have money. It may not be a huge amount of money. We may reduce our needs and keep expenses low, but we have not yet figured out how to live a decent life without money, whether we are poor or rich, married or unmarried

To keep busy

We need to do something. We may not be very creative or industrious. We may just watch TV, surf the internet, go out to events or to watch movies, or spend time with friends. All of these activities may be very entertaining, but there will likely still be a natural desire to accomplish something real.

For meaning

Many of us ask questions like 'Why are we here?' or 'What is the meaning of life?'. These questions may not have satisfying answers, but that doesn't stop us from asking them. We are all searching for purpose—any purpose—in life.

To contribute to society

We all feel connected to others. There are moments when we feel very close to some people. We want to take care of them. We understand that the individual is part of a larger whole. We want to feel connected to our neighbourhood, our community, our country or even to the whole of humanity. We hold down a job, perhaps working for a company, the government or even non-government organizations to contribute to the overall welfare of society in our way.

While engaging in such activities, we may start asking questions in critical moments, just like Arjuna: 'Why am I even doing this?'

Gita 1: 1

Dhritarashtra said: O Sanjaya, when my sons and the sons of Pandu, desiring to fight, assembled with their respective armies at Kurukshetra—the abode of Dharma—what did they do?

Setting the stage

It is the D-Day of the epic Mahabharata war. The war is being fought between the sons of Dhritarashtra, the Kauravas, and the sons of Pandu, the Pandavas. The Gita begins with King Dhritarashtra asking Sanjaya about the events at the battlefield. Dhritarashtra and Pandu were brothers born in the Kuru dynasty, descendants of the great King Bharat, by whose name India has been known for ages past.

Bhishma, Arjuna's grandfather, the eldest in the Pandava and Kaurava family, was a great warrior. He was considered to be invincible as he had never lost a battle. (Bhishma is known by this name because of the vow of celibacy he took as a young man. He vowed to never get married and to serve the throne for as long as he lived.) When Dhritarashtra (the patriarch of the Kaurava clan) and Pandu (the patriarch of the Pandava clan) came of age, Bhishma had to make one of them the king. Although Dhritarashtra was older than Pandu, he was not fit to rule because he was blind. So, Pandu was made king. He ruled well and extended the frontiers of his kingdom.

Once, Pandu went to the forest with his wives, Kunti and Madri, on a hunting trip. There, he came across a pair of deer. He shot at them with his bow and arrow and left them mortally wounded. However, it turned out that the deer were Sage Kindama and his wife in another form. The sage cursed Pandu that if he ever united with his wives, he would die. After this episode, Pandu renounced his kingdom and took to an ascetic way of life.

Pandu's wife, Kunti, used a boon she had been granted by Sage Durvasa so that she and Madri could have children. Thus, the five Pandavas—Yudhishthira, Bhima, Arjuna, Nakula and Sahadeva—were born. The eldest son of Dhritarashtra, Duryodhan, never liked them. Krishna (also known as Partha), who was Kunti's nephew, favoured the righteous sons of Pandu and helped them in many crises.

Seeds of conflict

Yudhishthira, the eldest son, became the crown prince when Pandu died. This was not appreciated by Duryodhan, the son of Dhritarashtra, Pandu's elder brother. Duryodhan began plotting for the throne. Once, Duryodhan asked the Pandavas to visit Varnavata to preside over a festival. He put them up in a palace built of flammable material. The palace was set on fire in the night, but the five brothers escaped because some of their well-wishers knew of the plot and saved them. After narrowly avoiding this disaster, the Pandavas lived incognito for some time.

To end the enmity between the Kauravas and the Pandavas, the elders of the family divided the kingdom into two halves. Despite the Pandavas getting fallow land as part of their kingdom, they made the land fertile and built massive palaces.

Duryodhan again resented this prosperity. He plotted once again to deceive the Pandavas and invited Yudhishthira for a game of dice. In those days, it was a custom not to refuse such an invitation. Due to the trickery of Shakuni,

Duryodhan's uncle, Yudhishthira lost everything, and all the Pandavas were sent to twelve years of exile. There was an added condition: The last year of exile was to be spent incognito, and if any of the five were to be recognized in that last year, they would have to repeat the entire cycle.

The Pandavas completed their twelve years of exile, successfully managing to remain hidden in the last year, and returned to claim the kingdom. Duryodhan refused to accept their claim, thus making this epic war inevitable. Following several more instigating events, both the Kauravas and the Pandavas gathered large armies of their well-wishers and loyal supporters and set for the battlefield of Kurukshetra.

As the Gita opens, the forces of Duryodhan and Yudhishthira are lined in front of each other. The opening statement of Dhritarashtra sets the stage for the teachings of the Gita.

Gita 1: 9

And there are many warriors, experts in warfare, who are armed with various weapons and are ready to risk their lives for my sake.

Exploiting the feelings of love and duty

Duryodhan, whose desire is to not part with even a portion of his kingdom, looks at the army on his side and proclaims that the Kuru army is very strong and far bigger than the Pandava army. He feels very satisfied that all of these people were willing to risk their lives for his sake.

Bhishma and Drona (the guru of both the Pandavas and the Kauravas) had joined Duryodhan's army. Bhishma and

Drona's support was his biggest advantage, and he thought that he could win this war with their help. He had one more warrior, Karna, who was almost as good as Arjuna. These three people were key to his decision to participate in this epic war.

In our desire to win, we take calculated risks. Some people side with us, even when we are wrong—some are bound by love, and some are bound by duty. Bhishma and Drona knew that they were on the wrong side, but Bhishma was bound by his duty to protect the kingdom, while Drona was bound by loyalty to the king and love for his own son. Duryodhan was a good friend of Drona's son, Ashwatthama, and because Drona loved his son, Duryodhan asked Ashwatthama to get Drona on his side.

We need to pause here, and consider: Are we exploiting love and duty—such fine sentiments—to bring people on our side for the battle?

Gita 1: 21–23

Then Arjuna said these words: O Hrishikesh, please draw up my chariot between the two armies.

O Achyuta (Krishna), I want to have a good look at those who have assembled here, desirous to fight, and with whom I should fight at the onset of this war.

I want to look at those who have come to fight against us and are eager to please the misguided son of Dhritarashtra (Duryodhan).

Evaluating the resources

All of us do this. Before any action, we like to evaluate the resources available to us and to others.

Arjuna is the best archer on the Pandavas' side. During his time in exile, he had once singlehandedly defeated the whole Kaurava army.

When the battle is about to start, Arjuna asks Krishna to drive his chariot into the neutral zone between the two armies so that he can take a closer look at both armies. He wanted to look at the people who had assembled for him and also those who would fight on the side of Duryodhan.

Arjuna is still quite the warrior, and he tells Krishna that he wants to see those who have come to fight for the 'misguided' son of Dhritarashtra. At this stage, there is no confusion. Arjuna is in full control of the situation. He knows why he is here.

The same thing happens to us. When we plan anything, we are in full control of the situation—on paper. It is only when we face the reality of the situation that the mind starts wavering.

Gita 1: 28

Clearly seeing all those who had assembled, Arjuna was overcome by deep compassion and said: O Krishna, I am filled with deep sadness and profound empathy when I see my own family and friends standing ready to fight against each other.

Empathy and compassion at the wrong time

In most families, family members have unique problems and issues of their own. Life does not give us time to solve these problems and issues in an orderly fashion. We get angry and frustrated when things do not seem to go the way we want them to. We lash out at each other. What we need is empathy and compassion towards each other. However, can this compassion be a problem?

While standing in the middle of the battlefield, Arjuna looks at both armies and finds that there are family members and friends ready to fight against each other. He tells Krishna that he is filled with 'profound empathy'. The situation hits him hard.

In a normal situation, this compassion is laudable. But what about the battlefield?

Misplaced empathy can be bad for us and others and may prevent us from helping the very people who need it. At the same time, we must stand up for the issues we believe in. For that to happen, we need to have confidence and belief in our capabilities and a clear sense of purpose.

Gita 1: 29–31

My limbs are losing their strength, my mouth is drying up, my body is trembling and the hair on my body is standing on its end (goose-flesh).

My bow, Gandiva, is slipping from my hands; my skin is also burning. I am not able to stand up and my mind is totally confused.

O Keshava (Krishna), I see bad omens and I only see misfortune from killing my own people in this battle.

The anxiety attack

Some of us may have experienced an anxiety attack.

An anxiety attack is a sudden occurrence of intense fear that triggers severe physical reactions in the body, even if there is no real danger or apparent cause. Anxiety attacks are very frightening. In the throes of an anxiety attack, we might think that we are losing control, having a heart attack or even dying.

This *shloka* describes Arjuna experiencing an anxiety attack. He is losing his strength, his mouth is drying up, and his body is trembling. He is not able to stand up, and his skin is burning. This is a reaction to his imagining the worst consequences of this war.

According to a report by The National Institute of Mental Health, USA, published in 2023, an estimated 31.1% of US adults have experienced an anxiety disorder at some time in their lives. Anxiety attacks end when the problem is resolved or when the stressful situation ends. Anxiety attacks themselves are not life-threatening, but they can be terrifying and may affect one's quality of life.

Here, Arjuna's anxiety has made him drift away from his natural disposition of a brave and skilled warrior; he becomes a scared and fearful person right in the middle of the battlefield. The reason for his anxiety attack is his attachment to his family members and friends, who are on opposing sides on the battlefield. He is also anxious about the consequences of the war and the destruction it would cause.

Anxiety disorders are very common. Typically, multiple factors, including genetics and environmental reasons, play a role. However, some events, emotions or experiences may cause symptoms of anxiety to develop or worsen. These elements are called triggers. These triggers may be due to health issues, negative thinking, financial concerns, conflict or stress.

Gita 1: 32

O Krishna, I do not wish for victory, kingdom or royal pleasures. O Govinda, what is the use of this kingdom, enjoyment or even life itself?

Why do we live?

We work very hard to earn a degree or learn a skill. We get a job so that we can support a family and enjoy the pleasures of life. When we have an anxiety attack, it is difficult to think clearly. We just want to escape the situation, whatever the cost.

While stricken by anxiety, Arjuna does not want anything, including this life. Arjuna is here to fight the war to regain his kingdom. But he says, 'I do not wish for victory, kingdom or pleasure'. How does he know that he will win the war? Even if he has defeated this army before, there is no guarantee that he will be able to defeat them this time.

The ultimate fallacy is that he is even questioning the purpose of this life. He does not even want to live anymore.

Some of us might have asked ourselves about the purpose of this life. On such occasions, we need to find meaning in our existence. Sometimes, there isn't a single thing that brings meaning per se, but the journey of life itself may help find the purpose of life. There will be moments of pleasure and moments of pain; we need to learn from all of these moments.

Gita 1: 33–34

When all those for whose sake we desire kingdom, enjoyment and pleasures, are geared up for a battle ready to lose not just their wealth, but their very life.

All these people are my dear ones: teachers, fathers, children, grandfathers, uncles, brothers-in-law, all my relatives and friends.

Why do we need friends and family?

Can we enjoy the pleasures of life alone? We need people with whom we can share the joy of experiencing such pleasures. When we are alone on a vacation or an official tour and we are enjoying ourselves thoroughly, we need someone around to share the experience.

Instagram and Facebook are filled with the joys of people who are itching to share their joy with others, known or unknown.

Arjuna is commenting here that if all of these friends and relatives were to perish in the war, what would be the meaning of enjoyment and pleasure? Arjuna is building an argument for not fighting this war, as we do when we don't want to do something. Arjuna's mind is in conflict: should he kill his family and friends in performing his duty, or should he refuse to fight them? The inability to resolve this conflict under the pressing situation of the war led to this anxiety attack. This is what many of us also do at critical moments. We want to run away from our conflicts and use logic, fate, destiny or other reasons to justify our actions.

Gita 1: 35

O Madhusudan (Krishna), I do not wish to kill them, even if they are intent upon killing me. I would not harm them to become ruler of the three worlds, let alone doing so for the earth!

False sacrifice

There is a popular perception that there are three worlds: *swargaloka*—the land where everyone performs *karma* for the welfare of others, *mrityuloka*—the world of humans where people perform their *karma*, and *patalloka*—the world of the *Asuras*—where people always think about sensual enjoyment.

When compassion strikes, it strikes with full force, sometimes even overcoming one's survival instinct. Self-preservation and survival are basic instincts in the animal kingdom, including in human beings. Only people driven by self-loathing try to harm themselves. In the present case, Arjuna is taking the argument from profound sympathy to ultimate non-violence leading to self-sacrifice. He declares he will not fight even if his victory could grant him the pleasures of the three worlds.

This is a case of false sacrifice. Many people try to hide their cowardice or ineptitude behind a show of self-sacrifice.

We find many people around us who talk about their defeat as a moral victory.

This train of thought of Arjuna shows us that if we decide not to act, then we will go to any extent to defend our inaction using moral arguments.

Gita 1: 36–37

O Janardana (Krishna), what happiness shall we derive by killing these sons of Dhritarashtra? *Paapa* alone will accrue to us by killing these oppressors.

Therefore, we cannot be justified in killing the sons of Dhritarashtra, who are our relatives. O Madhav (Krishna), how could we ever be joyful again after destroying our own family?

Taking a moral high ground

What is *paapa*? It is a Sanskrit word, and in the Gita, this word appears many times. In popular translations, *paapa* is translated as 'sin'. In my view, that is not a true translation of *paapa*. To understand that, let us see what 'sin' is.

Hamartiology, a branch of Christian theology, is the study of sin. It describes sin as an act of offence against God. A sin is committed by despising followers of God and Christian biblical law. Thus, sin is related to not having faith in God. Other scholars understand sin to be a loss of love for the Christian God. Therefore, when we use the term 'sin' while translating the word '*paapa*', we lose all the meanings intended.

Paapa in Hinduism has no relation to the love of God.

The author of Mahabharata, the great epic, Maharshi Vyasa says: '*paropakaara punyaaya paapaaya parapidanam*' (परोपकार: पुण्याय पापाय परपीडनम्।). It means: *punya* (virtue) is any act which benefits another and *paapa* is that deed which causes suffering to others. *Paapa* can be committed in four ways: With our body, we do evil; with our tongue, we speak untruths; with our mind, we think evil; with our money, we indulge in wickedness.

Here, Arjuna is giving another twist to his argument for not fighting the war by taking a moral high ground. He does not want to commit any *paapa*. The moral high ground—in ethical and political acts—refers to the desire to be respected for remaining moral under challenging circumstances to uphold the universal standards of justice and goodness. On the battlefield, however, the act of running away from the war does not appear to be an appropriate action. This behaviour can only be termed as false and unjustified righteous action.

Gita 1: 38–39

Although these people, whose mind is overpowered by greed, who cannot see the negative consequences of destroying one's family and the flaw in the betrayal of one's friends;

O Janardan, we—who can see clearly the *paapa* born in the destruction of the families—should we not withdraw from this *paapa*?

Wars destroy families.

Among the consequences of war, the impact on the civilian population is the most significant. Families are destroyed and women are more severely affected than men. Other vulnerable sections are children, the elderly and people with disabilities. There is a high degree of trauma and a lack of physical and emotional support.

One of the reasons for war is greed—for wealth, power and kingdom. Arjuna says that when we are overpowered by greed, we fail to see the negative consequences of our actions, which may destroy our family.

Now, Arjuna gives an emotional and intellectual twist to his resolve to not fight the war. He says that the war will destroy many families. He says that perhaps Duryodhan and his supporters do not realize the negative consequences of their actions, but we (that is, Arjuna and Krishna), who can clearly see such consequences, should withdraw from such heinous acts.

These are fine and appealing sentiments. With this argument, Arjuna is trying to appeal emotionally to Krishna to justify his decision. Most cultures in the world lay great emphasis on the family system. He tells Krishna that by fighting this war, many families will be destroyed. This will be a great *paapa* that should be avoided.

Arjuna is trying to justify his actions through several arguments. Let us summarize the reasons why Arjuna does not want to fight the Mahabharata war at Kurukshetra:

- Compassion
- Consequences of the war
- Destruction of families

- Non-violence
- Confusion and indecision

Gita 1: 40

The destruction of families results in the destruction of the *kuladharma*. When *dharma* is lost in families, will not *adharma* overwhelm the entire family?

Importance of family values and traditions

The family, in Indian society, is an important institution. It is a symbol of the collectivist culture of India right from ancient times. The family has been an important feature of Indian culture. Family values and traditions evolve with changing times, and they reflect progressive customs and practices.

Arjuna now talks about the consequences of the destruction of families. He says that when families are destroyed, there will be *adharma* all around, resulting in discord, disharmony, contradictions, injustice, wickedness and immorality in the society and community.

Family traditions are an accumulation of experiences and activities that are passed down from one generation to another. These traditions are unique and special to the family and the community. They establish a foundation for family values and also serve as special bonding experiences, while providing families with a sense of identity and belonging. They tend to inspire positive feelings and memories that can be shared by family members. Family traditions provide a sense of continuity across generations.

Gita 1: 45–46

Unfortunately, what great *paapa* we are prepared to commit by killing our own people just to enjoy a kingdom and its pleasures!

It would be better if the sons of Dhritarashtra, with weapons in their hands, were to kill me in the battle—where I am unarmed and do not even retaliate.

Non-violence or cowardice?

There is a very thin line between non-violence and cowardice, especially when a warrior talks about non-violence on the battlefield.

In a famous article, The Doctrine of the Sword, Mohandas Gandhi (1920) writes, 'I do believe that when there is only a choice between cowardice and violence, I would advise violence. ... I would rather have India resort to arms in order to defend her honour than that she should in a cowardly manner become or remain a helpless victim to her own dishonour.'

Non-violence, as mentioned in our traditions, means conscious suffering. It does not mean meek submission.

Here, Arjuna is willing to get slaughtered, unarmed, by the sons of Dhritarashtra. This is not non-violence; this is pure cowardice. A coward is a person who lacks courage when facing a grave and hostile situation and tries to avoid it. A person cannot practice non-violence and be a coward at the same time. There is no fear in the mind of a non-violent person. In the current situation, there is no fear in Arjuna's mind either. It is just an inappropriate time and place to talk of non-violent resistance.

Gita 2: 2–3

Shree Bhagwan (Krishna) said: O Arjuna, from where does this weakness come to you at the most inappropriate time? It is unbecoming of a noble person.

It will not lead you to heaven. It will lead you to disgrace only. O Partha, do not behave like a coward. Abandon the weakness of the heart, O Parantapa (nemesis of the enemies), and get up.

Abandon the weakness of the heart.

Krishna recognizes the crisis at hand. He has heard Arjuna's rant patiently. He has listened to Arjuna's compassion for his kin, friends, relatives and all other soldiers present on the battlefield. He has also witnessed the meltdown of a warrior experiencing an anxiety attack: He has seen Arjuna's limbs quivering, his skin burning, his mouth becoming parched, and his inability to stand on his own feet.

Krishna has listened carefully to Arjuna justifying defeat as a moral victory, his fear of the consequences of this war—the destruction of families and family traditions. He has also heard about Arjuna's desire to get killed unarmed without offering any resistance on the battlefield.

How many of us can handle a crisis of this magnitude?

Krishna is surprised to hear these words from Arjuna. He tells Arjuna that this attitude does not befit a man who is about to lead an army to war. He tells Arjuna that this is a weakness of the heart and that he must overcome this newfound magnanimity and sudden love for non-violence. Anyone would be distressed by this turn of events. The first words of Krishna in the Bhagavad Gita are very relevant to all of us who play critical roles in our given functions.

Wherever we are in life, we have reached there through focused actions and strategies. Many people have worked hard to realize their dreams and goals. The problem is compounded when a warrior argues in favour of defeat and justifies it as a moral victory. If we give up at the last moment, anyone would feel exasperated and speechless ... but not Krishna.

Krishna uses his words carefully. Let us look at the opening words:

- Don't become weak at the most inappropriate time.
- Quitting is not noble.
- It will be a cause of eternal damnation.
- It will only lead to disgrace.
- It is unmanly (cowardice).

Krishna addresses Arjuna by the title Parantapa, meaning the nemesis of enemies, reminding Arjuna of his past victories. He further appeals to Arjuna to abandon this weakness of the heart and get up.

Krishna is trying to challenge Arjuna's ego. If we have to motivate a person who is experiencing an anxiety attack, one who is willing to give everything away and justifies defeat as a moral victory, we need to paint the most horrible picture of the future. What is worse than eternal damnation, and being called a coward and a person with a weak heart?

At the same time, Krishna addresses Arjuna by the names *Parantapa*, i.e., the nemesis of enemies, and *Partha*, i.e., son of Pritha (Kunti), who will bring fame to Kunti. By using these names, Krishna is appealing to Arjuna's base nature as a son and a warrior, to remind him of his origin (his mother, Kunti) and his past (where he has defeated his enemies). Is it sufficient to goad Arjuna into action? We know that it is not, but it is a start.

After this monologue, Arjuna asks the first question.

QUESTION 1

WHAT IS THE RIGHT THING TO DO?

We have heard it many times: 'Do the right thing'.

But what is 'the right thing' to do?

Doing the right thing means acting in a way that is consistent with one's ethical values and beliefs. It also means adhering to social norms and treating people with kindness and respect, even in difficult times. Doing the right thing may involve speaking up against an injustice or helping those in need.

Doing the right thing is about making choices that represent one's values and belief systems while also contributing to the welfare of society.

The idea of doing 'the right thing' leads to an important question: How does one recognize 'the right thing' in any given situation? There are several ways of looking at justice and freedom, but any answer can look confusing and wrong. The search for truth is noble, and that is what Arjuna, in his confused state of mind, wants to do.

Arjuna realizes that his mind has been thrown off balance by thinking too much. He also realizes that because of this imbalance, it is possible that his decision to lay down his arms is not the right thing to do. By this time, Arjuna has regained some of his composure, and he tries to raise some ethical issues.

Luckily for him, his trusted friend Krishna is beside him. So, he asks for Krishna's advice.

Gita 2: 4–5

Arjuna said: O Madhusudan, how can I fight with arrows in battle with Bhishma and Drona? O Arisudana (slayer of enemies), they are both worthy of my reverence.

It is better to live as a beggar in this world than to kill these two most revered gurus. In fact, all our gains will be tainted by the spilt blood of these gurus.

Fighting against our own people

Arjuna is not satisfied with Krishna's response. He wants to convey that his decision to not fight is logical. He goes to the extent of saying that it is better to live the life of a beggar than to kill revered elders like Bhishma and Dronacharya.

In the real world, we compete with those we know most of the time, such as our friends or relatives. I have seen this in professional courses I have attended and taught— we compete against our own friends and colleagues for the same jobs most of the time. People make friends at their workplace and then compete against them when the opportunity for a promotion arises. If we look at the data in the court of law, most crimes have been committed by those who knew the victim. So, we are up against our own people, be it in a positive or negative sense.

Whether we are fighting with our spouse, friends, coworkers or family, a bitter fight can leave us feeling unhappy and overwhelmed for days. Quite frequently, this fight may also keep us from achieving the very goals we were trying to achieve.

Within a family, family members have to deal with each

other and their differences. There are different levels of growth and maturity and different goals, wants and needs. No matter how different family members are from each other, they share the bond of love along with the memories of all the good and bad times together. Living with family members so different from oneself is a challenge, not least due to all the conflicting desires and differences in life choices. However, in order to keep a family together, we have to forfeit some of our wants and freedom. Most family fights take place when there is a contradiction or competition between family members. The fight is triggered first in our mind due to some incident or event. A voice in our heads keeps nagging us to make a move. The love and bond we share cloud our judgement and actions at the same time. We hesitate to start a fight even when we think that our stand is the right one. Arjuna is struggling with the same thought process here.

Gita 2: 6

It is difficult to say which would be a worse outcome, defeating them or being defeated by them. If I kill the sons of Dhritarashtra, I will not want to live. And yet, here they are, standing before me on the field of battle.

Why do we fight with our own people?

Arjuna is in the middle of the battlefield. He is creating many scenarios in his mind. Unfortunately, this is war. Whether he wins or loses, many of his kin will die. One can see that he is beginning to move away from the all-or-nothing position of 'I will not fight', a response that was triggered by his anxiety attack. While he has calmed down somewhat, his hard-line position has morphed into a dilemma. And the dilemma is: How do I fight against my own people?

Some of the reasons for fighting against our own people can be summed up here.

First, we could be insecure. Sometimes our loved ones may perceive our actions as a threat. We may become vocal about it, which finally may turn into a bitter fight.

Second, a joke could have gone wrong. Many fights start simply when we are having fun and commenting on some idiosyncrasies, habits or silly actions of our loved ones. Even if there is no intention to harm them, situations may get out of hand.

Third, there could be a ticking emotional bomb. There are often unresolved issues between friends, coworkers and near relatives which keep building over a period of time. Any trigger at any surprising moment may turn these issues into a fight.

Fourth, a sense of drama: Some of us are simply more dramatic, and we sometimes make a mountain of a molehill because we enjoy doing so.

Fifth, a fight could also be to highlight our point of view. There are always issues where we have different standpoints and viewpoints. When one of us starts stressing the correctness of our stand over others, a simple discussion may take a turn for the worse.

Sixth, there could be small irritants in our behaviour towards others. All of us have some sharp edges in our character—bad habits, unintentional behaviour, perhaps not being able to understand the gravity of our comments and so on. Others may tolerate these for a while, but sooner or later, a time comes when the situation blows up.

Seventh, we could be taking our loved ones for granted. When we are very close to people, we start taking them for granted and indulge in silly behaviour. Sometimes, we go over the top while fully knowing that the other person will forgive us.

Next, we could also be looking for sympathy, admiration or attention. This happens very often—we believe we have done something remarkable and want to be admired for it. When that admiration is not forthcoming, we let ourselves go. It could also happen that you are in a miserable mood. When others do not sympathise with your plight, the result is obvious.

Finally, it could simply be bad timing. There are always good times and bad times in our life. When times are bad, nothing good seems to happen. We get frustrated and stressed, so much so that a drop of the hat could ignite us.

Gita 2: 7

Compassion, even if flawed, is my basic nature. With total confusion in my mind about my *dharma* (duty), I ask you, as your disciple, please instruct me on the correct path of action.

Ask for help when you need it.

Arjuna says that compassion is his basic nature, even if it is flawed. He does not want this kingdom by killing the people arrayed against him. Even though Arjuna does not know why he is behaving this way, he does not want to lower himself by saying so. He insists that he is confused because he is in essence a compassionate person and does not want to harm others.

We present such arguments and try to cover our weaknesses. We want to keep the focus on our basic goodness rather than on the problem at hand. Presenting an exaggerated account of oneself is also a sign of arrogance.

At the same time, Arjuna acknowledges that there is confusion in his mind about his *dharma* (the right thing to do), and he is looking for Krishna's guidance. This also shows his humility.

Do we have the same humility to ask for help when it is needed? It can be extremely difficult, even knowing that people are naturally inclined to help when asked. Many of us struggle to reach out for help when we are really in need.

Gita 2: 8

I do not know how to take care of this anxiety that is tormenting my *indriyas*. I do not want this kingdom, even if I gain an unrivalled and prosperous kingdom on the earth or gain power like the *suras*.

Dealing with anxieties

Anxiety is one of the most common mental health crises of modern times. While there are many types of anxiety disorders, they have one thing in common: excessive worry and fear.

Anxiety may be described as 'a feeling of worry, nervousness, or unease about something with an uncertain outcome'. Anxiety causes stress that can be triggered by a variety of factors, including relationship troubles, family conflict or work-related issues. Sometimes, the anxiety is so strong that it interferes with our daily activities.

Every person deals with anxieties at one time or another because it is part of our brain's response to a perceived danger—even if that danger isn't real. There are times when anxiety can become serious and turn into anxiety attacks that may feel manageable but may gradually build up. Some of the symptoms of anxiety attacks are as follows:

- Excessive fear and worrying
- Restlessness
- Agitation
- Irritability
- Rapid breathing
- Insomnia

Gita 2: 11

Krishna said: The words you speak are full of wisdom, but wise people do not grieve for either the living or the dead.

Wisdom—in words or action?

Wisdom can be understood as an action or behaviour aimed at achieving an altruistic outcome. Wisdom can also be understood as a quality that simultaneously engages both intellectual ability and prior knowledge which is acquired through experience and constant practice.

Krishna tells Arjuna that his words are full of wisdom but reminds him that wise people grieve neither for the living nor the dead. This is pertinent since Arjuna is distressed about the possible death of family members, friends and well-wishers and anxious about the outcome of the war.

Wise people know that the world is affected by suffering, death and decay. Therefore, they do not mourn for those living or dead, knowing fully well the facts of the world. One will gain no peace of mind by grieving or mourning.

Gita 2: 13

Just as people grow from childhood to youth to adulthood and then to old age, so after death, the *dehi* (immortal consciousness) migrates to another *deha* (body). Those who understand this are not confused by these changes.

Why do wise people not grieve?

Krishna points out to Arjuna that wise people do not grieve because they know that even when the *deha*—the body— dies, the *dehi*—the body dweller (*brahman*)—never dies.

The Indian knowledge system tells us that the eternal essence, the body dweller, the immortal consciousness (*brahman*) is imperishable and real, whereas human bodies and material objects are perishable and unreal. This immortal consciousness, called *dehi* here, is also called the *atma* or the soul. This *dehi* resides within the body of all beings and cannot be destroyed in any way. Therefore, one should not grieve for the death of anyone.

The theory of transmigration or **metempsychosis in the Indian knowledge system believes** in the rebirth of an individual. It states that what one does in this present life will affect the next life. In Hindu Dharma, the process of birth and rebirth, i.e., transmigration of souls, is endless until one achieves *moksha* or liberation ('release' from this process). *Moksha* is achieved when one realizes that the *atma* and the Absolute reality (*brahman*) are one. Thus, one can escape from the process of death and rebirth (*samsara*).

Since every wise person is aware of this process, Krishna's question to Arjuna is: Why are you grieving about it?

Gita 2: 14–15

O Kaunteya (Arjuna), the contact of senses with objects creates experiences like heat and cold, pleasure and pain. O Bharata, they are temporary, with a definite beginning and end.

One must learn to endure them. People who are not disturbed by the experience of pleasure and pain are exceptional individuals in society, and such wise people achieve immortality.

Who are wise people?

Cold air is pleasant in summer but painful in winter. Similarly, heat is pleasant in winter but painful in summer. Cold and heat, which give pleasure at one time, give pain at another. Our *indriyas* (sense organs) give rise to the sensations of heat and cold, leading to pleasure and pain. Therefore, pleasure and pain are impermanent in nature.

Objects come in contact with the senses or the *indriyas* — for instance, the skin, ears, eyes, or nose—and the sensations are carried by the nerves to the mind. It is the mind that feels pleasure and pain. Krishna says that wise people try to develop a balanced state of mind.

There is a story about two wolves, which conveys this process clearly:

An old man is teaching his grandson about life. He says to the boy, 'A fight is going on inside me. It is a terrible fight, and it is between two wolves. One is evil—he is anger, envy, sorrow, regret, greed, arrogance, self-pity, guilt, resentment, inferiority, lies, false pride, superiority and ego.

'The other wolf is good—he is joy, peace, love, hope, serenity, humility, kindness, benevolence, empathy, generosity, truth, compassion and faith. The same fight is going on inside you, and inside every other person, too.'

The grandson asks his grandfather, 'Which wolf will win?'

The old man smiles and replies, 'The one you feed.'

At such moments, we wish we had a grandfather to guide us, to make us understand what is happening in our life.

Identification of the Self with the body is the cause of pleasure and pain in the mind. The more we can identify ourselves with the *dehi* (*brahman*), the less we will be affected by pain and pleasure.

Gita 2: 16

That which is false (*asat*) will not endure, while that which is true (*sat*) can never cease to exist. To wise people, both these aspects of facts are obvious.

Wise people are also aware.

This world of names and forms, as we see it, is always changing. Hence, it is impermanent and temporary. Only what is constant and permanent must be real. The *dehi* is constant; it moves from one body to another in the cycle of birth and rebirth. Hence, it is real and never ceases to exist.

The feelings of cold and warmth are impermanent; hence, they are *asat*. Pleasure and pain are impermanent; hence, they are *asat*. Since the distinction between the real and the unreal is dependent on awareness, wise people are those who are always aware.

Arjuna is confused about the true nature of the body and the Self, so Krishna tries to remove his delusion. He tries to discriminate between these two—that which is *asat* (perishable) and *sat* (imperishable).

Gita 2: 24

This 'immortal consciousness' cannot be cut into parts, burnt by fire, drowned in water or dried by wind. It is eternal, all-pervading, subtler than matter, stationary and ancient.

What is the nature of *dehi (atman, eternal soul)?*

In Hindu Dharma, some words are used very frequently, such

as *atma* and *parmatma*. *Atma* is the soul and *parmatma* is the eternal soul. It is important to understand the nature of *atma* to believe in the theory of transmigration or birth and rebirth.

It is important to understand that the eternal soul is the essential constitution of all living beings, and this eternal soul is immortal. The eternal soul is unchangeable, everlasting and eternally the same.

Robert Lanza, currently head of Astellas Global Regenerative Medicine and adjunct professor at Wake Forest School of Medicine, USA, asserts that the human consciousness does not die with the body; it falls into a parallel universe. He has propounded the theory of biocentrism. According to this theory, 'Death does not exist as such; it is just an illusion that arises in the mind of a person.' He says that a person's consciousness exists regardless of time or space; it can be anywhere, either in the human body or outside it. This theory is intertwined with quantum mechanics, according to which an individual particle can appear in any place, and a certain event can develop in an innumerable number of ways.

The nature of the eternal soul is such that weapons are powerless to inflict any injury by cutting or piercing it, fire is powerless to burn it, water is powerless to drown it, and air is powerless to dry the eternal soul.

Gita 2: 25–26

O Mahabaho (Arjuna), it is said that this *atma* is invisible, inconceivable and unchangeable. Therefore, knowing this to be such, you should not grieve.

If, however, you believe that this *atma* is constantly born and constantly dying, you should not grieve.

Why should one grieve in either case?

Here, the nature of the soul is explained. We can all see the body, but we cannot see the soul. When we see the body, we can think about the nature and purpose of each organ, but we do not see the soul and find it difficult to imagine its nature. Since we cannot visualise the soul and cannot conceive it in any form, it is changeless. If you believe in this nature of the soul, you should not grieve because when the body dies, the soul does not die. It just moves from one body to another.

Krishna says that, however, if you believe that the *atma* is always taking birth and rebirth, then birth is inevitable to what is dead, and death is inevitable to what is born. So, you should not grieve.

Gita 2: 31

You should never abandon *svadharma*. To a *kshatriya* (one who is a warrior), nothing is more welcome than a righteous war.

We should choose a career based on our true nature.

Krishna now deals with the issue of *svadharma* or one's duty, or one's work based on one's true nature. Krishna points this out to Arjuna by reminding him that a true warrior would look forward to the challenge of fighting a war instead of running away.

Krishna advises us that as long as we are performing actions that are aligned with *svadharma*, our duty, then action is always preferable to inaction or procrastination. The outcome of acting in accordance with our duty will always be good. The good here refers to a future state where you will be happy after you have performed according to *svadharma*. Krishna says that we have authority only over our actions, but never over the result. In other words, we do not have complete control over the outcome of any activity.

One should never abandon *svadharma* (your own *karma*). To a *kshatriya* (one who is a warrior), nothing is more welcome than a righteous war. And if a warrior turns away from his *svadharma* (true nature or duty), he will suffer infamy. People will speak ill of that warrior for all time. For someone who is accustomed to being honoured, dishonour is worse than death.

Gita 2: 34–36

Further, people will speak ill of you for all time to come. For someone who is accustomed to being honoured, dishonour is worse than death.

Maharathis **who earlier spoke highly of you will assume you left the battlefield out of cowardice. They will ridicule you and will never again speak of you with respect.**

Your enemies will also taunt you with harsh words and belittle your ability. What could be more painful than that?

Honour and dishonour

Like pleasure and pain, honour and dishonour have a big impact on our lives. One of the reasons we want to do the right thing is to earn respect and honour from our family, friends and society. We are scared that if we don't do the right thing, people will ridicule us, taunt us and criticize us.

Honour is a fundamental attribute of character. Honour is a virtue which implies loyalty and courage, truthfulness and self-respect, and justice and generosity. Its underlying principle is truth. Honour relates to the perceived quality of worthiness of an individual, which affects one's social standing. On the other hand, dishonour is a state of disgrace. It involves a lack of respect. For example, sportspersons who cheat bring dishonour to themselves and the team.

One legendary story dealing with honour and dishonour has enthralled many storytellers for millennia: This is the story of the rape of Lucretia.

Lucretia was a Roman noblewoman who lived in the 6th century BCE. As it happens, the Roman prince Sextus Tarquinius visited her while her husband and her father were away at war. Tarquinius developed an intense longing for Lucretia and wanted to sleep with her. She repudiated his advances. He threatened to kill her, but she did not relent. Finally, Tarquinius said that he would kill Lucretia and a male slave and would arrange their bodies in such a way that it would appear that she was killed while in an adulterous relationship with a man of base condition. The threat succeeded in gaining Lucretia's consent.

Afterwards, Lucretia felt miserable and stabbed herself to death. Horrified and outraged, Lucretia's kin revolted against the ruling family and helped found the Roman Republic. Such is the play of honour and dishonour.

Krishna is reminding Arjuna that it is his duty to fight. If he runs away from the war, his honour will be lost forever.

Gita 2: 38

Treat pleasure and pain, gain and loss, victory and defeat as if they are all the same, and then engage in this fight. Thus, you will not incur any *paapa*.

The concept of duty

When we want to do the right thing, we need to rise above the feelings of pleasure and pain, gain and loss, victory and defeat. Otherwise, we will be worried about the outcome all the time. We will also be driven by our likes and dislikes, which will influence our course of action.

This aspect enjoins both knowledge and action: Such is the concept of duty. Duty involves a level of self-awareness: We must not only do what is right, but we must also stand for what is right. When we value our duty, we realize that we have an obligation to act, a commitment to grow, develop and evolve professionally.

In Western philosophy, Immanuel Kant talks about the concept of duty in the *Groundwork of the Metaphysics of Morals* (1785). For Kant, 'All humans must be seen as inherently worthy of respect and dignity.' He argued that 'All morality must stem from such duties. Consequences such as pain or pleasure are irrelevant.'

Krishna then addresses Arjuna's concern about incurring *paapa*. Krishna says that if Arjuna fights the war as his duty, he will not incur any *paapa*.

Gita 2: 41

O Kurunandana (Arjuna), the trained *buddhi* (intellect) is focused, and inept *buddhi* (intellect) continues to deliberate on various aspects and perspectives.

Work with a focused mind.

Focus is the ability to concentrate on something and direct mental effort towards it. Focus is critical for learning new things, achieving goals and performing well in various situations. To achieve focus, we need to train our minds and intellect.

When there is a lack of focus, the mind keeps wavering and deliberating on various aspects and we lose perspective.

There are unlimited options available to the mind because of the uncountable number of impressions it receives, leading to innumerable opinions. When the mind, one's intellect, is not trained, it loses focus and dwells on unnecessary and irrelevant subjects.

Gita 2: 42

**O Partha, inept people are confused by the flowery
and poetic language of the Vedas; they interpret
them in a literal sense and then conclude that there is
nothing more to them than that.**

Beware of flowery language.

We easily get influenced by flowery language. We are
often under pressure to showcase our understanding of a
subject through writing or speaking by using extensive and
supposedly eloquent prose and vocabulary. We want to join
the ranks of those we view as highly intelligent beings.

Some people use flowery language as a strategy to sound
more professional and intelligent. When elaborate words
and longer sentences are used instead of simple ones, you
can see flowery language in action. People who use flowery
language want to convey multiple ideas in a single long
sentence. This is an attempt to sound as though they know
more about a subject by using jargon and connecting
different concepts.

Since Arjuna had been using lots of intellectual concepts
to avoid the war, Krishna is cautioning him about the use
of the flowery language of the Vedas. Many people talk
about the Vedas by interpreting them in a literal sense and
concluding that that is all that they contain.

Krishna is calling the use of flowery language a fallacy
because flowery language has an adverse effect.

Gita 2: 43

Those desirous of sensual pleasures, aiming to reach *swarga*, perform result-oriented, specific actions.

Beware of pretenders.

When we are ignorant, we easily get influenced by people who promise us the pleasures of heaven. We are told to do certain rituals to attain enjoyment and power. This looks attractive at first sight.

People whose mind and intellect are untrained, but who are well read about the scriptures, impress common people like us easily. Whether we attain heaven or not, these people earn immense wealth and gain power in society. They are driven by desires, but they hide behind flowery language. Such people will not be able to achieve the mental disposition needed to gain true knowledge and wisdom.

Gita 2: 44

For those who are extremely attracted to pleasure and wealth, their *buddhi* (intellect) is absorbed in gaining pleasure and wealth. For such people, *samadhi* (a state of meditative consciousness) is not possible.

Why do we seek pleasure?

We are all engaged in the pursuit of pleasure. Sometimes we seek intellectual pleasure, and sometimes, sensuous pleasure. Many a time, we seek pleasure in cultural activities or even in reforming society.

We take pleasure in telling others what to do. We feel joy when eradicating the evils of society and doing good. Some gain pleasure in seeking greater knowledge, greater physical strength and varied experiences, or in developing a better understanding of life.

We pursue pleasure from childhood until death. Seeking pleasure guides and shapes our lives. It is a basic demand of life, and without it, existence would become dull, lonely and meaningless.

We may ask: Why should life not be guided by pleasure? The answer is very simple. We all know that when moments of pleasure are over, there will be pain, frustration, sorrow, fear and violence. The choice is ours. If we want to live that way, we can, of course, make that choice. But if we want to be free from these dualities and achieve a state of meditative consciousness and eternal bliss, we need to understand the right thing to do.

Gita 2: 45

The Vedas deal with the three *gunas* (*trigunas* or three modes of *prakriti*). O Arjuna, rise above these three *gunas*, established in your true Self, free from any confusion, committed to goodness and without any concern for results.

What is our true nature?

There is an emphasis throughout the Bhagavad Gita on acting according to our nature. For the first time, Krishna refers to the construct of our true nature.

There are three modes of nature called *guna*. *Guna* means an attribute or quality. These three *gunas* are *sattva* (purity, light or harmony), *rajas* (passion or emotion) and *tamas* (inertia or resistance to change).

Purity, passion and resistance to change are the three drivers of our life. They create the pairs of opposites: heat and cold, pleasure and pain, gain and loss, victory and defeat, honour and dishonour, praise and censure.

Those who are anxious about acquiring new possessions, or about preserving their old possessions, cannot have peace of mind. They are ever restless. Therefore, Lord Krishna advises Arjuna that he should rise above the play of these three *gunas*, these drivers, to be free of confusion, and in so doing, commit to goodness. There will be no concern for the results of actions when he rises above these three *gunas*.

Gita 2: 46

As much as there is the use of water in a reservoir when there is a flood, that much is the use of the knowledge in the Vedas to a wise person.

Knowledge and wisdom

Knowledge is gained through the study of textual information. However, wisdom has more to do with having insight, understanding and acceptance of the fundamental nature of things in life.

Thus, to a wise person who has realised the Self, the Vedas are of no use because the person has infinite knowledge of the Self. This does not mean that the Vedas are useless. They are useful for beginners and aspirants who have just started on the path.

The example here is very clear. During a flood everywhere, the water in the reservoir is of no use. So, if one rises above the three *gunas*, there is no desire left for pain and pleasure or gain and loss.

Gita 2: 47

You only have the rights over *karma*, not over the results. Let the fruits of action not be your motive. Let there be no attachment to inaction.

Rewards should not be the motive for action.

Everyone has the right to perform actions, but we should not perform actions only for their rewards. When we perform actions to gain rewards, we get attached to both the actions and the rewards. Krishna emphasizes that even when we are performing actions, we have no right over the rewards. Rewards should not be the motive for doing the right thing.

When someone is performing an action, they may or may not receive a reward. There are so many factors and variables involved.

In other words, it is not that they will not receive rewards, but the focus should not be on those rewards.

It is a fact that when we are concerned about the rewards associated with an action, there will be anxiety and worry about the outcome: 'If the outcome is not along the expected lines, will I be punished?' Such thought processes impact the efficiency and effectiveness of one's actions.

It is also likely that if there is a possibility of not achieving a certain result, one may simply procrastinate and avoid action altogether.

Gita 2: 48

O Dhananjaya (Arjuna), perform your *karma*, established in *yoga*, without any attachment. *Yoga* is defined as remaining the same during success or failure.

What is *karma yoga*?

If the rewards are not the driver for performing an action, then why should someone work? When we act, we often do so after asking, 'How will this benefit me?' We always expect results or appreciation for our efforts. *Karma yoga* suggests that we overcome this attitude and act without anticipating any credit or result. In other words, we act simply for the delight and joy of action.

When we are attached to the outcome of our actions, we suffer if we fail. In order to truly practice *karma yoga*, we must act with no expectations and work without thinking of results.

Karma yoga is one of the most popular concepts in Hindu Dharma. Krishna is asking Arjuna to perform all his actions without any attachment to the fruits of action. He defines *karma yoga* as the ability to remain the same regardless of the success or failure of one's actions.

Gita 2: 49

O Dhananjaya, selfish action is far inferior to unselfish action. If you take refuge in your *buddhi*, you would consider inferior those who work for results.

Be selfless.

Selfish action is motivated by a concern for one's interests. Undoubtedly, most of our daily actions are selfish actions. For example, when I fetch a glass of water only for myself, it is a selfish action. All of us work to reduce pain or satisfy a desire. A certain amount of selfishness is needed to live and survive in this world. However, if everyone focuses on selfish gains, society will not survive.

Krishna says that selfish action is inferior to selfless action. What is selfless action? Here are some examples:

- When we are driving and stop on the road to help someone whose car has broken down
- When we give money to charity
- When a soldier falls on a grenade to protect others from the explosion

When we act selflessly, we think less about ourselves and more about others. These qualities are called being generous and kind. Selfless action deals with what is good for others, not just for one's own benefit. Selflessness helps in conquering our ego because we are not acting out of pride or a desire to be noticed.

Gita 2: 50

They who act according to their *buddhi* (wisdom) discard both good and bad deeds. Therefore, remain established in *yoga*; *yoga* results in excellence in action.

Yoga is excellence in action.

These are some of the most quoted words from the Gita.

When work is performed with a focus on the results, there will be a loss of efficiency and effectiveness. Some of the energy is lost in anxiety and worry about the result. When one starts following the doctrine of *karma yoga*, one rises above the desire for the rewards of action. Such a person does not look at an action as good or bad based on the outcomes of that action.

When someone is a *karma yogi*, one hundred percent of their energy is used for the action. When we work with such focus continuously, we will excel in those actions.

Therefore, *karma yoga* brings out excellence in action.

Gita 2: 51

Thus, wise people trying to achieve perfection use their discriminative power of intellect and give up the result of action to get liberated from the entanglements of birth.

Doing the right thing is natural.

Can our actions be the means of liberation?

When we follow *karma yoga*, we are on the path to excellence and perfection. A *karma yogi* relinquishes the desire for results in their actions. Performing actions with equanimity is the way to wisdom and the means of assured liberation from birth and rebirth.

A *karma yogi*'s actions are full of generosity. Generosity means sharing one's power, joy and love with others. The life of a *karma yogi* is a life that is aware; it is meaningful and useful to others. A *karma yogi* is full of patience and does not get angry. Such a person does not want to lose the good energy at work for others and oneself by being angry.

A *karma yogi* is full of joyful energy, ensuring constant growth. There is an immense joy inherent in constant growth, in never allowing anything to become dull. Real growth happens beyond one's comfort zone. It pays well to demand little from others and much from oneself.

Constant growth happens through generosity with one's body, speech and mind. Joyful energy exudes through skilful thoughts, words and actions. Joyful energy also gives the extra momentum which opens new dimensions.

When we follow *karma yoga* with wisdom, by recognizing the true nature of the mind, we develop an intuitive understanding that doing the right thing is natural.

Gita 2: 52

When your intellect transcends the dense forest of ignorance, then you will become indifferent to what is heard and what is yet to be heard.

Beware of external judgement.

When we follow the path of *karma yoga*, we become indifferent to things heard or yet to be heard. Such things will appear to be of no use. A *karma yogi* does not care a bit for them.

Most of us get affected by what others say. We want to listen when good things are said about us. However, if we transcend the forest of ignorance, we should not be worried about what is heard and yet to be heard.

We always fear external judgement and what other people think of us. Such fears stop us from fully being ourselves. We need to belong and be accepted.

Gita 2: 53

When your *buddhi* (intellect) remains steady without being influenced by the results of what you hear, absorbed in *samadhi* (meditative consciousness), you will be able to attain self-realization.

What is self-realization?

Self-realization is the truth of who we are and what we are. When we understand that, we will not hesitate in doing the right thing.

For many, self-realization is a term that means the same as 'enlightenment'—a word which is difficult to define. Self-realization is the realization that we are not the physical body, but the energy within that physical form which gives us life. We realize that we are not the body, and we are not the mind; indeed, we are life energy itself. Life energy is immortal; it never dies. The body dies and disintegrates, but life energy, the *dehi* or the immortal consciousness, can merge with the cosmic consciousness—this is self-realization.

When we begin training our intellect to understand this concept of action without the expectation of results, we are on the path to self-realization. If we want to achieve perfection, we have to use the discriminative power of the intellect and give up on the result of the action.

When our *buddhi* (intellect) is trained to be steady and unwavering, we are no longer distracted by what we hear. This state of *samadhi* (meditative consciousness) is needed to attain self-realization.

HOW DO I BECOME A CALM AND WISE PERSON?

In the last chapter, we saw Krishna telling Arjuna that he should not grieve for the death of the body because the *dehi* never dies. He also tells Arjuna that one should always work according to one's true nature without getting affected by the results of one's actions. By using the discriminatory power of one's intellect, one can attain perfection in their work. Whatever the result, one will be happy performing work based on one's true nature.

This state of understanding is described as self-realization. When one attains self-realization, one attains total balance in life and is not affected by pleasure or pain. This state of living life is described in the scriptures as the state of *sthitpragnya*. In modern parlance, we can describe such a person as the ultimate 'cool' person, someone who is calm and wise.

Being a calm and wise person means keeping a calm demeanour in high-pressure situations. Staying calm is important for the following reasons:

1. Our mind works smoothly in a calm condition. We can analyse and understand any problem to find a solution for it.

2. We can analyse the external world in a state of calmness.
3. Everyone can sail a boat in a calm ocean, but a calm mind can sail a boat in a stormy ocean.
4. A calm mind creates positive energy around us, so more people are attracted to us.

When people are calm, they can better understand a situation and are more apt to devise a solution. When you are calm, you are able to combat challenges more confidently. Being calm is great because no one wants to be stressed or fearful all the time.

How can one be such a calm and wise person? That is the question Arjuna asks in the following verse.

Gita 2: 54

Arjuna said: O Keshav, what is the disposition of a *sthitpragnya* (a calm and wise person)? What is their body language—how do they sit, talk or move?

Being calm and wise

A wise person is one who manages their emotional, physical and mental well-being. Such a person is calm and composed in every situation. Being calm and wise, such a person can consider various alternatives even in challenging situations.

Wisdom does not come from reading books, but it comes from handling challenges and gaining first-hand experience. Such a person goes beyond their comfort zone and is not afraid of making mistakes.

Krishna describes such a calm and wise person in the Gita and says that such people are on the path of self-realization and can attain perfection in their field of action.

Arjuna wants to know the characteristics of such a person.

Gita 2: 55

O Partha, when people give up all desires of the mind and are self-satisfied and contented, they are called *sthitpragnya*.

Being self-satisfied and contented

A calm and wise person is self-satisfied and content. These two words are generally used as synonyms, but 'content' is more general than 'satisfied'. In other words, 'to be content' means to be generally fulfilled. However, satisfaction requires the fulfilment of a more specific need. For example:

'Did you get enough to eat?

'No, but I'm content.'

'Was the answer good enough?

'No, I'm not satisfied yet.'

We may be content, yet dissatisfied. When one is content, one does not want to pursue an area further, whereas satisfaction is the degree to which one has fulfilled one's wants.

In simpler terms, being satisfied is when we achieve what we want. Being content is being happy even if we don't achieve what we want. To make it clearer, let us take an example: We have a bike but want a car. When we buy a car, we are satisfied. But we could also be content with just a bike, without the desire to buy a car.

Being satisfied supposes various degrees of satisfaction. It is time-dependent and experience-dependent. Being content reflects the mind and behaviour of a human being who lives in happiness. Contentment coming out of a negative achievement, however, may never make a person happy.

In the Bhagavad Gita, *sthitpragnya* refers to a person of steady wisdom. A person is described as being *sthitpragnya* when one 'renounces completely all the desires of the mind, when one is fully satisfied with a mind fixed in cosmic consciousness'. According to the Gita, a *sthitpragnya*:

- is free from worldly attachments and aversions;
- does not need to seek the truth because they see the truth;
- is free from motives and ego;
- has attained self-realization;

- does good deeds with no expectations of reward; and
- is aware of the oneness of the universe and its elements.

Gita 2: 56

Those whose mind is not agitated in sorrow, remains indifferent in joy and is free from attachment, fear and anger; such contemplative individuals are known as *sthitpragnya*.

Develop an even-minded mental state.

Contemplation, a natural ability that everyone possesses, allows one to observe sensations, emotions, thoughts, sights and sounds. However, we are not consciously aware of this process, for a certain mental and physical calm is required for the contemplative dimension of our being. When we are aware, we are limited in our ability to settle on one object of observation at a time.

When the mind is busy, it moves from one object to another almost without interruption. It keeps moving from one experience to another. So, when the mind is not calm, or when it is agitated, it moves from one pleasant or unpleasant experience to another. However, those who are contemplative remain indifferent to joy and sorrow. They are not attached to the results of their actions, and they do not fear the outcome or lose their energy in anger.

Our emotions—attachment, fear, anger and others—are the physical manifestation of the mind. Fear, anger, sorrow and joy are all physical experiences expressing themselves through various organs of the body. The degree of calmness reflects the experience and the maturity of that moment.

Those who are calm and wise achieve a higher degree of equanimity in any given situation. Equanimity can be explained as an even-minded mental state towards all experiences, regardless of whether they are pleasant, unpleasant or neutral.

Gita 2: 57

Those who are without likes and dislikes are not jubilant in gain and are not dejected in loss; such people are *sthitpragnya*.

Likes and dislikes

Likes and dislikes arise as a result of emotional responses, which may include positive emotional reactions (such as elation) or negative emotional reactions (such as anxiety). These likes and dislikes develop without conscious thought as we interact with the world. Positive responses are to situations that we *like*, and negative emotional reactions are to situations we *dislike* (or fear or hate).

Different likes and dislikes develop over a period of time. Sometimes, we also like or dislike a person based on the thoughts that person has about us and the aura of his personality. When a person thinks negatively about us, we instantly develop hostile vibes towards them.

There was once a king in India. One day in the court, the king saw a merchant whom he had never met, but simply after seeing him once, the king thought about punishing him. The king was shocked at this instinctive response. After the court session for that day, the king called his minister and asked him to investigate the merchant.

The minister went to that merchant undercover and asked him about his reasons for visiting the city. The merchant said that he sold sandalwood. During the conversation, the merchant off-handedly mentioned that when he was in the king's court, a thought had occurred to him: If the king were to die, the merchant could sell his entire sandalwood stock for use in the king's last rites, and the merchant would become rich.

The minister revealed himself and told the merchant that king was very happy to have him here and had ordered the minister to buy a large amount of sandalwood for religious purposes. Hearing this, the merchant was very happy. The next day, the happy merchant once again went to the king's court. When the king saw him again, he no longer had a negative unconscious response; in fact, he felt nice about the merchant and praised him in public.

After the day's court session, the king asked his minister about this change in his behaviour towards the merchant. The minister narrated the whole story.

Calm and wise people are not influenced by such likes and dislikes.

Gita 2: 58

Those who are able to withdraw their senses from sense objects in all situations, as a tortoise draws in its limbs, such people are *sthitpragnya*.

Restraint over senses

In most households, when people go shopping for monthly utilities and groceries, they prepare an extensive list and firmly decide not to buy anything beyond that list. But when we leave the store, we leave with a bag of goodies such as chocolates, potato chips and ice cream—goodies that were never on the list.

Why does this happen? We neglect to guard our sense faculties. The visuals, the memories of the test buds and overt corporate branding lead to desires being triggered in the subconscious mind.

If we want to prevent this, we need to gain control over our senses. Krishna says that a calm and wise person is able to restrain their senses like a tortoise that draws in its limbs when sensing danger. Restraint of the senses means making sure that they are in harmony with their objects.

We have a lot to learn from tortoises. Every time a tortoise senses danger, it withdraws its limbs into its shell, which is strong enough to withstand any adverse situation. Once it senses that the situation has passed, out come the limbs again. Similarly, if we detect that an object, person or situation is about to disturb our equanimity, we should bring our discriminatory intellect to bear and completely withdraw our attention from that object, person or situation.

Gita 2: 59

People, when fasting, restrain the desires of the body. For such people, even the longing to enjoy the senses goes away. When this happens, they are called *param drishtva* (people who have seen the ultimate reality).

How fasting helps

Fasting means choosing not to eat food—sometimes not even drinking water—for a period of time. We may not eat for several hours, only have one meal a day, have no meal at all for 24 hours or eat nothing for several days. Some people may drink only fruit juices or warm water during a fast. Fasting may offer unexpected health and mental benefits.

When we fast, our body goes through autophagy, which has been linked to mental clarity. While fasting, the energy we normally use to digest food is available to be used by the brain.

It is likely that we won't notice this mental change until the first few days of a fast because our body takes time to adjust. But once the body is clear of toxins, our brain has access to a cleaner bloodstream, resulting in clearer thoughts, better memory and increased sharpness in our senses. Krishna says that by fasting, we may even stop longing for the enjoyment provided by the senses.

A calm and wise person fasts regularly to develop such restraint over the senses.

Gita 2: 60

O Kaunteya, the *indriyas* (senses) are so intense that they can tempt the mind of even the *sthitpragnya* who is ever striving (to restrain the *indriyas*).

Don't fall for temptation.

The word 'temptation' is often used to indicate that we are craving something that we are better off avoiding.

Temptation is about desiring something that is not right or good. Temptations force us to fulfil some desires in the short term without thinking about the consequences. When we give in to temptation, we may feel guilt or dissatisfaction about our own vulnerability.

Temptations overcome the do's and don'ts and provide strength to the underlying thought that it is fine to indulge just once. Krishna says that temptations are so strong that even a calm person may fall for them.

Gita 2: 61

Having restrained them all, they sit contemplating on the Supreme. For those who have all their senses under control, their *prajna* is steadfast.

Dedicated and devoted

A calm and wise person is dedicated to the task and devoted to a higher being. Dedication refers to commitment to a task or purpose. When we are dedicated towards something, we put a lot of effort into that task.

Devotion represents a strong feeling of love or loyalty towards another—a person, an ideal or a higher being. Since such persons have restraint over the senses, their mind and intellect are unwavering and steady. This helps in moving towards total dedication and devotion.

Gita 2: 62

When people constantly think about sense objects, they develop a temptation for them; this temptation grows into desire, and any obstruction in fulfilling desires triggers anger.

Why do we become angry?

When we continue to think about the enjoyment we can gain from worldly objects, we become attached to them. We want to acquire them and possess them. If the fulfilment of the desire is frustrated for some reason, we become angry. This anger is directed at the reasons or the people who have obstructed the attainment of our desires. Here are some reasons why people become angry:

- They desire respect but are treated unfairly.
- They feel violated, threatened or attacked.
- They are frightened.
- They are interrupted when they are trying to achieve a goal.
- They feel powerless or hopeless.
- They desire to acquire or possess things and are unable to do so.

We witness different types of anger in people, such as physical anger (violence), stress anger (rage), passive-aggressive anger (controlled rage), verbal anger (abusiveness), retaliatory anger (revenge) and repressed anger (bottled-up rage).

Our turbulent senses can ruin the mind. What we need to do is set a goal that is higher than ourselves and channel our mind and senses towards that higher goal. The senses, along with the mind, will detach from material objects only when they are shown a higher goal. They cannot detach without attaching themselves to a higher goal. Otherwise, we end up forcibly suppressing the senses, which is not healthy.

Constant thinking about material objects leads to a fall from equanimity. If the mind and senses constantly wander, our psyche is agitated. An agitated psyche will never allow the intellect to focus.

For most of us, the world of material objects is our end goal. We are always attracted to them. But if we constantly strive for equanimity, the world of material objects loses its importance.

Gita 2: 63

From anger comes delusion, and delusion leads to disregard for *smruti* (established rules and regulations). A disregard for *smruti* destroys *buddhi* (discriminative power of intellect), and destruction of *buddhi* leads to total breakdown.

Consequences of anger: total breakdown

Many people don't see anger as a problem. When frustrating things happen, for example, a disagreement in relationships or criticism at work, we think we can handle the situation. But if the anger is not expressed by blowing up, we may suffer consequences later.

When there is anger, we feel deluded, deceived, conned or duped. From this delusion comes the disregard for established rules and regulations. When there is disregard for rules and regulations, our discriminatory power of intellect vanishes and we start justifying the unjustifiable. There is a total breakdown.

A 'total breakdown' or 'mental breakdown' means a period of intense mental distress or illness that occurs suddenly. During this period, we may be unable to function in our everyday life.

Gita 2: 64

But those with a restrained mind remain peaceful and free from passion and revulsion, even while moving through sense objects.

Are you a passionate person?

There are certain qualities of passionate people:

- Passionate people are typically very opinionated, and they are not afraid to share their views with others.
- Passionate people are curious by nature, and they want to know more about everything.
- Passionate people are very excited about their work and hobbies, and they derive a lot of enjoyment out of them.
- Passionate people have certain standards of performance, and they are never satisfied with mediocrity.
- Passionate people are very competitive, and they always want to win.
- Passionate people are never content with what they have.
- Passionate people don't wait for opportunities; they create them.
- Passionate people are often willing to take disproportionate risks.

- Passionate people understand that pursuing their passions will make them happy, and they are willing to do whatever it takes to achieve that.

Though this is very exciting to read, passionate people are susceptible to the dualities of pleasure and pain, gain and loss, or victory and defeat. They cannot remain calm. It is difficult for them to decide the right thing to do.

A person with a restrained mind and intellect develops strong willpower. Even if a lot of tempting objects are nearby, such a person remains unaffected.

Gita 2: 65–66

Such people whose sufferings are destroyed are surely at peace and of joyful mind. Soon, the intellect becomes steady. People whose senses are not restrained cannot have a focused *buddhi*.

Without a focused *buddhi*, they cannot contemplate, and without contemplation, there is no peace. How can there be happiness without peace?

No happiness without peace

Peace of mind, or inner calm, is an internal state of tranquillity. When we have mental peace, we might feel at ease with ourselves and are prepared to welcome whatever life throws our way. The feeling of internal peace can boost overall contentment and happiness, regardless of the challenges we face.

We can find peace of mind by accepting what cannot be controlled. Peace of mind is a feeling of being safe and protected. It also indicates the mental state of being without worry, anxiety and stress. Peace begins in the mind and happiness is its parallel. Thus, one who has peace of mind finds happiness in every place.

Happiness depends on external objects and the fulfilment of desires. Peace is quietness and inner feeling. We want to share our happiness with others, whereas in peace, we want to remain alone.

A monk used to walk from one place to another with a few of his followers. In one such journey, they came across a lake. The monk was feeling thirsty, so he told one of his disciples to get some water from the lake.

When the disciple reached the lake, he saw that some people were washing clothes in the water and a bullock cart was also crossing the lake. He saw that the water was very muddy. He returned and told the monk about the muddy water, which he said was unfit to drink.

The monk waited for half an hour and asked the same disciple to go back to the lake and get him some water. This time, he found that the water was clean. The mud had settled down. So, he brought some water in a pot to the monk.

The monk told the disciple to learn from this observation that when time was given for the mud to settle, the water became clean. Our mind is also like that. When it is agitated in sadness or excited in joy, just let it be. It will settle down on its own. It will become quiet. You will discover peace. We don't have to put in any effort to calm it down. It is effortless. Having 'peace of mind' is not a demanding job; it is an effortless process.

When the mind and intellect are quiet and focused, we

can be free. This inner freedom helps to free one's mind of undesirable motives like greed, hatred and delusion.

Gita 2: 67

For, when the mind follows the *indriyas* (senses) to experience sense objects, the *prajna* is carried away by them as the wind carries away a ship on the waters.

We are prisoners of our senses.

In the book *The Republic* by Plato in 360 BCE, Socrates describes a group of prisoners who have lived chained to the wall of a cave for their entire lives, unable to move their heads. Every day, they watch shadows projected on a blank wall from things passing in front of a fire which is behind them. This is their reality.

If one prisoner is freed and allowed to turn his head, he would realise that the shadows which he thought were real were just illusions cast by the fire. If the prisoner were to walk out of the cave and into the sunshine and then see his reflection in the water reservoir nearby, he would be even more confused. If he came back to the cave and talked about the sunshine and his own reflection, would the other prisoners believe him?

A wise person is like a prisoner who has been released from the cave. He has seen reality in a completely different way from other people. This allegory describes our limitations as human beings. We are the prisoners, and the cave is the human condition. We are deceived by what our senses experience.

When we experience sense objects, our mind is carried away like the wind carries a ship on the water.

Gita 2: 70

Just like the ocean remains unmoved though water enters it from all sides, so do those people remain undisturbed by desires who have no desire for desires.

Let there be no desire for desires.

Once we delve into desire fulfilment, we cannot escape being touched by it. That feeling of wanting, or having a desire, is a restless, dissatisfied feeling. We are moved by the feeling of how we would react when we get the thing we want. We think we will finally be happy and satisfied. But this is an endless cycle of pain and pleasure and gain and loss.

It is not the desire itself that causes suffering; it is the attachment and craving for what is desired that causes suffering. Letting go of desires (as best as we can) can be a very freeing experience.

We may continue to have everyday desires for our survival, but we should not be affected by them. Krishna gives an example of the ocean, which remains unmoved and unchanged though water is continuously entering it from many sides.

The state of *sthitpragnya* is like a deep, large ocean that has many streams of water entering it. No matter how many streams enter the ocean, regardless of how gently or how forcefully they enter it, the ocean always remains calm and undisturbed.

There are four lessons for us from this question of Arjuna:

1. Give up selfish desires.
2. Give up cravings for things we already possess.
3. Eliminate even the slightest trace of selfishness.
4. Give up the sense of 'I-ness' and 'mine-ness'.

Gita 2: 71

People who live by abandoning all desires, free from longings, devoid of mine-ness (ownership) and devoid of false ego, they attain peace.

How to attain peace

In the frantic pace of everyday life, we need serenity the most. There are ways to experience inner peace:

- We need to know which things are within our control. Anything beyond those things can distract and create stress in our life.
- We should spend some time in nature, with birds and trees.
- We should have no pretensions. We should make our own decisions based on our true nature rather than to impress others.
- Follow the golden rule: 'Do unto others as you would have them do unto you.'
- We should stop trying to change others. We will have as much success as we would if we tried to change the weather.
- When we have abandoned all desires, are free from temptations and have moved away from the ego of I, Me, and Myself, Krishna says that we can attain peace.

Why are we unable to stay calm? What stands between us and our inner peace and tranquillity?

The answer is very simple. Our *indriyas*—senses—have the power to destabilize the mind and consequently destroy the intellect's capability to make proper judgements. Our senses create desires in us. If we are not careful, then even a stray thought about a material object will escalate into a chain of events that will bring about the destruction of peace.

Krishna advises us to monitor our desires, that is, track how they are arising, how they are being fulfilled and so on. Continual harbouring of material desires has the effect of destabilizing our mental balance, which takes us further away from a state of equanimity. Therefore, a man of steady wisdom is one who has learnt to monitor all such desires.

QUESTION 3

IS KNOWLEDGE SUPERIOR TO ACTION?

This is the era of the knowledge economy. We believe that knowledge is power and that success depends on how much a person knows. Knowledge is indeed power, but knowledge without action can be useless.

In our modern education system, we spend all of our childhood and the early part of our young age acquiring information and knowledge. We don't need most of it, but it helps us in understanding the world around us. Knowledge is power only when it is turned into a skill through action.

There is an enormous appetite for acquiring information. We use the internet and can access most of the information we need. The smartphone has replaced newspapers and libraries, which were sources of information earlier. Many of us have become experts through WhatsApp university and Instagram. But how much of that information is truly actionable? There is a big difference between knowing something and understanding it. Knowledge is power only when we truly comprehend it. Wisdom involves internalising a concept.

When we understand something, it changes the way we think and behave, whereas merely knowing something makes no difference to our life. Knowledge is power only when it changes our life.

At the beginning of his argument, Krishna emphasises action based on one's true nature and the need to act without expecting any rewards. While explaining the importance of action without expecting any results, Krishna points out the importance of knowledge.

Now, Arjuna says he is confused and wants to know whether knowledge is superior to action.

Gita 3: 1–2

Arjuna said: O Janardana, if knowledge is superior to action, then why are you advising me to engage in this horrible action, O Keshava?

You confuse my *buddhi* with statements that seem to contradict each other. Tell me for certain that one way by which I could attain *shreyas* (highest good).

Why do we get confused?

Intellect is our capacity to think through reason. It is not intelligence, which can be acquired from books, teachings or life experiences. Intellect can be trained by self-discipline. It enables us to take decisions with integrity and clarity. It has its own discriminatory power, but this discrimination cannot be developed on its own and is often attained with practice.

There are plenty of external experiences that contribute to the functioning of our intellect. Different situations influence us when we use our intellect. Contemplation is one such activity, where the discriminatory power of intellect guides us to do the right thing.

Many inept people—those who have not trained their intellect—tend to resort to gaining control of the situation by any means possible. The natural response is the intuitive reaction, which happens without any reasoning or deep assessment. In this process, we remain complacent with the way we are and derive comfort in proclaiming, 'This is the way I am'.

In situations where we lose control of the narrative, we become more attached to our own arguments. We continue to do that even if it means behaving irrationally. When we are not in control of events, our mind becomes increasingly anxious and stressful, resulting in an anxiety or panic attack.

Arjuna is confused because Krishna's arguments are contrary to his thought flow.

Gita 3: 3

O Anagha (Arjuna, the sinless one), I have created a two-fold path in this world, *jnana yoga* (the path of knowledge) for those who are interested in *Samkhya* (principles of *prakriti* and *purusha*) and *karma yoga* (the path of action) for the *yogis*.

Path of action and path of knowledge

There are two distinct paths: the path of knowledge and the path of action. Both paths are important based on the true nature of a person. Krishna rightly understands the confusion in Arjuna's mind. Essentially, Arjuna wanted to know which of the two paths is superior. Krishna addresses that question here. According to him, neither of the two is either superior or inferior.

Jnana yoga begins as an intellectual enquiry into the true nature of reality. A person on the path of knowledge sees the Self in all and all in the Self. In *karma yoga*, a person works without any attachment to the fruits of their action. This requires the cultivation of knowledge in the intellect. Hence, knowledge is also necessary for success in *karma yoga*.

Gita 3: 4

People do not attain freedom from action by abstaining from action, nor do they attain *siddhi* (self-actualization) merely through renunciation.

Self-actualization

One cannot reach self-actualization by merely following one path. Those who follow the path of knowledge must act, and those who follow the path of action must contemplate.

One cannot achieve freedom from the cycle of birth and rebirth by merely abstaining from work, nor can one attain perfection of knowledge by mere renunciation. Our mind continues to engage in fruitful thoughts. Since mental work is also a form of *karma*, it binds us, just as physical work.

There is a story in the Mahabharata. This is the story of a disciple who left his home and parents to engage in deep spiritual practices. Once, when he was sitting in meditation under a tree, some bird droppings fell on him. He looked up towards the bird in anger. To his amazement, he saw that the bird dropped down dead, burnt to ashes.

Later, he went for *bhiksha* in a nearby village. He went to a house and asked for some alms. There was a delay, and he started getting angry. Suddenly, he heard a voice from inside the house: 'I am a housewife and doing my duty. When my work is over, I will attend to you. However, I am not a bird who will drop dead and burn to ashes.' The disciple was surprised. He asked the housewife later how she had attained this high state of knowledge. She said she just performed her duty, and if he wanted to know more, he was welcome to go and meet her guru.

He left for the address given. To his surprise, the guru was a butcher. When the disciple started to ask a question, the butcher said that he knew he had been directed there by the housewife. He asked to be given some time to finish his work first, and then they could go home and talk. Sitting there, the disciple realised that the housewife and the butcher were doing their *karma* without any attachment or any expectation of reward. They had attained this high spiritual state through *karma yoga*. On the other hand, he was just a slave of anger and full of pride in his knowledge. He realised that there was no need to run away from home and go to a forest—shirking responsibilities—to attain that high spiritual state.

Gita 3: 5

There is no one who can remain without action even for a moment. Indeed, everyone is compelled to act by their *gunas* (mental tendencies) born out of *prakriti* (Mother Nature).

We cannot live without action.

It is our nature to perform actions. We cannot remain without action for even a moment as our mind cannot remain still.

Action does not only refer to professional work. Action also refers to our daily activities, such as eating, drinking, sleeping, waking and thinking. All activities performed with the body, mind and tongue are actions. Therefore, Krishna tells Arjuna that inactivity is impossible even for a moment. When we sit down, it is an activity. If we lie down, that is also an activity. If we fall asleep, the mind is still busy dreaming. Even in deep sleep, the heart and other organs are functioning.

Krishna points out to Arjuna that all of us have no choice but to act because all beings are governed by *trigunas*. He explains that *prakriti* is nothing but the three *gunas*—energies or forces that make up this entire universe. These three energies are *rajas*, which causes movement, *tamas*, which causes inertia, and *sattva*, which maintains harmony between movement and inertia.

Gita 3: 6

Those who restrain the *karmendriyas* (sense organs of action), while continuing to think about the sense objects in the mind, may be called misguided, stupid characters.

Who is a stupid person?

Attracted by the lure of renunciation, some people renounce their work, only to find that their renunciation is not supported by an equal amount of mental and intellectual withdrawal from the enjoyment of the senses. This is total hypocricy, where one displays an external show of spirituality while internally living a life of despicable base motives.

The Puranas tell the story of two brothers, Tavrit and Suvrit. The brothers were walking from their house to listen to a spiritual discourse at the temple. On the way, it started raining, so they ran to take shelter in the nearest house. The house was part of a brothel. Tavrit was disgusted and walked out to go to the temple. The younger brother, Suvrit, remained there for the rain to stop.

Tavrit reached the temple and was listening to the discourse, but in his mind, he became regretful. 'I should have remained at the brothel', he thought. 'My brother must be enjoying himself there.' Suvrit, on the other hand, was thinking, 'My brother is so pious. I too should have braved the rain and listened to the discourse.'

The brothers met when the rain stopped. But the moment they met, lightning struck them, and they died on the spot. The *yamdoots* were taking Tavrit to hell. Tavrit complained, 'You are making a mistake. I was at the spiritual discourse. It was my brother who was sitting at the brothel.' The *yamdoots* replied, 'We are making no mistake. He was sitting there, but he was thinking of the Divine, whereas you were sitting in the temple but thinking of the beautiful women at the brothel.'

Krishna calls such a person as stupid. Most of us tend to repress our emotions or try to give up actions in our life. Repressing our urges and giving up actions does not work. Krishna says that we should not give up actions; instead, we should give up attachment.

Gita 3: 7

O Arjuna, but they are unique, who restrain their senses by the mind and perform their actions without attachment.

Performing actions without attachment

When we perform actions with attachment, the reactions of ill-will and hatred are born from our attachments to worldly pleasure and happiness. Similarly, thoughts of greed and lust and resulting actions also arise from acting upon a desire for the things or people we like.

A *karma yogi*, even when performing worldly duties, keeps the mind attached to a higher being, the Supreme Brahman. Such a *karma yogi* is not bound by *karma* even while performing all kinds of work. This is because what binds one to the world is not actions, but the attachment to the results of those actions. A *karma yogi* has no attachment to the rewards of action.

There is a story about a man who had gone travelling, and upon his return, finds that his house is on fire. This loss saddens him. Suddenly, one of his three sons comes running and whispers to him that he had sold the house the day before at a very good price. Since the offer was good, the son had gone ahead without waiting for the father. With this news, everything changes about the man. He is relaxed and becomes a silent watcher just like the others.

Then, the second son comes running and says, 'We took only the token amount for the sale. I doubt that the purchaser will pay up now.' The father's mood changes, and he starts crying for his loss.

Then the third son comes to tell the father, 'That man is a man of his word. I have just met him. It didn't matter to him that the house was on fire; he said it was his. He will pay us the price that he had settled for. After all, nobody knew that the house would catch fire.'

Again, the joy is back on the father's face. Just the feeling that 'I am the owner of the house' made all the difference.

Gita 3: 8

You must perform your *niyata karma* (mundane everyday actions). *Karma* is superior to *akarma* (inaction). Even the sustenance of the body is not possible if you remain inactive.

Karma, akarma and *vikarma*

Hindu scriptures explain three types of *karma—karma*, *akarma* and *vikarma*.

Karma means movement in the external world, and cessation of any such movement amounts to *akarma* (inaction). However, many learned people have explained the meaning of 'action' and 'inaction' differently. According to them, the thinking process too is 'action'. Any 'action' performed without the notion of ownership, where the doer is not affected by the fruit of action, can also be understood as *akarma* (inaction).

Hindu scriptures have classified actions into several categories. There are two main classifications: *niyatam*, or prescribed actions, and *nishiddha*, or forbidden actions (*vikarma*). Prescribed actions are those that are enjoined in the scriptures. In today's context, we may interpret them as one's duties.

Niyat karmas include performing one's *svadharma*, attending to one's parents and family, and working for the development of one's nation. Forbidden actions include killing another being, stealing, cheating and so on. Krishna urges Arjuna to perform prescribed actions but without any attachment to the action or its fruit.

Gita 3: 9

All actions other than *yajnaarth karma* (actions for the welfare of others) bind us to this world. Hence, O Kaunteya, perform actions free from attachment.

Work for the welfare of others.

Work in itself is neither good nor bad. Depending on the state of mind and the motive, it could turn out to be good or bad. A knife in the hands of a murderer is a weapon, but in the hands of a surgeon, it is an instrument to save people's lives. The act of the knife in itself is neither murderous nor benedictory, and its outcome is determined by how it is used.

All actions can be either binding or elevating. Any work done for enjoyment through one's senses is the cause of returning to the material world, while work performed for the welfare of others, without attachment, liberates one from the world.

Gita 3: 10

At the beginning of this world, Prajapati (originator of this world) created *yajna* (*yaj* means worship, and *yajna* means work as worship), and said, 'The performance of *yajna* will fulfil all your desires'.

Work as worship

When we do the right thing, work becomes worship.

In *karma yoga*, we perform our actions without attachment, without expecting any results, and we perform them selflessly. Individuals who work selflessly seldom think about themselves. Their vision is broad. Such actions, performed with devotion and undertaken for the welfare of others, comprise *yajna*. The output of this *yajna* is an environment that is charged with the potential to create almost anything.

Gita 3: 11

When you gratify *Deva* (good spirits, divinities) by this (*yajna*), they will be pleased with you. Thus by making each other happy, you will attain *shreyas* (the highest good).

What is the highest good?

In the beginning, Arjuna wanted Krishna's advice to clear his confusion and show the path to the attainment of *shreyas*—the highest good. *Shreyas* can be for an individual or the whole world.

Shreyas symbolizes the good and deals with virtues, strengths and right actions. *Shreyas* is a Sanskrit word meaning 'that action which brings happiness'. It also means 'auspicious' or 'conducive to well-being and prosperity'.

Karma yoga deals with the good of all or absolute good. For example, universal health care is good-for-all *shreyas*, whereas the effort of an individual to take care of their own health is *shreyas* at the individual level.

At the mental level, *shreyas* is peace of mind. We all aspire to have a calm and peaceful mind. *Shreyas* at the intellectual level is clarity of thought. At the spiritual level, *shreyas* is joy in the mind and heart. This joy is not dependent on any factor, thing, being, time, place or situation.

Therefore, being at peace in the body, mind and intellect in every situation is *shreyas*.

Gita 3: 12

Pleased by the performance of *yajna*, *Deva* will give you desired *bhoga* (basic needs of your existence). Anyone who enjoys them without sharing them with others is a thug.

Need to share and care

The human race has flourished in all fields because it shares knowledge, resources and experiences. We have been sharing food, water and shelter right from the beginning of the known history of humankind. By sharing, we save time and energy.

Sharing helps in building trust, confidence and security. When we share our moments of joy, it multiplies happiness.

All actions should be performed for the welfare of others. We need to make our contributions to society. A person who perform actions for only selfish gains is described here as a 'thief'. Such selfish persons do not care about anyone but themselves because of their large egos.

Gita 3: 13

Sants (pious people) share their food with others first and then enjoy them; so, they are free from any *kilbish* (guilt, remorse, shame). Those who cook food only for their own needs commit *paapa* (crime).

Not sharing is a crime.

Sharing food is an act of humanity, care, consideration and compassion for others in any way, shape or form. We share food with the poor out of compassion—the feeling that arises on witnessing another's suffering and motivates a subsequent desire to help.

Sharing happens also because of empathy—the natural ability to perceive and be sensitive to the emotional state of others, coupled with the motivation to care for their well-being.

I read a story of a man who used to buy fruits and vegetables from a lady who was more than 80 years old. A vegetable vendor sitting next to her observed that the man would tell her that the fruits she was selling were rotten and that she must taste them. The old woman would take a bite and tell the man that the fruits were good. The man would then buy the fruits.

The incident was repeated for several days. Curious, the vegetable vendor asked the old lady, 'Why do you entertain this fellow?'

The old woman replied, 'I know that he cares about me. He wants to ensure that I eat a fruit every day from the fruits he has bought. He thinks I am not aware of his kindness, but I am.'

Sharing and caring go together. Krishna says that if we cook food for only our own consumption, it is a *paapa*. We must share it with others.

Gita 3: 17

But for those who are *atma-rati* (rejoice in the Self), *atma-trupta* (self-satisfied) and *atma-santushta* (self-contented), nothing remains to be accomplished.

Enjoy the Self.

Only those who have given up desires for external objects can rejoice and be satisfied and content in the Self. This may also be called self-actualization.

The state of self-actualization means 'becoming everything you are capable of becoming'. It can also be explained as the 'ability to become the best version of yourself.'

How can one achieve self-actualization? There is no unique way. We have to find our own way to hear the inner wisdom that can help us live a life of truth.

Karma yoga is one way to achieve self-actualization.

Gita 3: 18–19

For such people, there is no anxiety about doing or not doing any action. They also do not depend on other living beings to fulfil their needs.

Therefore, always perform your *karma* without attachment, because by performing your *karma* without attachment, you can attain the highest good.

Perform your karma without attachment to attain the highest good.

Karma is not just work or action. It is a deeper understanding of our actions along with their effect on our body, mind and intellect. *Karma* includes all actions—work, speech, and thoughts—as well as the motives and intent behind them. It also includes the reaction of our *karma* that remains in our minds in the form of impressions and memories.

Therefore, right from our childhood, we should learn to manage our thoughts and emotions. We need to learn how to move away from the cycles of pain and pleasure as a result of *karma*.

If we learn to be free from attachment to our *karma* and its results, we will be free from pain and pleasure. We will be free from the reactions in our minds, such as greed, anger, lust and so on. Those who are attached to their actions and the results of those actions—good or bad—can focus on the performance of their actions and attain perfection in their field of action. We become steadfast in our actions. With continuous practice and focus, we attain the state of perfection.

Gita 3: 20

Janaka achieved self-actualization by performing his *karma* for others. Therefore, you should perform your actions for *lokasangraha* (welfare of society).

Work for *loksangraha*—the welfare of society.

Krishna says that King Janaka, the father of Sita, was a self-actualized king who worked for *lokasangraha*. He is the best example of a leader who works for the welfare of all.

Lokmanya Bal Gangadhar Tilak, the visionary freedom fighter, wrote a commentary on the Bhagavad Gita, *Srimad Bhagvad Gita Rahasya* (1936). He laid great emphasis on the concept of *lokasangraha* in the Gita.

Loka means humankind or the world, and *sangraha* stands for protection. The word *lokasangraha* means social harmony and welfare of the world. *Lokasangraha* means welfare for all. It is the duty of every individual to work towards social integration and a peaceful society. The philosophy of *lokasangraha* was interpreted by Tilak as a dynamic doctrine for action for the welfare of the world.

Lokasangraha has three components:

1. Creating and maintaining harmonious relationships between people
2. Being kind and compassionate to all, treating all with respect and dignity and giving a helping hand whenever the opportunity arises
3. Preserving the environment from pollution and avoiding the exploitation of natural resources

Gita 3: 21

The way a great leader behaves, people behave in the same manner. Whatever standards such a leader sets, people start following them.

People follow the leader in every aspect.

Leaders are the heroes of the people. They motivate us to go places that we would never otherwise go. Followers may fall into two categories: rational and irrational. The rational ones are conscious and hope to gain money, status or power; irrational followers just imitate what leaders do.

Most followers have some basic needs:

- Trust
- Compassion
- Stability
- Hope

Leaders need to behave in a consistent, reliable manner, be open with information and walk the talk when it comes to ethics and values. Krishna has given an important leadership lesson here: The best way to lead is to lead by example.

Gita 3: 26

Wise people should not create conflict in the mind of ignorant people who are attached to the results of *karma*. They should inspire them by performing their own *karma* diligently.

Avoid conflict with ignorant people.

We often encounter people who choose to ignore the facts or refuse to understand the situation. We may find their ignorance frustrating. It becomes very difficult to deal with them. In such situations, we try to train them or teach them. But the best way is to inspire them with our own example rather than creating a conflict.

Those who are leaders of society need to set an example by their actions and behaviour. Krishna gives his own example: Even he has to perform *karma* like everyone else.

When we are working with others, we should learn to work in harmony. We should not thrust our ideals on others, who may have not yet understood the concept of action without attachment and without expecting any results.

Gita 3: 27

All *karma* is performed due to the influence of the *gunas* of *prakriti* (Mother Nature). But because of the ego and false identification with the body, you think, 'I am the doer'.

I am not the doer.

We identify ourselves with the body. When we do something, we say, 'I am doing, I am eating, I am drinking'. It is 'I' who takes credit for all the actions that are being done by our body. Krishna says that it is the *guna* which is the cause of all our actions. Due to false identification with the body, we think, 'I am the doer'.

The 'I' which we think of is not the Self. The 'I' which we use is the ego which claims ownership of the body and mind. What we call 'I' cannot do anything. But once the action is done, the ego will immediately claim that it has done that particular action.

Who is the doer?

Samkhya philosophy states that *prakriti* (Mother Nature) is constituted of three *gunas: sattva* (goodness), *rajas* (desires and emotions) and *tamas* (inertia, that is, resistance to change). We need to understand that 'I don't do anything'. The *guna* energy (*sattva, rajas* and *tamas*) within this body is making things happen. The composition of these three *gunas* influences the uniqueness of our thoughts and behaviour. Our personality is influenced by these three *gunas,* and their composition affects our physical, mental and intellectual competence.

We believe that we are performing our *karma,* but Krishna says that it is the composition of *trigunas* which drives us to act. He says that when we don't understand this, we think that 'I am the doer'. When we begin to understand this relationship, we will not get attached to our actions. When we understand this, we will be able to perform our actions without expecting results because we know that 'I am not the doer'. Finally, while emphasizing the importance of performing actions, Krishna says the following:

Gita 3: 28

O Mahabaho! those who understand correctly the relation of the *gunas* to *karma* (action) are not attached to the act. They understand that it is merely the action and reaction of the *gunas*.

Relationship of *guna* to *karma*

Krishna explains why it is difficult to follow the path of action. Our sense organs are like agents that send messages to the mind when they perceive an object. For example, if we hold a rose in our hand, the eyes, skin and nose send different signals to the mind. The mind creates a picture of the rose from all those signals: 'This is a red rose'. The signal goes to the intellect. The intellect analyzes that information and makes a decision: 'I want this rose', after consulting its memory of past pleasant experiences with roses. Krishna says that a wise person understands that all the above actions take place because of the nature of *trigunas*.

Those who understand 'I am not the doer' are not attached to *gunas* and their influence on our actions.

Gita 3: 29

Those who do not understand the nature of the *gunas* are attached to the results of their actions. The wise, who understand the relation of *gunas* and *karma*, should not upset such people till they understand the truth.

Understand the play of *trigunas*.

The Sanskrit term *guna*, in its ordinary sense, means the 'quality', 'energies' or 'characteristics' of nature. *Sattva* defines goodness—the energy that is spiritual in nature. *Rajas* is concerned with passionate action—the emotional energy that drives action. *Tamas* is associated with inertia—the inertia of the body. These three energies are eternally bound to one another and are in a constant state of flux. They each try to overpower, support, produce and intimately mix with each other.

Once we understand this, we realize that all the results of our actions are merely the play of *triguna* in our body, mind and intellect. Since we are not the doer, we cannot take credit for the results. Once we understand this, we will not be attached to the results of our actions.

Krishna says that those who don't understand this, or are not willing to understand this, should not be pressurized to accept this reality and get upset, till they understand the truth.

Gita 3: 30

Therefore, renounce all *karma* unto Me completely. With a focused mind, free from desires and selfish motives, fight without any nervousness.

Be free from any nervousness and anxiety.

There is a story in the Chhandogya Upanishad (6:14), which is a parable of the blindfolded man. The robbers blindfold a man and rob him. After robbing him, they leave him outside the city of Gandhara in a forest. The man has no idea how to get back to his house and his family in the city of Gandhara. He is helpless, nervous and full of anxiety. At this point, a wise man meets him and gives him instructions to reach the city. The blindfolded man follows these instructions and reaches home. The man appreciates that even though the robbers had robbed him and ill-treated him, there were people who were willing to help him without any desire of gain or any selfish motive.

We should follow the life of the wise man and not that of the robbers. We should not work with a selfish motive but always dedicate the action to a higher ideal. It can be any higher ideal, such as supporting our family, giving our best to our employer or dedicating ourselves to the nation, or surrendering our life to the Divine.

We should use our intellect and knowledge to follow a righteous way of life and perform our duty without expecting any results. Actions that are unethical or illegal should be discarded by the intellect.

Our mental energy and focus get weakened through three sources: memories of the past, excitement for the present and anxiety of the future. Once we overcome this anxiety, we can perform our actions without being nervous. A *karma yogi* always lives in the present moment and gives complete and undivided attention to the task at hand, no matter what kind of task it is.

Gita 3: 31–32

People who follow this philosophy of Mine with sincere faith and without doubt become free from the results of their *karma*.

But those who criticize My point of view and do not follow it are totally ignorant and live in a state of constant confusion.

Act with faith and without any doubt.

Krishna has explained the path of knowledge (*jnana yoga*) and the path of action (*karma yoga*) in an answer to the question: 'Is knowledge superior to action?' We can follow either of the paths to do the right thing.

But even before we follow anyone, we need to have faith in the person who is teaching us. If we doubt the content and the concept, we will not fully apply what we have learnt and understood.

Krishna says that those who have faith in him will be free from the results of their *karma*, but those who criticize and doubt will remain in a constant state of confusion.

Therefore, once we learn something from a guru, we should follow it with faith and without doubt, unless proven otherwise.

Gita 3: 33

Even wise people act according to their true nature because all living beings are driven by their true nature (*guna*—mental tendencies). What, then, can self-restraint do?

We are driven by our true nature.

When we are under the influence of desires, our actions will be prompted by selfish motives. These motives are expressed as negative emotions, such as jealousy: 'I will do things to make others jealous', anger: 'I will destroy this person', or greed: 'I will earn immense wealth even if it means I compromise on ethics'. When we dwell on such negative emotions, our intellect knows that what we are doing is wrong. But since our desires have overpowered the intellect, it stops guiding us.

Explaining the play of *triguna*, Krishna points out that these tendencies manifest as likes and dislikes for material objects. These likes and dislikes reside in our sense organs. The tongue is attracted to the taste of certain food and is repelled by other food. The eyes like a certain kind of form and are repelled by another form.

Therefore, Krishna says that mere self-restraint will not result in the eradication of desires. Direct suppression of thoughts is almost impossible. When we try to repress thoughts and desires in the hope of progressing spiritually, the strategy may backfire very easily.

Gita 3: 34

There is inherent attraction and repulsion for each sense organ and corresponding sense object. One should not come under the influence of either of these two forces.

Beware of the feelings of love and hate.

Love and hate, attraction and repulsion are very basic human feelings. Love has been explained as an action, attitude, experience and even as a classical emotion. Hate arises mainly from a personal betrayal, with negative attitudes, anger and fear.

Attraction is a very important component in the development of love. We have different emotional reactions towards different people in the context of love and hate. There is always a thin line between love and hate.

Krishna cautions that we should not fall into the trap of love and hate. They create intense feelings and may take us away from the path of *karma yoga* or *jnana yoga*.

Gita 3: 35

It is better to do your own *karma*, however lacking it may be in importance, than to do that of another, even though it looks glamorous. It is better to even die doing one's own *karma*, since performing someone else's *karma* has serious consequences.

Do your own *karma*.

If we have strong likes and dislikes, it is possible that we may love some type of work and hate another type of work. Sometimes, we don't like the work we are doing because we feel that our work is inferior to that of others. We might even get attracted to other professions because they look glamorous.

When we don't like our work, there is a possibility of jealousy, anger and greed. If we have to avoid that, we should be aware of our true nature and our *svadharma*.

A person with a strong desire to fight can become a soldier if they use their *svadharma* in the service of their country. But the person can also become a gangster if their *svadharma* is not dedicated to a higher ideal. Therefore, once we have selected a strong desire as our *svadharma*, we should not let weaker likes or dislikes distract us from the *svadharma*.

Krishna says that it is better to do our own *karma*, however lacking in glamour, than to do the *karma* of another person, however trendy that might appear.

QUESTION 4

WHY DO PEOPLE COMMIT AN IMMORAL ACT?

The struggle to do the right thing is a lifelong struggle. The battle between right and wrong is a continuous one. The basic questions are: How is it that immorality manages to enter our lives? Why do we commit an immoral act?

The biggest difficulty is that we are driven by our senses. We hardly have any time for reflecting on our actions, which are driven by our senses. Driven by our desires, we act to satisfy our natural impulses. It is the passing interest or pleasure which determines our immediate action. The excitement of the present shields from our view the immorality involved.

Why does this happen? Why do we ignore the higher ideals and purpose of our life?

One of the causes is ignorance about the outcome of our actions. Even when we have the knowledge and wisdom, the impulse to ignore the advice being given by our discriminatory intellect could be strong. We could instead be driven by greed, passion, intense need, fear, attachment or optimism. The desire may be so strong that we are willing to do anything to satisfy it.

Another reason for committing an immoral act could be the influence of our friends and companions. If we keep bad company, there is a higher likelihood of getting involved in immoral acts. We tend to do as others do without weighing or considering the consequences of what we are doing. These social influences include the influence of parents, friends, relatives and other people close to us.

Let us see what Krishna says.

Gita 3: 36

Arjuna asked: O Varshneya (Krishna), what is it that drives people to commit *paapa* (an immoral act), even against their will and as if by compulsion?

Why do we commit *paapa* (an immoral act)?

So far we have understood the path of action and the path of knowledge. We have also been told about the importance of following one's *karma*. The path of knowledge should be able to lead us to the highest moral activity. Krishna also says that the path of knowledge in its way becomes the life of devotion, and extends out into the path of action.

The Indian knowledge system (comprising Shada Darshan—Samkhya, Yoga Darshan, Nyaya, Vaisheshika, Purva Mimansa and Uttar Mimansa, which is also called Vedanta) has a unique understanding of the term *paapa* (generally translated as 'sin'). Here, *paapa* is explained as a person's experience resulting from *dushkarma* (an immoral act) and *punya* (merit) as an experience resulting from *satkarma* (a moral act).

Paapa means impurity in action, which causes hurt, harm and suffering to oneself, to others or to the world. *Paapa* may arise from physical, mental or verbal actions, because of impurities such as selfishness, desire, attachment, egoism, ignorance, delusion and negligence of one's essential duties (*dharma*). If you harm or hurt others or yourself by any means, you infuse your body with the poison of *paapa* and bind yourself to the cycle of birth and death.

Arjuna says that even with all their knowledge and wisdom, people continue to commit *paapa*, even against their will and as if by compulsion. What is it that drives them to commit *paapa*?

Gita 3: 37

Bhagwan said: Know that the desires born from *rajas guna* are the enemy for this all-consuming *mahapaapa* (great immoral acts).

Our desires are our biggest enemy.

We are all born with a particular composition of *trigunas*. These *trigunas* influence our mental tendencies. Our mind gathers data from the senses, responds with emotions, and generates thoughts based on current and past impressions. These thoughts influence our intellect, which makes decisions based on analysis and rationality. When we begin to justify and rationalize our likes and dislikes, it indicates that desire has permeated into our intellect. Then, it becomes extremely difficult to tackle such desires, because they have completely taken hold of us—our senses, our mind and our intellect.

Krishna says that desires born from *rajas guna* are the main cause for people committing immoral acts. Even wise people engage in immoral acts when they are driven by their desires.

When we make decisions based on our likes and dislikes, it increases the proportion of *rajas guna* in our system. When this happens, our likes and dislikes turn into strong desires. Strong desires create more *rajas guna*, which in turn makes the desires even stronger. When such desires remain unfulfilled, they turn into jealousy, anger and hatred, and we start turning a blind eye to morality and values.

Earlier, Krishna stated that likes and dislikes turn us into highway robbers, but now he uses the term 'enemy' to refer to desires. What is the difference between a highway robber and an enemy? A highway robber does not care who we are. But an enemy knows us and knows our weaknesses well. Therefore, desires are much more dangerous than likes and dislikes.

Gita 3: 38

As the fire is covered by smoke, a mirror by dust, an embryo enveloped in the womb, so is this (*paapa*) concealed in that (desire).

Immoral acts are concealed in desires.

Our challenge is to deal with our desires. When desires are fulfilled, we experience peace and happiness. However, most of us wrongfully attribute that temporary moment of happiness to the achievement of our goals. We then move towards fulfilling other desires, which always crop up once we have fulfilled one desire. We go through life fuelling our desires in the hope that we can recreate that experience of happiness. Desires arise from the deeper, subconscious aspects of our mind and conceal this wisdom. When this happens, we lose our ability to differentiate right from wrong.

In this *shloka*, Krishna explains the way *paapa* is hidden and concealed in our efforts to fulfil our desires at any cost.

Wisdom, or the ability to discriminate, is a quality of our intellect. Knowledge of what is right and what is wrong is called discrimination. However, the force of our desires is such a formidable adversary that it clouds the judgement of many people, and they indulge in criminal acts. Here, Krishna describes three levels of loss of discrimination based on our three types of desires—*sattvik* desire to do good, *rajasic* desire to fulfil our wants and *tamasic* desire to resist change. When fire, which is the source of light, is covered by smoke, it obscures the light as if there is a thin cloud over the sun. This is the influence of our *sattvik* desires over our intellect.

The next example is that of a mirror. A mirror, in which we can see our image, stops showing a clear image when it is covered by dust. This is the effect of *paapa* due to *rajasic* desires on the intellect. We stop seeing things clearly. The third example is that of an embryo which is concealed in a womb. We are not even aware of its existence unless it is brought to our notice. This complete failure of discrimination occurs because of *tamasic* desires. Here, *paapa* totally subverts the power of discrimination. Krishna says that we should be extremely careful of the rise of our desires.

Gita 3: 39

O Kaunteya, the knowledge of the wise gets enveloped by this desire, which is the persistent enemy, like an insatiable fire.

Desire is a constant enemy of the wise.

Krishna uses two words to describe desire: enemy and fire. Desires become our enemies when we fall prey to them. Also, once we are in the trap of fulfilling our desires, they never get satiated. The trap of desire fulfilment is like a fire whose intensity keeps increasing. It is the power of likes and dislikes which fuels our desires and makes them stronger. Even the knowledge of the wise gets enveloped by these desires once they rise.

Desires can never be quenched or cooled down through the enjoyment of sense objects. We know that fires keep burning when we feed them with ghee (clarified butter) and wood, and similarly, desires grow when we feed them with objects of enjoyment.

Even a person who owns all of the earth, all precious metals and all living beings would still not be satisfied if they are full of desires. Such a person would consider desire as their friend if they keep craving more objects.

A wise person knows from experience that desires only bring suffering, trouble and misery. We should understand that desire is a constant enemy of the wise but not of the ignorant.

Gita 3: 40

The senses, the mind and the intellect are its (desire's) sanctuary. Everybody is influenced by these (senses, mind and intellect), which in turn clouds the knowledge so acquired.

Desires reside in our body, mind and intellect.

How is a desire born? Desire arises from contact with sense objects by seeing, hearing and touching. The mind is agitated and forces us to make a determined effort to enjoy the sense object.

The desire for the object manifests itself from within

the mind, completely overpowering the intellect and the discriminatory faculties. The person is controlled and deluded and becomes a slave of their senses.

All desires per se are not bad. When we are hungry, appetites and needs that are natural to our bodies have good and healthy purposes. But that same desire, when not properly controlled, can lead to overindulgence. Natural desires are not in themselves *paapa*. The way we fulfil them makes them good or bad. Without desires, our lives would be practically useless. Many times, desires serve as motivating forces in our lives. That is why we need to use our intellect to discriminate between what is good and what is bad. We need to train our mind and intellect to bring in restraint in the way we fulfil our desires.

Gita 3: 41

Therefore, O Bharatarshabha (Arjuna—the best among the Bharatas), first restrain these senses, which are the destroyers of knowledge and wisdom and the source of *paapa*.

Restrain your senses first.

How do we control our desires? Here is a simple rule: By taking care of those who shelter the enemy, the enemy can be conquered. The shelters of desires are our senses, the mind and intellect.

Let us look at an example of two friends who were preparing for an examination. Around midnight, one of the friends said that he needed a cup of coffee to stay awake and wanted the other friend to accompany him. The other friend said, 'I don't need a cup of coffee to stay awake. I am deeply involved in solving a problem, and I am wide awake.' So, the first friend went out in search of a cup of coffee. He kept searching for a coffee shop in the middle of the night. At last, he found a shop and had a good cup of coffee. When he returned, his friend was asleep. It was late, so he went to sleep too.

In the morning, the friend who had gone for a cup of coffee was a little jittery about the examination because he had not prepared for it to his satisfaction. The other friend explained to him, 'You created a desire for a cup of coffee, and to fulfil that desire, you wasted a lot of time. When you had a cup of coffee, you fulfilled the desire which you created. I, on the other hand, did not create any desire and slept peacefully after solving my problem.'

This is the way we create various desires to satisfy our senses. There are five senses: smell, sight, taste, touch and hearing. There are five sense organs to satisfy our senses: nose, eyes, tongue, skin and ears. Some students cannot study unless they are listening to music. We create a desire for music and then get agitated when our preferred music is not available. Krishna calls these sense-driven desires our biggest enemy.

The senses are difficult to restrain, but they are easier to conquer than the mind and the intellect. Therefore, we should try the easy one first. To begin with, we should try to restrain our senses by carefully monitoring our desire for sense objects, such as music, coffee or tea. By restraining the senses, we can cut off the line which feeds the mind and intellect.

Gita 3: 42

The *indriyas* (senses) are superior (to the body), the mind is superior to the *indriyas*, and the intellect is superior to the mind. But what is superior to the intellect is that (willpower).

Your willpower to the rescue

We should not try to restrain the mind and intellect first because of the unlikelihood of controlling them without restraining the senses. The senses are considered superior to the body because all our bodily functions are driven by our senses.

However, the mind is superior to the senses. The mind continues to function even when we are asleep. Compared to the mind, the intellect with its power of discrimination is stronger. During deep sleep, the mind may rest, but the intellect remains active.

Compared to the intellect, willpower is superior in strength because our willpower remains even when one trains the intellect through the practice of *jnana yoga*.

Our willpower is the most powerful instrument of all of them—the body, the senses, the mind and the intellect. We can use our willpower to restrain our senses.

Gita 3: 43

O Mahabaho, even though it may appear extremely difficult, once you know that willpower is superior to the intellect, restrain yourself by your willpower and destroy this enemy (desires).

Restrain your senses with your willpower.

Our senses, mind and intellect are the sanctuary of our desires. These senses are the biggest source of our desires. We should never underestimate the senses, for they are very powerful. The mind is stronger than the senses, and the intellect is stronger than one's mind, but our willpower is stronger than even our intellect. Therefore, Krishna advises that even if it may seem difficult, one must try to restrain one's desires through willpower. That is the only way for us not to commit immoral acts.

Krishna, here, provides a method of taming desire. He advises Arjuna to control desire at the level of the senses. Desires originate in the likes and dislikes present in the senses, and therefore, that is where we should begin. Krishna also mentions here that desire envelops not only knowledge but also wisdom. Essentially, wisdom is knowledge combined with experience. When we read something in a book, then it is knowledge. But when we experience something on our own and reflect on it, it becomes wisdom.

Controlling our desires requires us to be constantly aware of when our desires arise. For example, we can detect anger towards someone we dislike. Then, we need to use our willpower to restrain our mind and sense organs not to react impulsively. Krishna urges us to take our focus away from our likes and dislikes as soon as we are aware of them.

Gita 4: 1–3

Bhagwan said: I had declared this *yoga* to Vivasvaan. Without any omission, he told it to Manu, and Manu told it to Ikshvaaku.

**O Parantapa, thus handed down in succession,
rajarshi (royal sages) knew about this (*yoga*).**

**Due to the passage of time, this *yoga* has been lost
here. It is the same secret, ancient *yoga* being told
to you today by me. That is because you are my best
friend and even a devotee.**

The source of all knowledge and wisdom

Krishna says that this *karma yoga* and *jnana yoga* explained
to Arjuna is not being taught for the first time. Krishna
himself had taught it to Vivasvaan, who taught it to Manu,
who in turn taught it to Ikshvaaku.

Vivasvaan is one of the Adityas, the offspring of Aditi,
the goddess who represents infinity in Hindu philosophy.
The name Aditya refers to the sun god, Surya. There are
12 Adityas: Vivasvaan, Aryaman, Tvashta, Savitr, Bhaga,
Dhata, Mitra, Varuna, Amsa, Pushan, Indra and Vishnu (in
the form of Vamana). The Mahabharata and the Puranas
mention sage Kashyap as their father. Manu is the son
of Vivasvaan. Ikshvaaku is the son of Manu, who was king
of the earth in ancient times.

The royal sages knew this *yoga*, as it was passed on to
them by tradition. Over time, however, this knowledge was
lost. Krishna says that this knowledge has come to him from
various authoritative sources and Arjuna should believe in
what he is saying.

QUESTION 5

WHY SHOULD I BELIEVE IN YOU?

When someone asks this question—why should I believe in you?—it could be because someone is unsure of your credibility or trustworthiness. To address this, you try to provide evidence or examples that prove your knowledge or expertise on the topic in question. You may try to assure them that you always provide correct and truthful information and that you value honesty and integrity. Ultimately, you will try to build your reliability and credibility in order to gain and maintain the trust of others.

Why do we ask this question: Why should I believe in you? It is because we are scared of the unknown. When we are faced with an unfamiliar situation, we seek guidance. We seek guidance from people we trust, people whose good intentions and helpfulness we believe in. Such people provide us with the answers to our questions. We tend to follow their instructions because, in truth, no one actually knows how to live. They provide us with various alternatives and make us believe in things that we like. They tell us ways to achieve success in our life.

We all want to make our life easier, so we tend to believe these things. We like the advice if it provides us with an easier way. We also need someone to blame if things go wrong.

We have a lot of faith in spiritual gurus because of their life of renunciation. When everyone in this world is out to gain something, acquire something, or achieve something, such gurus command extra respect. We have faith in them, and we believe that they have nothing to gain by misguiding us.

Krishna is Arjuna's friend. Arjuna completely believes in him, but in the current state of anxiety, he is finding it difficult to accept what Krishna is saying.

Therefore, he asks: Why should I believe in you?

Gita 4: 4

Arjuna asked: Vivasvaan was born much before you. How then could you reveal it to him?

The genuineness of a teacher is essential.

In the *shloka* 4: 1 of the Gita, Krishna said that he had revealed this knowledge to Vivasvaan, Manu and Ikshvaaku. Since Krishna is Arjuna's contemporary and Vivasvaan, Manu and Ikshvaaku were born in a different era, Arjuna naturally wonders how Krishna could have revealed this knowledge to these three ancestors.

Arjuna does not directly ask: Why should I believe you? He asks the question indirectly by raising suspicion about an obvious fact: These people were born ages ago, so how could Krishna have revealed this knowledge to them? By raising this question, Arjuna has not raised doubts just about Krishna's authenticity but about all of Krishna's arguments. This is a very clever question. Any teacher would be thrown off balance when the teacher is shown to be inflating their claims. If this is a false claim, then like the fruit of a poisoned tree, everything else is similarly false and need not be acted upon.

'Vivasvaan was born much before you. How, then, could you have revealed it to him?'

The way Arjuna asks this question is very striking. He could easily have said, 'I don't believe you; how is this possible?' He could have said, 'My mind cannot understand this point. Please help me understand it.' But the question is asked with sincerity.

This question enables Krishna to reveal his true identity to Arjuna.

Gita 4: 7–8

O Bharata, whenever there is a decline of *dharma* and growth of *adharma*, at that time, I manifest myself.

I take birth to protect the virtuous and destroy the wicked, to establish *dharma* in every era.

The source is authenticated.

Arjuna leaves Krishna with no option but to reveal himself as Ishvara. If he does not say so now, the authenticity of his teaching is at stake. He says the entire universe is the body of the supreme person known as Ishvara. Since he has already established the doctrine of transmigration—the cycle of birth and rebirth—he does not find it difficult to put forth this argument.

Krishna says that he manifests himself whenever there is a decay in *dharma* and a rise in *adharma*. *Dharma* means righteousness, but it also means universal harmony. *Adharma* is disharmony. Krishna points out three reasons: protecting good people, destroying wicked people, and establishing *dharma*. This decay is not a one-time occurrence. It happens in every age when the harmony of the world is disturbed.

Gita 4: 12

Those who long for immediate results of *karma* in this world worship *devata* (deities) because people want worldly success by performing *karma*.

Deities for worldly success

Krishna says that most of us do not desire self-realization.

We want material objects for instant happiness. We strive for worldly success by obtaining tangible goods, assets, money, recognition and popularity.

Hindu Dharma has many deities, each representing a particular form and characteristic. We have Mother Lakshmi for gaining wealth, Mother Saraswati for gaining knowledge, Mother Durga for courage and valour, Ganesha for removing obstacles, and many more deities.

Krishna says that those who don't want liberation but want worldly gains can worship deities accordingly by performing *karma*.

Gita 4: 13

I created four types of *varnas* according to the interplay of *guna* and *karma*. Even though I have created this system, understand that I am the *akarta* (non-doer) and eternal.

Four types of *karma* orientations

There are four types of *karma* orientations: knowledge, power, wealth and skill. When they are combined with the three gunas—*sattva*, *rajas* and *tamas*—it results in the formation of various combinations and types of occupations. Krishna says: 'I created four types of *varnas* (*karma* orientation based on true nature) according to the interplay of *guna* and *karma*. Even though I have created this system, understand that I am the *akarta* (non-doer) and eternal.'

The most significant advantage of identifying our career choice based on our true nature is that there is a higher possibility of attaining perfection in the profession we have determined for ourselves. There is no denying that by performing one's *karma* and working devotedly, one can reach perfection in one's occupation.

Gita 4: 16

What is *karma*? What is *akarma* (non-action)? Even the wise are perplexed by these. I shall declare to you what *karma* is, knowing which you will be liberated from suffering.

What is *karma* and *akarma*?

In the Indian knowledge system (based on Shada Darshan of Hindu Dharma), *karma* is the fundamental causal law by which good or bad acts decide the future modes of an individual's life. *Karma* explains the birth and rebirth cycle, which is accepted widely throughout Hindu Dharma. The *karma* doctrine applies to all deeds and their consequences and is used to advance the soul and cause enlightenment. *Karma* works by holding us accountable for our actions and intentions.

The concept of *karma* is based on the following idea: 'When we do good, we receive good, and when we do bad, we receive bad back.' For example, suppose we drive carelessly and injure others. In that case, we will face negative consequences in the form of legal action. However, if we plant trees, there will be positive consequences for the environment.

I came across a fascinating story while reading about *karma* and its consequences. A manager started from his home for his office and opened the car door. There was a dog under the car. The dog was startled and tried to bite the manager. The manager became angry and lifted a stone to hit the dog, but missed as the dog ran away. He felt frustrated and started shouting at his subordinates when he reached his office. Those subordinates, in turn, shouted at their own subordinates.

Finally, this reached the peon of the office. No one was working under him, so he vented his anger on his wife when he arrived home. The wife shouted at her son, who was watching TV. The son angrily switched off the TV and left the house. In anger, he picked up a stone and threw it at a dog passing by. He hit the dog, and the dog cried in pain and ran away.

It was the same dog who had tried to bite the manager in the morning.

So, this is an example of *karma* and its consequences. *Karma* means action performed by the body, mind and intellect. But what is *akarma*?

Akarma is action performed without the notion of doership. *Akarma* can be understood in many ways. It is often referred to as *karma* without the expectation of any fruit of the action performed. *Karma* can also evolve into *akarma* when we surrender to the Divine and perform it on behalf of the Divine. Then, there is no *karma*.

Gita 4: 17

It is essential to understand what *karma*, *vikarma* (forbidden action), and *akarma* (non-action) are since the law of *karma* is very complex.

Karma, *akarma* and *vikarma*

Karma means the performance of prescribed duties. *Akarma* means the performance of prescribed duties without a sense of doership. Gita 4: 16 explains both concepts.

Akarma means doing something which has no reaction. When we perform *karma* without attachment and ownership, we are not bound by those *karmas.* In simple words, the attitude towards a deed is more important than the deed. Inaction does not mean abandonment of work. It rather implies doing one's duties without a sense of attachment. Such a person does not consider themselves the sole doer of work. All the actions of such a realized person fall in the category of *akarma* (inaction).

Vikarma means going against the prescribed duties. The performance of *vikarma* is unethical and illegal. One can be punished by law for performing *vikarma.* Examples of *vikarma* are robbery, rape and murder, which are legally punishable. Also, unethical actions like white-collar crimes, financial fraud and taking bribes are types of *vikarma.*

Gita 4: 18

Those who see *akarma* (inaction) in *karma* (action) and *karma* (action) in *akarma* (inaction) are wise among people. They are able to engage in all their *karma.*

Action in inaction and inaction in action

Karma yoga helps in attaining freedom through unselfish work. Every selfish action reduces that freedom because the focus on results creates our boundaries of action. The goal of all nature is freedom, not bondage. This freedom can be obtained only by total unselfishness.

Let us understand what is meant by 'seeing inaction in action'. The action here refers to an activity of any sort: thinking, feeling or working. Even thinking a thought is an action. The word 'inaction' here refers to the constant awareness that 'I am not the doer'. There, the 'I' is inactive. It means complete detachment from the work and detachment from a sense of doership. That will happen when we are attached to a higher ideal. Krishna then goes on to say that one who constantly uses the discrimination to eliminate all sense of doership from every action is a wise person. That person will accomplish any task because it is not a desire-prompted activity. This is inaction in action. Krishna advises us to contemplate a higher ideal. When that happens, our mind and our body become quiet and subdued.

Gita 4: 19

Those who initiate all their *karma* without any desires, purified by the fire of knowledge, *pandits* (scholars) call them wise.

Wise people perform *karma* without desires.

We believe that wise persons are those who educate themselves. They don't wait for others to teach them but educate and train themselves to solve problems on their own. There are some well-accepted characteristics of wise people: discipline, patience, consistency, willingness to learn from their mistakes, trustworthiness. We can identify these qualities of wise people, but how does one become wise?

Krishna also says *karma yoga* is not difficult for a 'wise' person. The question is, who is wise? Krishna says that those who see *inaction* in *action* and *action* in *inaction* are wise among people. They can engage in all their *karma* and initiate all their *karma* without any desires, purified by the fire of knowledge.

Gita 4: 20

Those who have abandoned attachments to the fruits of *karma*, always contented and independent, do not act at all, even though engaged in action.

Unselfish actions

Most of the time, we act out of selfish motives. We are willing to engage in immoral or unethical actions to achieve our goals. No yardstick or method distinguishes such a person from a *karma yogi*. It is only during continuous interaction with a *karma yogi* that people start realizing the depth of the personality and serenity in appearance. A *karma yogi* works with unselfish motives, which becomes apparent over time.

This *karma yoga* slowly makes us lose identification with the body, mind, intellect and material objects. As our attachment recedes, we become liberated individuals. Krishna assures us that the fire of knowledge burns the binding of the *karma* we have accumulated, provided that our actions are entirely unselfish.

Gita 4: 21

Without a desire for the result, being self-restrained, and having given up all possessions, with just the body performing *karma*—such people do not get a guilt complex (*kilbish*).

Why do we feel guilty?

Guilt is our way of recognizing that we have not lived up to our values and standards. On the other hand, shame is the intensely painful feeling of believing we are flawed and, therefore, unworthy of belonging. Here are some of the reasons why we might feel guilty:

- I think I am a selfish person.
- I did not fulfil my responsibility.
- I am not as good as others.
- I am unable to understand others' needs.

Our guilt shows us where we went wrong. But Krishna says that when we work without a desire for results, having given up all possessions and acting with self-restraint, we will not feel guilty at any time.

Gita 4: 22

Those content with what comes to them without complaining, free from confusion and envy, balanced in success or failure, do not get entangled even when engaged in action.

No complaints, confusion or jealousy

When we are contented, we accept the results without any complaints. When we follow *karma yoga*, there is no confusion about doing the right thing. When we are contented, we do not compare our status in life with that of others, so there is no envy. We remain calm in victory or defeat and success or failure.

Doing something with total involvement without expecting any results is what breaks the karmic cycle. *Karma* means action. For *karma yoga*, action is liberating. We bind ourselves if our activity creates an attachment to the act, process or result. *Karma yoga* means to discover your true self through action. *Karma yoga* helps attain liberation by not getting entangled in the mind and personality of a person.

Gita 4: 23

Those who are not attached, who are liberated, whose minds are established in knowledge, performing *karma* as *yajna* (welfare for all)—they merge entirely.

Service orientation

Karma yoga helps in developing an attitude of serving others. We work for the welfare of all. Our focus shifts to serving society. We start loving the people around us and accept them as they are. We develop skills to help us interact with others and understand different thoughts and ideas without judgement. We start being a part of the same universe. We become conscious of the universal energy—*prakriti*—that binds everyone to this world while adjusting and adapting to different people and cultures.

Karma yoga takes us on a path of absolute purification of the heart. We start developing good qualities while becoming aware of the negative ones. We all need to practice *karma yoga* to develop, harness and use the power of our inner spirituality and strength.

Gita 4: 24

Brahma (the Self) is offering. *Brahma* (spiritual nature) is the offering. *Brahma* (the spiritual kingdom) is the fire where *brahma* (spiritual nature) is offered. *Brahma* (the Supreme) is the final goal. *Brahma* (blissful) is *karma* when done in total awareness (of body, mind and intellect).

Attaining divine bliss

In this *shloka*, Krishna explains the process of attaining total bliss. It also describes the approach to attaining perfection in any field of activity.

This approach can be termed the Unified Theory of Consciousness. When we get involved in any activity, we become totally unaware of ourselves, the time, the place and the action. All of these elements become one. This total unawareness of the situation or setting makes the activity blissful.

There is a story of a monk explaining to his disciples how to eat an orange with consciousness. He says that even before eating the orange, look at the colour of the orange, the texture of its skin, its aroma, and how soft it feels in your hand. Look at the juices coming out as you start peeling it, enhancing the aroma. Enjoy the taste of the orange in your mouth, its smell through your nose, its texture through your skin. Appreciate the sound of peeling it. Submerge yourself completely in the process with full awareness of the body, mind and intellect.

In this *shloka*, Krishna says that while performing a *yajna*—a fire ritual— imagine yourself to be the person performing the ritual; become one with the offering being put in the fire. Imagine yourself to be the fire engulfing the offering. Become one with the entire process.

Such is the way to attain perfection in any of our activities. As a *karma yogi*, we should offer ourselves as the offering in the action we perform. Our spiritual nature is the offering as ghee in the fire of our actions. The whole world, the spiritual kingdom, is the field of action, the fire where we offer our virtuous deeds.

We do this because ultimate bliss is the final goal—liberation from the cycle of birth and rebirth. When we act according to this spirit, with total awareness of the body, mind and intellect, our *karma* becomes blissful and divine.

Gita 4: 25

Some *yogis* worship by performing *yajna* to *deva* (deity). Others worship by offering *yajna* (selfless dedication) in the fire of *brahma* (the spiritual kingdom).

Different forms of worship

Some *yogis* worship deities with devotion to gain material rewards. Ideally, *yajna* is performed in divine consciousness as an offering to the Supreme Being. However, different people understanding these concepts in different ways; hence, they offer worship in different forms with dissimilar perceptions.

Others with a deeper understanding of the meaning of *yajna* offer themselves as an offering to the Supreme. This is called *atma samarpan*, or *ātmāhutī*, or offering oneself to *paramatma*.

How do we offer ourselves to the Divine? This is performed by surrendering oneself entirely to the Divine.

Gita 4: 26

Some offer senses, such as the organ of hearing, in the fire of restraint (self-control). Others offer sense objects, such as sound, in the fire of the senses.

Restraint of senses and sense objects

Fire consumes everything when things are consigned to it. In ritualistic Vedic *havans*, it physically consumes the oblations offered to it. Fire is symbolic in the internal practice of spirituality. The fire of self-discipline burns the desires of the senses.

One example of such an offering is the negation of senses followed in *haṭha yoga*. In this type of offering, the actions of the senses are fully restrained, except for the bare maintenance of the body. By using willpower, the mind is completely withdrawn from the senses and sense objects.

In *bhakti yoga*, the senses are surrendered to the glory of the Creator. They no longer remain instruments for material enjoyment; rather, they are used to perceive Brahman in everything. Accordingly, *bhakti yogis* observe the Divine through all their senses—in everything they see, hear, taste, feel and smell. This path of devotion is more straightforward than the path of *hatha yoga*. Devotees are full of joy, and there is a negligible risk of deviating from the path.

Gita 4: 27

Others offer all *indriya karma* (functions of the senses) and *prana karma* in the fire of self-control ignited by knowledge.

The practice of *prana karma* (life force)

On the path of *jnana yoga*, *yogis* take the help of knowledge to withdraw their senses from the world. While on the path of *hatha yoga*, the *yogis* strive to restrain the senses with willpower, *jnana yogis* accomplish the same goal with the practice of *prana karma*, i.e., enhancing the flow of *prana* (life force) throughout the body.

Prana karma is an intense means of accessing the life force's intrinsic wisdom (*jnana shakti*) to make intelligent, well-defined, sincere and necessary corrections. These corrections are performed by the life force and not by the *yogi*.

Gita 4: 28

There are other enlightened people, taking strict vows, who offer *dravya* (objects, materials, wealth) as *yajna*, *tapa* (austerity, self-denial) as *yajna*, *yoga*

(devotional service) as *yajna, swadhyaya* (self-study)
and knowledge as *yajna.*

The offering of *dravya* (material), *tapa* (austerity) and knowledge

We all differ in our natures, motivations, activities, professions and aspirations. There can be various spiritual practices which can take hundreds of forms. All these practices are means of purification of the body, mind and intellect. In addition to the practices mentioned above, three more practices are highlighted here.

The offering of *dravya* can be described as charity. One can offer various objects or money for charity. Even when involved in worldly affairs, one can offer to serve the Divine as it is manifested in all human beings. In this manner, people share their money or other materials as an offering to the Divine.

Yogis offer their practice of *yoga*—in the form of *karma yoga, jnana yoga* or *hatha yoga*—to the Divine as total surrender. To attain perfection in *yoga*, we need to surrender to the Divine. This results in the practitioner's physical, mental and spiritual purification.

The offering of knowledge is the third practice described here. Some people are inclined towards acquiring knowledge. Such people acquire knowledge of the Divine with the spirit of devotion.

Gita 4: 29–30

Others offer inhalation into exhalation and exhalation into inhalation. Others, who are so inclined in the process of *pranayama*, restrain the flow of inhalation and exhalation.

Other people, by regular practice, offer *prana* into *prana*. All these performers of *yajna* cleanse imperfections.

Practice of *pranayama* and *kriya*

Some of us are attracted to the practice of *pranayama*, translated as 'regulated breathing'. *Pranayama* involves:

- *Pūrak*—the process of drawing the breath into the lungs;
- *Rechak*—the process of emptying the lungs of breath;
- *Antar kumbhak*—holding the breath in the lungs after inhalation. The outgoing breath gets suspended in the incoming breath during the period of holding; and
- *Bāhya kumbhak*—keeping the lungs empty after exhalation. The incoming breath gets suspended in the outgoing breath during the period of holding.

The practice of *pranayama* should only be done under the supervision of qualified teachers. *Yogis* inclined towards the practice of *pranayama* utilize the process of regulated breathing to tame the senses and restrain the mind.

Prana is not exactly breath; it is a subtle life force energy that permeates the breath. The Indian knowledge system talks about five kinds of *prāṇas* in the body—*prāṇ, apān, vyān, samān,* and *udān*—that help regulate various bodily functions.

Samān is responsible for digestion. When one fasts, the diet is curtailed; the senses become weak; the *samān*, responsible for digestion, is made to neutralize itself. Some people perform this offering.

The offering of *prana* into *prana* is the process of *kriya yoga*, as explained by Paramahansa Yogananda, the author of *Autobiography of a Yogi*.

We perform various kinds of austerities for the purpose of purification. All these austerities aim to restrain the senses, mind and intellect from pleasure-seeking in sense objects.

Gita 4: 31

O Kurusattam (Arjuna), those who have tasted the nectar of the *yajna* go to *sanatan brahma*. Even this world is not for them who do not perform *yajna*; how then can they have the other (worlds)?

Taking everything as *prasada*

This is a Hindu tradition. Whatever food we eat, it is first offered to the Divine. After cooking the food, we place it on the altar and pray to the Divine to accept the offering. In our mind, we meditate on the sentiment that the Divine is eating from the plate. After the food is offered, the food becomes *prasada*. Consuming such nectar-like *prasada* leads to illumination, purification and spiritual advancement.

Many devotees offer clothes to the Divine and then wear them as His *prasada*. Many install the deity in their house and then live in it with the attitude that their home is the temple. When objects or activities are offered to the Divine, the remnants, or *prasada*, are a nectar-like blessing for the soul.

Krishna says that those who do not perform such offerings remain entangled in the fruitful reactions of the world and continue to experience the dualities of pain and pleasure.

Gita 4: 33

O Parantapa, *jnana yajna* (offering of knowledge) is superior to *dravya yajna* (offering of wealth). O Partha, all *karma* finally culminates in knowledge.

Don't be a ritualist.

It is good to do ceremonies, fasts, *mantra* chants, and holy pilgrimages, but if they are not performed with knowledge, they remain just empty rituals. These rituals are better than not doing anything at all. Still, insufficient to restrain the mind since the cause of bondage and liberation is the mind.

Devotional sentiments are nurtured and sustained by knowledge. Therefore, Krishna explains to Arjuna that offerings performed in full knowledge are superior to those performed as rituals.

Gita 4: 34

Know that by submissive enquiries and by rendering *seva* (service) to a spiritual master, who is self-realized and who has seen the truth, you will gain the knowledge.

Qualities of a good student and a teacher

This *shloka* explains in brief what the attitude of a student seeking knowledge should be. The *shloka* also describes the qualities of a good teacher.

For a student, the *shloka* mentions two qualities: asking questions politely and having an attitude of service.

A student who takes the initiative and reads may gain knowledge by *svadhyaya* (self-study). Some brilliant students develop arrogance of knowledge, which is on display when they ask their teachers questions as if they are testing the teachers' knowledge. Students should always be humble and should have an attitude of service.

Similarly, Krishna says that before we accept someone as our guru or teacher, we should look at two essential qualities: being self-realized (proficiency in the field) and understanding every aspect of the subject matter.

Gita 4: 36

Even if you are the worst crook among all crooks, you can cross the ocean of miseries by using the raft of this knowledge alone.

The raft of spiritual knowledge

Krishna says that even if we are the worst *paapi* (crook) among all *paapis* (crooks), we can cross the ocean of miseries using the raft of spiritual knowledge.

Perhaps this is just a glorification of spiritual knowledge. How can we get spiritual knowledge if we are the worst crooks? However, it is not possible for one who has attained knowledge to commit wrongs. These words are used here to show the impossible hypothetical: though the commission of *paapa* would be impossible for a realized person, the assumption is made to show the results of attaining knowledge.

Gita 4: 37–38

O Arjuna, as the blazing fire reduces the fuel (woods) to ashes, the fire of knowledge similarly reduces all *karma* to ashes.

Certainly, there exists nothing as purifying as this knowledge. One who has attained perfection in this *yoga* discovers this over time.

Purifying effects of the fire of knowledge

We know that once we roast seeds, they cannot germinate. Similarly, our actions, once burnt by the fire of knowledge, cannot bear fruit. When the knowledge of the Self is acquired, all actions—with their results—are burnt by the fire of that knowledge.

There are three types of *karma* we bring along with us when we take birth:

1) *Prarabdha karma*, or past actions which have given rise to the present birth;

2) *Sanchita karma*, which is accumulated actions that will give rise to future births; and

3) *Agami karma* or *Kriyamana*, which are the acts being done in the present life.

The fire of knowledge can burn all three *karmas*.

There exists no method of purification comparable to knowledge. If we follow the spiritual path, we will understand this ourselves.

Gita 4: 40

Ignorant, unfaithful and sceptical people suffer a downfall. There is no happiness for such sceptical people in this world or in any other.

Don't be a sceptic.

Krishna says that there are obstacles that prevent us from gaining that knowledge. There are three main obstacles: ignorance, lack of faith and being sceptical. Ignorance, selfishness and scepticism is our natural condition. This ignorance causes us to question our relationship with the world.

A sceptic is a person who always has doubts about things that other people believe. Such a person is prone to question all accepted opinions. They cannot just accept ideas, proposals, opinions or even facts as offered—they need to be convinced. Sceptics like to weigh and measure and draw their own conclusions.

Once our doubts are destroyed, we should stop being sceptical. We should see the same eternal essence in the actor, the action and the result. Ultimately, we rise not just physically but also spiritually to a new level of consciousness.

Gita 4: 42

Therefore, with the sword of knowledge, cut asunder the doubts in the heart born out of ignorance. O Bharat, take shelter in the *yoga* and arise.

Cast all doubts aside.

When the heat is on, when life gets tough, we often raise questions. We have many doubts, even about the person who is guiding us. We are no more confident about their credentials. Accusatory thoughts flood our minds.

Arjuna had asked: Why should I believe you?

Amid Arjuna's doubts, Krishna explains various methods of *yoga*, *pranayama* and other spiritual practices. He says that you will get what you are looking for by following these practices. Learn these practices with humility and from a self-realized guru. These words give a promise, a reminder that Krishna is who he claims to be. You need to trust him. Can you cast aside all doubts?

At the outset, Krishna tells Arjuna that he is Ishvara, the ruler of this world. He takes birth to protect good people whenever there is a rise in *adharma*. Krishna explains several types of *karma* which need to be burnt by the fire of knowledge. Krishna urges Arjuna to cast away all his doubts and return to fighting the war.

The lesson for us is to not only gain knowledge but also to act on it. Once we understand this, our questions concerning who we are, what our relationship is with the world, what our duties are, and what is the right thing to do will be answered.

WHICH PATH IS BETTER: *SANYASA OR KARMA YOGA?*

When we act with the impression that 'I am the doer', we are not liberated from *karma*. The ego is involved, and we look forward to a favourable result. In the process, we get into an endless circle of *karma* creation, responsible for the cycles of birth and rebirth. Krishna tells Arjuna about performing his duties without ego so he can be free from every type of attachment.

When actions are performed without expecting results and without attachment, over time, we are freed from the effect of *karmas*. For a *karma yogi*, the object of performing *karma* is self-purification. We should understand that *karma yoga* is all about doing our duty without thinking about our self-interest. The main outcome of *karma yoga* is letting go of your ego.

We all have duties according to our station in life. We have a duty as a citizen, a member of society and a family member. We chose some duties based on the profession or occupation, such as our duty as a doctor, engineer, bureaucrat, lawyer, skilled worker, teacher or progeny. A *karma yogi* performs all their duties without attachment and expecting results.

The difference between *karma yoga* and *karma sanyasa* is one of importance. A *karma yogi* focuses on performing their worldly duties, and a *karma sanyasi* wanders in search of wisdom and knowledge of the Divine and the eternal Self, renouncing all earthly *karma*.

Arjuna wants to know which path is better: *sanyasa* or *karma yoga*?

Gita 5: 1

Arjuna said: O Krishna, at one moment, you praise renunciation of *karma (karma sanyasa)*; at another, you praise *yoga (karma yoga)*. Which of these two is better? Please tell me conclusively.

Confusion about the renunciation of *karma*

Even though Krishna said that one should not be sceptical, Arjuna finds variations in the assertions made by Krishna. At one place, Krishna praises the renunciation of actions. At another place, Krishna says that *karma yoga* alone should be practised. How do renunciation of *karma* and *karma yoga* fit together? They are contradictory to each other. Let us review the context of this question.

The first chapter of the Gita describes the nature of Arjuna's grief. In the second chapter, Krishna explains that since the soul is immortal, nobody would die in the war; hence, it was foolish to cry. He then tells Arjuna that it is his duty to fight this war. Since *karma* binds one to the fruits of actions, Krishna tells him the importance of doing one's duty without expecting any results. This approach is called *karma yoga*.

In the third chapter, Krishna explains that performing one's duties is necessary because it helps to purify the mind. In the fourth chapter, Krishna explains the different kinds of *yajnas* to achieve specific goals and purposes. Finally, in verse 4.41, Krishna introduces the principle of *karma sanyasa*, in which duties and obligations are renounced to engage in devotional service with the body, mind and intellect.

All of this advice perplexes Arjuna. He thinks that *karma*

sanyasa (renunciation of work) and *karma yoga* (work in devotion) are opposite in nature, and it is impossible to perform both simultaneously. Hence, he raises his doubt before Krishna.

Gita 5: 2

Bhagwan said: Renunciation and *karma yoga*, both lead to *nihshreyas* (highest good). But of these two, *karma yoga* is superior to renunciation of *karma*.

Karma yoga is better than renunciation.

Some people are competent in the practice of *jnana yoga* alone. It is also true that *jnana yoga* and *karma yoga* can be practised independently to pursue a higher good. Still, Krishna categorically says that of these two, *karma yoga* is better than the renunciation of actions.

When we continue to focus on *karma*, we start understanding the finer and subtler points which only we can experience. *Karma yoga* helps deliver the best of our capacities and capabilities while using these subtle experiences. We begin to understand that there is scope for continuous improvement and the task can be performed better. There is no need to fear about achieving our goals or success or failure. We do not worry about the effort it takes or about external criticism. *Karma yoga* helps us reach perfection in whatever we do without any worry.

Karma yoga keeps us aware of why we wanted to do what we are doing in the first place. Due to this, we continue to be aware of our duty and obligations. We may still be passionate about the work, but there is no harm in that.

The play of *rajas guna* will keep us emotionally charged. The play of *sattva guna* will help us be aware of inward calm and balance.

Gita 5: 3

It should be known that a renunciate is one who does not hate, does not desire. O Mahabaho, there is no doubt that such a person is beyond sense enjoyment.

Who is a *sanyasi*?

Sanyasa is a form of asceticism observed by renouncing desires and prejudices. A state of disinterest represents itself in detachment from material life. The purpose of a *sanyasi* is to spend one's life in peaceful, spiritual pursuits. A *sanyasi* is a *karma yogi* who does not hate and does not desire. Such a person has restrained the body, senses, mind and intellect to move beyond sense enjoyment.

Sanyasa does not mean giving up actions out of laziness, ignorance, a family dispute or disaster, or unemployment. A *sanyasi* is not a coward.

A *sanyasi* neither hates pain nor the objects which give pain. They neither desire pleasure nor the objects that provide pleasure. There is neither attachment nor aversion to any sense object. A *sanyasi* rises above the dualities of heat and cold, joy and sorrow, success and failure, victory and defeat, gain and loss, praise and criticism, honour and dishonour.

Even though a *sanyasi* is engaged in action, there is no attachment to the action. *Sanyasa* may be formalized under a specific sect of the practice of spirituality. Even a householder may be a *sanyasi* at heart because of their attitude to life. *Sanyasa* is a way of living, dwelling amongst life's luxuries, yet remaining unaffected by them.

Gita 5: 4–5

The immatures, not the scholars, speak of Samkhya and *yoga* as different. Those who are truly established in any one of them enjoy the results of both.

That place which Samkhya reaches is also reached by the *yogi*. Those who see Samkhya and *yoga* as the same truly understand this.

Samkhya and *karma yoga* give the same result.

Only immature and ignorant people say that the paths of knowledge and action are different forms of *yoga*. Such people do not know the Self and have only a theoretical knowledge of the Indian knowledge system.

Wise people know that both paths produce the same results. They know the Self and know that both paths will lead to liberation. Anyone who is established in one, who truly follows the one—whether Samkhya or *karma yoga*—obtains the fruits of both.

Gita 5: 7

Those who are established in *yoga*, with the purity of the Self, self-controlled and senses restrained, identify themselves with everyone and do not get attached to actions.

Sanyasis do not get attached to actions.

There are certain qualities of a *sanyasi*:
- A *sanyasi* is established in *karma yoga*.
- A *sanyasi* has purified the Self with the sword of knowledge.
- A *sanyasi* has control over actions and thoughts.
- A *sanyasi* has restrained the senses.
- A *sanyasi* is inclusive and identifies with everyone.

Due to this understanding, such persons are not bound by actions, although they perform all types of *karmas*.

Gita 5: 8–9

Those steadfast in *karma yoga* always think, 'I am not the doer', even while seeing, hearing, touching, smelling, eating, moving, sleeping; or breathing, speaking, giving, receiving, opening or closing eyes; thus convinced that the senses move amongst the sense objects.

I am not the doer.

Krishna is still talking about the thought process of a *sanyasi*, a renunciate. A *sanyasi* has realized the nature of the soul and knows the true nature of the world.

A *sanyasi* has realized that the Self is separate as an individual consciousness from the senses of perception, such as eyes and ears, and the senses of action, such as the voice, life breaths and physical body functions. The concept of doership is derived from identifying the Self with the body.

The liberated *sanyasi* remains a witness to the activities of the senses, identifying with the Self or Brahman. The *sanyasi* truly understands the idea of action in inaction and inaction in action, as they have immolated their actions in the fire of knowledge.

Gita 5: 10

Those who act without attachment, offering all *karma* to *Brahma*, are untouched by *paapa*, as a lotus leaf by water.

Why does *paapa* not touch a *sanyasi*?

In the Gita, *sanyasa* does not refer to the life of a drifter who retires from family and community responsibility to lead a life of seclusion and thinking. In the Gita, *sanyasa* is referred to as a selfless sacrifice, not hankering after the results of one's actions.

We can compare the attitude of a *sanyasi* to a camera that watches the happenings around it without getting involved. It is the attitude of detached engagement in the evolution of life. A camera does not make any distinction between desirable and undesirable. The *sanyasi* regards the senses as merely mingling with sense objects without relish or distaste, remaining a dispassionate, aloof observer.

Therefore, the *sanyasi* is untouched by the results of the *karma*, whether good or bad, like a lotus leaf which is in water but remains unaffected by it.

Gita 5: 15

Vibhu (the Supreme Being) is not responsible for anyone's immoral or moral deeds. Because wisdom is clouded by illusion, people get confused.

We are responsible for our actions.

Many people neglect the responsibility of their actions. They may blame destiny, the bad times, others, or even God when things go wrong. Krishna says that, at the very least, the Supreme Being is not the one who is responsible for anyone's moral or immoral deeds.

In the Indian knowledge system, the work of the Supreme Being in this regard is threefold:
1) He provides us with the power to act.
2) He watches us perform our actions.
3) We get the result of our actions based on what we have done.

We have the freedom to perform good or bad actions by exercising our free will. That free will is the basis of the play of creation and accounts for various actions.

One may ask why we have been given free will. It may be helpful to think of it as downloading an app on our mobile: We are free to use it any way we want. The creator of the app cannot be held responsible for how we use it.

Gita 5: 18

Those who have understood this are wise, humble and do not discriminate between a cow, an elephant, a dog, a scholar or even a chef.

Don't discriminate.

When we treat some people less favourably than others, it is called discrimination. Discrimination occurs between groups or categories of people. Discrimination may occur because of age, disability, ethnicity, origin, political belief, race, religion, sex or gender, language, culture or on other grounds.

Krishna says that wise people are humble and do not discriminate between living beings. They treat scholars and the ignorant alike. They do not even discriminate between a cow, an elephant and a dog.

For example, the sun's reflection falls on the river Ganga, the ocean and a dirty stream without distinction. The type of body of water does not make any difference to the sun.

Gita 5: 20

Those who are self-realized, self-aware and steadfast are not hampered by delusion. They neither rejoice on getting something pleasant nor grieve on experiencing the unpleasant.

Don't rejoice when things are going your way.

Wise people do not rejoice when an enemy experiences misfortune. They don't feel any disappointment when things are not going their way. Krishna says that one should not feel joy when there is a pleasant experience or grief when there is unpleasantness.

How can that be done? If the mind is steadfast and free from delusion, it is possible. If someone is self-realized and self-aware, it can happen.

Gita 5: 21

Those who are not so attached to external objects find internal joy. Such people who are absorbed in *Brahma* (the spiritual nature) enjoy eternal bliss.

Find internal joy.

We can find inner joy in every small thing in our lives. Inner joy is a state of mind. We can find inner joy by doing the right thing. We can find inner joy by working for the welfare of all.

When we perform our *karma* without attachment or expectation of results, we can be at peace with ourselves. Those who have understood this become wise and humble. Such people do not discriminate between people.

Once the mind is unattached and has withdrawn internally, it ceases to crave, yearn and desire to indulge in the objects of the senses. Having attained the wonder of self-awareness, the soul is in never-ending bliss.

Gita 5: 22

O Kaunteya, the pleasure arising from senses and sense objects is not everlasting. Therefore, wise people do not take delight in them.

Sense enjoyments are not everlasting.

Every living being is the king of their body because they are given total freedom to use this body as they like. Such a person will use their body for sense gratification because they feel that the ultimate goal of life is to serve the senses.

Most of us search for enjoyment and find external objects for our happiness. The enjoyment of sense objects has a beginning and an end. We feel a lot of pain when we are separated from the sense objects. There is a feeling of vacuum in the interval between one enjoyment and another. We try to fill this vacuum by looking for another form of sense enjoyment.

A wise person does not rejoice in these sense objects. Krishna says that sense organs are potent. They drag the mind to encounter one sense pleasure after another, and we become our own enemy if we keep running from one material object to another. We have to bring contentment to our life. This contentment will stop the chase for more and more pleasure.

Gita 5: 23

Those who can withstand the forces of desire and anger before giving up the body are alone happy in this world.

Withstand the forces of desire and anger.

We possess the faculty of discrimination. Krishna says that this power of discrimination should be exercised to restrain the impulses of desire and anger. When we do not get the object of our desire, we get angry. The forces of desire and anger are very powerful. Even animals have these urges, but they do not have this refined power of discrimination. Here, Krishna tells us to withstand the urges of desire and anger.

The resolute intellect should be used to check the mind. As soon as the thought of enjoying a pleasure comes to mind, one should use the intellect to look at the consequences of that enjoyment before taking the plunge.

Gita 5: 26

Those who are self-restrained, free from desire and anger, who have calmed their minds, are self-realized and experience eternal bliss.

Experience eternal bliss.

When there is absence of subject-object duality, there is bliss. Bliss is also called *ananda*, which comes from the word *ananta* or 'infinite'. Duality creates finite pleasures. So, when we are not seeking finite pleasure, bliss happens. Who can experience eternal bliss?

- Those who are free from desire and anger
- Those who are practising self-control
- Those whose mind is restrained
- Those who have conquered their mind

Eternal bliss is the state of complete happiness which encompasses unconditional, selfless love and total peace full of positivity. It is far from worries, misery, illusion and negativity.

Gita 5: 27–28

External sense objects do not influence such people; they focus between their eyebrows, balancing inhalation and exhalation in their nostrils.

These *muni*, with sense organs, mind and intellect restrained, free from desire, fear and anger, and striving for eternal bliss, are always liberated.

How to steady the mind

When we fix the gaze between the eyebrows, the eyeballs remain fixed and steady. At that point, we should breathe rhythmically by balancing inhalation and exhalation. Further, when we are restless, the length of the breath is long. Consciously, we should try to slow down the breathing—inhalation and exhalation—within the nose. With this process, the mind becomes steady. When the breath becomes rhythmical, there is perfect harmony in the mind and the whole system.

This is the yoga of meditation or *dhyana yoga*. When the mind becomes steady, external objects such as sound, smell and other sense objects do not agitate the mind. If the mind does not think of external objects, they are shut out from it.

Krishna says that a *muni*—a person of contemplation— masters this art of meditation, of balancing the breath. With contemplation, they understand that sense pleasures are temporary. Desires of the senses do not drive them. They are always thinking of the Divine. Such people have calmed their minds, are self-realized and experience eternal bliss.

Gita 6: 1

Bhagwan said: Those who perform *karma* without desiring the results of their actions are actual *sanyasis* (renunciates) and *yogis*, not those who do not act or have no fire (energy).

Who are actual *sanyasis* and *yogis?*

Some people assume the title of a *yogi* because they practice *yoga*. People in society may accept a person who practises any *yoga* as a *yogi*, be it Patanjali *yoga* or *jnana yoga* or *karma yoga*. However, according to Krishna, a true *yogi* has renounced desires. The practice of *yoga* is incomplete without renouncing the results of actions. A *yogi* has to be a *sanyasi* to achieve liberation.

A person cannot be called a *sanyasi* just by renouncing action, and a person cannot be called a *yogi* without the fire of knowledge to burn their *karma*.

Gita 6: 2

O Pandava, that which they call *sanyasa*, know that to be *yoga*, for nobody who has not given up expectations can be a *yogi*.

Karma sanyasa yoga

Karma sanyasa means renouncing all action. At the same time, *karma yoga* is performing action. These two concepts sound like exact opposites, but both lead to liberation. *Karma yoga* is performing acts (*karma*) as a *yoga*, without attachment or caring about the results. In *karma yoga*, one is not disappointed if the results are bad or ecstatic if the results are good.

Karma sanyasa yoga is the practice of performing our actions with detachment and without desire for their results. Instead of renouncing worldly actions or obligatory duties, we renounce desires and attachments and perform such actions as an offering without any expectations.

The best option for householders is practising *karma sanyasa yoga* along with knowledge, discernment and devotion.

Gita 6: 3

For the *muni* who wishes to ascend to *yoga*, action is said to be the means. For a *karma yogi*, inaction alone is said to be the means.

Advancement tips for a *muni* and a *yogi*

We all believe that worldly objects, people and situations bring happiness. A contemplative *muni* spends enough time observing the world and understands that this notion is false. Even without going to a mountain or a forest, if we contemplate enough, we will know from our daily experiences that the world cannot give joy.

Those of us who are contemplative need to act in order to experience the outcome of our contemplation. For a *yogi* who is always performing *karma*, inaction is said to be the means for moving towards liberation and eternal bliss.

Gita 6: 4

When people are not attached to the sense objects or to *karma*, having renounced all desires, then they are said to have attained the *yoga*.

When are you established in *yoga*?

Yogarudha is a person who is established in *yoga*. A person is established in *yoga* when the *yogi* keeps the mind steady by withdrawing it from the objects of the senses; they have an attachment neither to sense objects nor to actions. Such a person knows that these sense objects are of no use to them when they have already renounced all thoughts of enjoyment of senses. Such a person has overcome the desires for the objects of this world.

Krishna says that if you do not think of sense objects, the desires will die on their own. Renunciation of such thoughts implies that all desires and all actions have been renounced.

Gita 6: 5

One must uplift oneself; one must not degrade oneself. Since one is the friend of oneself, one alone is the enemy of oneself.

Have positive thoughts about yourself.

We should never undermine our capabilities. You alone are your friend, and you alone are your enemy. To progress in any undertaking, we must lift ourselves by our efforts. If we do so, we become our own friend, and if we don't, we become our own enemy.

We can do this if our mind is put to proper use. The mind must detach itself from the obsession with sense objects. In this way, the mind will be elevated and will gravitate towards spiritual objectives. But if the mind is pointed towards worldly pursuits and engaged in sense objects, then the mind will become agitated and stressed. The mind has the potential to give the most benefit as the greatest friend if it is restrained. At the same time, the mind has the potential to be the most destructive enemy if it is allowed to wander among sense objects.

Gita 6: 6

One is a friend when one has won over oneself, but one becomes an enemy of oneself if one treats oneself like an enemy.

Are you your friend or enemy?

If we are asked to name a friend, we will most likely name at least one person. If we are asked to name an enemy, we will think harder, but we would still be able to come up with a name. We always believe that our best friend or worst enemy is someone outside of ourselves.

But that is not true. Krishna says that we are our own

friend, and we are our own enemy. No one will stay with you as a friend or enemy forever. It is our own body, mind and intellect that will stay with us our entire lives.

So, Krishna says that if we nurture these three, they will become our best friends. And if we do not nurture them, they will become our worst enemies.

Gita 6: 7

The one who is self-restrained, self-realized and peaceful maintains equilibrium in cold and heat, pleasure and pain, as well as in honour and dishonour.

Maintain your equilibrium.

There is a connection between our body and mind. Our thoughts and feelings influence what goes on with our bodies. With a hectic life schedule, our lives can often become highly chaotic. Our mind gets overwhelmed with scores of thoughts and emotions. Therefore, finding peace and balance in our daily life is important.

When the mind is well focused and under control, it cannot be affected by dualities such as heat and cold, joy and grief, or praise and ridicule. When the mind is in equanimity, we feel a balance in our lives.

Gita 6: 8

One who is acquainted with suitable empirical and scientific knowledge, who has won over *indriya*, and is spiritually inclined, such a self-realized (*yukta*)

person is called a *yogi* (*dhyana yogi*), who treats alike a
lump of earth, a stone and gold.

Who is a *dhyana yogi*?

Dhyana is a Sanskrit word meaning 'meditation'. It is
derived from the root words *dhi*, meaning 'the mind'
and *yana*, meaning 'moving' or 'going'. An alternate root
word, *dhyai*, means 'to think of'. In the Indian knowledge
system, *dhyana* is a refined meditative practice that requires
deep mental concentration.

As Patanjali explained, *dhyana* builds upon the
practices of *asana* (physical posture), *pranayama* (breath
control), *pratyahara* (control of the senses) and *dharana*
(concentration).

This process results in a complete detachment of the
mind from worldly bindings and a deeper understanding of
the object of meditation.

A person who follows this process becomes self-realized
and treats a lump of earth, stone and gold in the same way.

Gita 6: 9

**One who gives the same attention to the good-
hearted, friends, enemies, relatives, the indifferent,
the neutral, the hateful, the righteous and the
unrighteous stands out.**

Treat everyone equally, without nepotism.

A friend is one whose heart remains good towards us on
its own accord. An indifferent person does not care about

us. A neutral one has no fixed opinion—they may be partly a friend and partly an enemy. A relative is one who is connected to us by birth or the marital bond.

A wise person, a *yogi*, treats everyone equally, whether a good-hearted person, a wicked one, a friend, an enemy, a relative, an indifferent or neutral person, a hateful person, a righteous one or an immoral person.

Such a person is without bias.

Gita 6: 11–12

In a clean spot, having established a firm seat of one's own, neither too high nor too low, made of cloth, deerskin and *kusa* grass, placed one over the other;

There, with the mind focused, desires and senses restrained, sitting alone, practise *yoga* for self-purification.

How to begin meditation

Here, Krishna describes the seat for practising meditation. Choose a clean spot that is neither too high nor too low, where the *kusa* grass is spread on the ground first. Then, spread a tiger skin or deerskin over this. Finally, spread a white cloth.

That was the type of seat preferred in those days. Nowadays, we can use a *yoga* mat or a woollen blanket covered with cloth. We can use a cushion placed on the floor. If one cannot sit on the floor, sitting on a chair with feet flat on the floor works too.

Once we sit for meditation, our mind should be focused, with no desire for sense enjoyment. We should sit alone for meditation for self-purification.

Gita 6: 13–14

Holding the body, head and neck erect and still, being steady, looking at the tip of one's nose and not looking around;

At peace with oneself, fearless, remaining with the sound of *brahma*— *aum*—mind steady, the *dhyana yogi* should meditate on Me, having Me alone as the supreme goal.

The process of meditation

Krishna provides a comprehensive introduction to the process of *dhyana*. He says that the goal of meditation is to purify the intellect. The process is to sit down, observe the mind and senses, and focus the mind, making it single-pointed on *brahma* or the sound of *aum*. We should continuously chant *aum* even when we are not meditating. Whenever we are free, and the mind is straying, we should bring it back to chanting *aum*. *Dhyana* is an inward journey into the Self.

Whether we are a *jnana yogi* or *karma yogi*, *dhyana* is crucial because it brings focus and calms our mind. Our personality is like a bundle of beads spread everywhere. When we do *dhyana*, it acts as a string that combines all aspects of our personality into a cohesive garland.

Gita 6: 16–17

O Arjuna, *dhyana yoga* is not for one who eats too much or fasts excessively, neither is it for one who sleeps too much or keeps awake.

Dhyana yoga is the destroyer of all sufferings for the
one who is moderate in eating and recreation, puts
moderate efforts while performing *karma*, and is
moderate in sleep and wakefulness.

Be moderate in eating and sleeping.

Practising moderation allows us to appreciate the things we
already possess. We maintain a good balance in life when we
follow moderation. A moderate lifestyle is one where we do
everything in the right amount. In short, we try to find the
middle ground in life.

We have often been advised to eat in moderation
because too much eating is bad for our health. The term 'in
moderation' does get used a lot in relation to healthy food
and a healthy lifestyle.

Our body is like an instrument which needs to be healthy
for a happy life. A perfect instrument is vital for perfect
music, so a light and healthy body is essential for meditation
of good quality. Bad food habits and a lack of knowledge of
what is suitable for our system destroy our health over time.

Krishna says that we must observe moderation in eating
and sleeping. If we overeat, we will feel drowsy and sleep
while meditating. When we overeat, we get indigestion and
flatulence. If we eat too little, we will become weak. We will
not be able to sit for a long time in meditation.

Gita 6: 18–19

When the mind is always free from longings and
desires, then it is called a perfectly disciplined mind.

As a lamp does not flicker when there is no wind, the same is true for a *dhyana yogi* whose mind is disciplined and who is self-realized.

Characteristics of a disciplined mind

A disciplined mind is a sound mind. Principles and prudence discipline the mind over time. A disciplined mind is a rational mind that does things based on reason instead of emotions and views issues from an unbiased point of view. A disciplined mind shows empathy for others.

Krishna says that when the mind is entirely free from longings and desires, it is a perfectly disciplined mind. Krishna compares the mind of a meditator to the flame of a lamp that is burning in a windless room. Just as candlelight is steady in the absence of wind, so too is the mind of a meditator unruffled in the absence of desire. Krishna says that supreme joy comes to the meditator whose mind is quiet and free from *paapa*, who has calmed the passions and identified with the eternal essence.

Gita 6: 26

Wherever this restless and unsteady mind wanders, one should bring it back from those subjects and objects by self-control.

How does one steady the wandering mind?

A wandering mind leaves us unable to focus on the task at hand. It is the habit of the mind to wander and move from one thing to another. When we sit quietly for a few minutes trying to think about something or just relaxing, we will find that our mind is going from one thought to another. If we observe the mind, we will find that it keeps thinking, worrying, asking questions, answering, imagining, creating and solving problems.

When we meditate, and the mind wanders, it takes time to realize that our mind is no longer focused on the breath. Once we have this awareness, we try to bring the mind back by disengaging from the thought that drew our mind away. We again steer our attention back to our breath.

This is a repeating cycle, but we have to keep practising without giving up.

QUESTION 7

HOW DO I CONTROL MY MIND?

Sometimes, I ask, 'Can you locate the mind in your body? Is it inside or outside of the body? If it is in the body, then where exactly is it? Does it permeate throughout the body—head, arms, legs, and other parts—or is it in a particular part—the head or torso, the upper part or the lower part? If it is outside of the body, then where is it exactly? Is it in any specific part?' I have never received clear answers to this line of enquiry. The point is to investigate and see things for what they are. The best and strangest part is when we say our mind wanders, it always seems to come back to our body, not to our neighbour's body.

The reality of our mind may seem challenging to understand. However, it may also be straightforward because it is simply not someone else's mind but our own. It is right here with us. Only we can know where it is.

We need to be aware of the mind, of our thoughts and perceptions. When there are thoughts, mental images or perceptions, we get absorbed in what is happening instead of taking a clear look at the perceiving mind. If we don't do that, we don't know whether we are thinking or simply imagining things.

Whether we are a *karma yogi* or a *jnana yogi*, we must do *dhyana* or meditation. Krishna says that *dhyana* is essential to control the mind. Arjuna brings it to Krishna's notice that the mind is very restless, turbulent and obstinate by nature. So, he asks, 'How do you control the mind?'

Gita 6: 33

Arjuna said: The system of *yoga* (*dhyana yoga*) that you have described, O Madhusudan, appears impractical and unattainable to me because of the restless mind.

Our thoughts are expressions of our minds.

Cognizance is when the mind is not involved in any thoughts, neither blatant nor subtle. Cognizance means there is a readiness to perceive, think and experience.

Next are thoughts. There are many types of thoughts, some subtle, like ideas or assumptions, and others quite strong, like anger or joy. We may think that the mind and our thoughts are the same, but they are not. Further, perceptions have two aspects: the perception of so-called external objects through seeing, hearing, smelling, tasting and touching, and the perception of mental images. These mental impressions are not perceived through the senses but occur to the mind as memories.

Our thoughts and perceptions are nothing but the expressions of the mind. Thoughts can be of many types and also include our emotions. The most obvious and familiar examples of thoughts are hate, attachment, compassion and moods.

When such thoughts arise, we try to find the direction they came from and where they go when they subside. Whether it is a thought, emotion, feeling or mood, we should analyze where it comes from, resides and goes. We will realize that they came from nowhere. Most of the time, we create them. If we want them to go away, they disappear.

The same is true of our memories. When we feel happy, we want to cling to that experience. On the other hand, we don't want to remember our painful experiences.

The mind is moody.

The mind experiences a variety of moods. There are feelings of happiness, sadness, exhilaration, depression, anger, attachment, jealousy, pride or close-mindedness. On the other hand, sometimes one feels blissful, clear or without thoughts. A variety of feelings can occupy this mind. One may think these moods are provoked by a material cause in the external environment, but this is not true. All of these states are based on the mind itself. We must look into this mind and discover various mental states of anger, attachment and other mental poisons. They continue rising and dissolving.

The mind is restless.

By its very nature, the mind is very restive. It constantly jumps from one place to another. The mind has been compared to a drunk monkey stung by a *bichhoo* (scorpion), which pointlessly jumps from one branch to another. Therefore, Arjuna is right when he says that the mind is unsteady, fickle, restless, turbulent, strong and obstinate. These attributes of the mind make it very unpredictable and difficult to control. The mind is always in flux.

Gita 6: 34

The mind is restless, turbulent, strong and obstinate, O Krishna! It appears to me that it is more difficult to control than the wind.

Controlling the mind is difficult.

Constant restlessness ultimately leads to unhappiness and distress. The mind experiences turbulence due to forceful currents of fear, anger, jealousy, attachment, lust, greed and the play of the ego. This turbulence destroys the faculty of discrimination and clouds one's power of judgement.

The mind is also stubborn because when it forms a particular view, it refuses to let it go even when proven otherwise. Arjuna says controlling the mind is like trying to control the wind.

Gita 6: 35

O Mahabaho, undoubtedly the mind is fickle and restless. O Kaunteya, but by practice and self-restraint, it can be disciplined.

Use self-restraint and discipline.

Krishna agrees with Arjuna. Krishna concedes that the mind is restless and very difficult to control. But he says that one can discipline the mind by self-restraint and practice. It is challenging, but one can tame the mind-monkey with practice and restraint.

The Bhagavad Gita says that one's thoughts, which constitute the mind, are rooted in past experiences and expected future events. The mind has infinite power, whether for good or bad. The mind can make or break a person, depending on which path you follow.

Krishna answers very simply and firmly while agreeing with Arjuna that the mind is fickle and restless. He says that you can discipline the mind by practice and self-restraint. If you are a person of uncontrolled desires, it will not be possible for you to discipline the mind.

Gita 6: 36

I feel that *dhyana yoga* is difficult to practice for a person of uncontrolled desires. It is possible only for a person who has good self-control and who practises it regularly.

Discipline the mind.

Now, what does disciplining the mind mean?

Discipline is the technique of constant observation, contemplation and internalization of knowledge that helps control the activities of body, mind and intellect. We need to observe ourselves to remain in control of our actions continually. Discipline does that. Disciplining the mind will help us give up our attachment to people, objects and situations so that our mind stops becoming agitated. Discipline will help us check the mind each time it rushes out into the world and examine whether we would truly get joy through the object that is the target of the mind. It will help determine when the mind gets excited or worried. Such a constant, disciplined investigation automatically brings forth calmness.

Practice *dhyana yoga.*

Dhyana, or meditation, is common for all *yogis*. If you want to follow *jnana yoga*, it is *jnana* plus *dhyana*; if you want to follow *karma yoga*, it is *karma* plus *dhyana*. Finally, if you want to follow *bhakti yoga*, it is *bhakti* plus *dhyana*.

Dhyana, or meditation, has become very popular across the world. There are various popular techniques taught in India and abroad. Some of them are mindfulness meditation, *mantra* meditation or chanting, transcendental meditation, Vipassana, and Chakra meditation. These are some of the methods of *dhyana*. There are many gurus teaching methods and techniques of meditation. Whatever the technique, the essentials of *dhyana* practice remain the same as Krishna describes in Chapter 6.

One should meditate early in the morning when one's mind has awakened and is clear and one's senses are not yet fully operating. It also helps because there is a gap of at least six to seven hours since your last meal. Gradually, the mind will become more and more stable and clear. If you do this, you will find that your mind is more alert throughout the day.

Suppose you are able to meditate a little before going to bed. In that case, you will be able to clear the mind of fresh impressions from your daily activities. It will help you clear out cobwebs before they become complex.

So, with the two-pronged approach of constant practice and self-restraint, we can slowly clear the mind of unwanted desires.

QUESTION 8

WHAT HAPPENS IF I LOSE MY PATH MIDWAY?

Arjuna wants to know what happens to a person who deviates from the path of *yoga* because of an unsteady character of mind and lack of faith. Does such a person lose both the material world and the spiritual world? Arjuna asks Krishna to dispel this doubt because only he can do it. Krishna answers this question by breaking it down into five segments.

First, he assures Arjuna that no harm will come to such a person in this world or any other. They will be born again in pious families or families of *yogis*. They will regain the lost knowledge in their early years and will continue again on such a path. They will keep improving with every birth, so there is nothing to worry about.

In the second segment, he asks, 'Why should one be lacking in faith?' One should not have any confusion about the Divine.

In the third segment, he gives glimpses of the play of *trigunas*—*sattva*, *rajas* and *tamas*—deluding the whole world. Krishna says that he has created these *trigunas*, but he is beyond them. All humans act based on the *trigunas* but think they are conscious doers with complete free will and get attached to their *karma*.

In the fourth segment, Krishna talks about people who don't have faith in the Divine—people who are miscreants, stupid, inhuman, misguided or those who torment others. Then, there are four types of people who seek divine help: *arta* (distressed), *jijnasu* (inquisitive), *artharthi* (one in need of money) and *jnani* (wise).

In the fifth segment, Krishna explains that people believe in different forms of the Divine with faith to fulfil their desires. In spite of the restless nature of the mind, those who strive for liberation keep following the path of *yoga*.

Gita 6: 37

Arjuna said: O Krishna, what happens to a person who strives for *yoga* but whose mind is unsteady due to lack of faith and is unable to reach the goal of *yoga*?

Lack of faith

When we are in trouble, hearing the following is very common: 'Just have faith!' We might also have heard people discussing their faith in a political candidate or a scientific breakthrough.

If faith is not a strong feeling, wishful thinking or a positive mental attitude, what is it?

There are many ways one can look at faith. The following definitions crop up when you start looking for an explanation of faith:

- Complete trust or confidence in someone or something
- Firm or unconditional belief in something for which there is no proof

Faith and belief are often used interchangeably but are not quite the same. Belief is a firmly held opinion about an idea or worldview. Beliefs can change over time as you grow and learn new things. Faith is not something you start and build from.

We are confident and perform well when we have faith in our capabilities. Having faith in myself means that I believe in myself as an able being; I believe in my wisdom, knowledge, potential and strength. It also means that I trust in myself and think I can fashion my life in the way I want.

Gita 6: 38–39

O mighty-armed Krishna, doesn't such a person, who deviates from the path of *yoga*, get deprived of both material and spiritual success and perish like a scattered cloud?

O Krishna, please dispel this doubt of mine completely, for who other than you can do so?

What happens if you have weak faith?

The journey towards self-realization begins with *shraddha* (faith). We develop faith in the divine knowledge of the scriptures and put in the necessary effort. Most of us get distracted from this path for various reasons. Arjuna compares this position to that of a broken cloud, a cloud that breaks away from the storm due to the wind and becomes worthless. It offers neither sufficient shade nor enough rain. It merely blows in the wind and perishes in the sky.

In Hindu Dharma, faith (*shraddha*) is referred to as a commitment to scriptures and practice. Faith refers to your belief or conviction. The object of your faith may be anything which appeals to your values and desires. Faith is an essential aspect of Hindu religious duty and practice. However, in matters of faith, Hindu Dharma is not dogmatic or rigid. Faith is regarded as the reflection of a person's essential nature, choice and *karma*. Faith may vary in strength due to different levels of knowledge, ignorance or delusion.

There is always a possibility of having no faith, weak faith or full faith. In the Gita itself, various types of faith have been explained in Chapter 17. Therefore, Arjuna asks: What happens to a person of weak faith who, because of an unsteady mind, stops following the path of self-realization after a while?

Gita 6: 40

Bhagwan said: O Partha, there is no downfall for such a person in this world or the other, for no one who does good ever comes to any harm.

One who does good never comes to harm.

There is good news for all those who strive to do the right thing. Even if the seeker fails to achieve perfection, they do not suffer destruction in this world or the next. It is one of the most positive things one can hear about doing good work.

People doing good often start doubting whether any good would come to them by being and doing good because we see bad people enjoying more comforts and seeming to be far happier than the good and the righteous.

It is only when we come close to such evil people that we realize that the wicked and the evil-minded are undergoing destruction in their hearts. The good live and thrive in the sunshine even though material riches may not come to them easily. These people need not doubt their present or future because Krishna declares here that they will never come to grief.

Gita 6: 41–42

One who has fallen from the path of self-realization goes to the worlds of pure souls and, after staying there for some time, takes birth in families who are pious and prosperous,

Or takes birth in a family of *yogis* endowed with great wisdom. Such a birth is very difficult to get in this world.

Rebirth in a pure and prosperous home

Krishna says that seekers who die without attaining perfection while following the path of *yoga* go to the realm of the good souls. When the time comes, they take birth in a virtuous and prosperous home.

They pick up the path of *yoga* where they left it in their earlier birth. Their new home is full of purity and prosperity. Such a spiritual home is free from poverty because if the home is poor, the person will have to spend much of their life and efforts on maintaining their livelihood. If the home is too wealthy, the person may lose themselves in material pleasures. Therefore, pure and prosperous homes provide the best training ground for spiritual practice.

Krishna says that such pure and prosperous homes are rare.

Gita 6: 43

O Kurunandan, there, s/he comes in contact with the knowledge acquired in the earlier birth and strives more than before to achieve perfection.

The theory of reincarnation is explained.

After death, the soul carries with it all the impressions acquired in previous births and lives on. Former mental tendencies come back to the soul when it takes another body. So, the *yogi* continues on the path precisely from the point where it came to an end when the body departed. There is no loss in death except the flesh and the body. There is a continuity from birth to birth, and the march continues until liberation is attained.

The theory of reincarnation is the only conceivable explanation for the differences in the mental makeup of different individuals. Whatever good we have done in the past creates a natural propensity for good things in the next life. Similarly, the evil thoughts and deeds done in the past create a natural tendency to do evil in the next life.

So, we have to be careful of what *karma* we are performing at the present moment.

Gita 6: 44–45

After birth, due to the influence of their earlier practices, one becomes interested in the path of *yoga* and completely remains absorbed in *shabda-brahma* (*aum*).

Those *yogis* continuously strive to remove all imperfections, keep improving in every birth and finally attain eternal bliss.

Strive continuously.

The impressions of the previous birth, called the force

of *samskaras,* influence the present birth. Even without any extra effort, the *yogi* is drawn to *yoga.* This is due to the mysterious power of *prakriti,* expressing itself as the composition of *gunas.*

They say as the fish takes to water or the bird takes to the air, the *yogi* in this birth takes to *yoga.* The impressions of past thoughts and behaviours, whether good or bad, start expressing themselves in the present birth. We often find that some people are born with certain natural talents. Some people are born with certain natural qualities. We find some people involved in the world's affairs, despite all of life's tragedies and misfortunes.

The *yogi* finally attains the highest abode by continuous practice through birth and rebirth. There are three things to note: diligent effort, continuous practice, and purity of effort. The *yogi* remains absorbed in *shabda brahma* and finally attains liberation.

Gita 6: 46–47

The *yogi* is better than a *tapasvi* (ascetic), a *jnani* (wise) and a person who is result oriented.

Therefore, O Arjuna, become a *yogi.* Of all *yogis,* those whose minds are always absorbed in Me and who are devoted to Me with great faith, I consider them to be the best of all.

Devotion and faith make the difference.

Krishna has described three types of spiritual disciples: the *taspasvi,* who practices austerities; the *karma yogi,* who works selflessly; and the *jnani*, who studies scriptures. Although each practice moves the seeker forward on the spiritual path, it may not lead the seeker to the goal of liberation. Such practices will result in worldly gains, and one should not get stuck in any of these practices.

Krishna says that the *yogi* who worships the Divine with faith is the greatest of all *yogis*. The *yogi* who worships Ishvara, the Absolute, is greater than those who worship the deities.

All spiritual practices aim to free the mind from impure tendencies binding it to the material world. The devotion to the Divine is of primary importance. It is important to have faith in the Divine to succeed in any *yoga—karma yoga, jnana yoga* or *dhyana yoga*.

If we look at the vegetable kingdom, the seed which is put in the earth and watered sprouts into life and grows. Similarly, the devotion to Divine is the water that nourishes the individual's mind and creates the ultimate success of all endeavours.

Gita 7: 2

I shall now reveal to you, in whole, this *jnana* (knowledge) and *vijnana* (practical application of knowledge), knowing which nothing else remains to be known in this world.

The essence of all knowledge

In the modern education system, there are many subjects in arts, performing arts, sciences, social sciences, technology, medicine and law. Even when a person acquires knowledge about them, this knowledge is not complete. We say that we have to continue learning all the time, and Krishna says that he will impart such knowledge that **there will be nothing left to be known in the world.**

A *yogi* does not waste time in learning a hundred mundane things but aspires to true knowledge, the essence of all knowledge.

When we water a plant, we water its roots. We don't water the trunk, branches, flowers or fruits. Even then, the water reaches everywhere in the plant's system. Krishna says he will impart knowledge through which one can understand all knowledge systems.

There are two words used here: *jnana* and *vijnana*. *Jnana* means knowledge derived from the study of texts and scriptures. It may also refer to the quality of that knowledge—knowledge derived through words. *Vijnana*, on the other hand, means scientific knowledge—knowledge based on experiences and understanding the truth.

Gita 7: 3

Among thousands of people, very few strive for perfection; even among those who strive for perfection, very few know Me.

Very few strive for perfection.

We all seek knowledge and skills to be able to earn our livelihood. Very few people have the disposition to know the truth. Most of us engage in action for the sake of some gains and results, but very few strive for perfection.

Even of those who strive for perfection, very few attain it. Let's take an example from the field of sports, say running a marathon. We find many at the starting point, but some people drop off on the way and very few strive to reach the finishing line.

When we look at a tree, there are many branches with many flowers, but only a few of those flowers grow into fruits. All the other flowers wilt away. Even among those flowers which turn into fruits, very few become ripe.

Gita 7: 4–5

Prakriti is comprised of eight different entities: earth, water, air, fire, ether, *manah* (mind), *buddhi* (intellect) and *ahankara* (egotism).

O Mahabaho, besides this lower *prakriti*, there is a *para-prakriti*—the life element that sustains the world.

Nature and the life element

The world of natural phenomena is made of five elements: earth, water, air, fire and ether. These are gross elements which we can see and experience. There are three other subtle elements: the mind, the intellect and the ego. These eight elements together constitute the phenomenal nature. *Prakriti* (the world of natural phenomena) is gross, and so it is inert. Without life in the body, the body, the mind and the intellect do not function.

Para-prakriti is the life element. You can see *prakriti*, as it is objective creation, but the life element is an unseen element, in the realm of the oracle or the seer. *Prakriti* is prone to destruction, but *para-prakriti* is everlasting.

Prakriti, which is inert, also includes the mind, intellect and ego. Just as the gross elements are not sentient, the mind, intellect and ego are not sentient either. When we understand them as such, their power is lost. They can be restrained and controlled like any other material object. All eight inert elements can never have power or command over the life element.

Gita 7: 6–7

Know that I conceived all these living beings. I am the source of the creation and dissolution of the entire universe.

O Dhananjaya, there is no one higher than Me. All this (the universe) is interwoven in Me as a string threads gems.

Purusha, the Brahman

Prakriti, in its two aspects as inert elements and the life element, is the womb of all beings. *Purusha,* or the Brahman, is the cause of the universe's creation, sustenance and destruction. *Prakriti* is the mechanism by which the Brahman creates, maintains and destroys the universe.

Therefore, if we trace back to the root cause of all things, we are told that the Brahman creates the manifested universe and the unmanifested one, which finally get dissolved in the Brahman. The omnipotent, omniscient Brahman is the material and efficient cause of the universe.

Krishna gives the example of a string here to help us visualize the theory. A thread holds gems together; without the thread, the gems would not stay together and would spread everywhere. Even though the gems could be of different shapes, sizes and colours, the string that holds them together is the same. Thus, the presence of the Brahman holds the world consisting of different beings, races, classes, religions and creeds.

Gita 7: 8–9

O Kaunteya, I am the taste in water. I am the light in the sun and the moon. I am the word *aum* in all the Vedas. I am the sound in the ether and virility in men.

I am the pure fragrance of the earth and the heat in fire. I am the life force in all beings and the ritual of the ascetics.

Decoding the essence

The essence of anything is what makes a thing what it is. The essence of a person could be his virility (virility is to men what fertility is to women). Everything that exists has an essence; things without it don't exist. Therefore, Krishna says that the Brahman is the string that holds together all the gems, where the string is the essence of the necklace.

Krishna now gives various examples to explain the concept of essence. Brahman is the taste in water, the light in the sun and the moon, *pranava* (*aum*) in the Vedas, virility in men, the pure fragrance of the earth and the heat in fire. The Brahman is the life force in all living beings. Rituals define an ascetic, and the Brahman is in those rituals.

Thus, one can experience the presence of the Brahman in all things. Conceptually and in reality, taste, water, light and the sun are inseparable. The essence of the Vedas is in *aum*. No one can study all the Vedas if the syllable *aum* is not understood and contemplated.

Gita 7: 10

O Partha, know that I am the seed of all beings. I am the intellect of the intelligent. I am the valour of the powerful.

The cause of everything

The Brahman is the seed and the cause of all beings. As the tree grows from a seed, the life force of the tree is rooted in the seed, which manifests with its life force in the new form of the tree.

A wise person transcends all separateness that appears to exist between one thing and another. He realizes that the seed of every being is the Divine.

The Brahman is the cause and also the effect; so, the effect is the cause in a different form. Once we know this, we will not imagine ourselves to be weak, neglected, forlorn and wretched. It is only because of ignorance that we have misunderstood ourselves as a limited body and personality.

Gita 7: 11

I am the strength of the strong that is free from desire and passion. O Bharatarshabha, I am the desire in all living beings that is not in conflict with *dharma*.

All desires are not bad.

The Brahman is the strength of the strong. But this strength is free from desire and passion. We should not use our strength to satisfy sensual desires and the greedy acquisition of worldly possessions. We should use it to do good and benevolent acts and to pursue spiritual progress.

We may have intellectual or physical strength, but we should not use it for selfish purposes to serve our desires and passions. Ravana had physical and intellectual strength, but he used it to fulfil his desires and passions, leading to his destruction.

All desires are not bad. For example, there may be a desire to do the right thing. Krishna says that the Brahman is also the desire in living beings that does not conflict with *dharma*. We may desire to maintain our family in good condition, to support our society without becoming a burden on others and to alleviate the suffering of others. Such desires are not in conflict with *dharma*.

Gita 7: 12–13

The three *gunas* of *prakriti*, *sattvic*, *rajasic*, and *tamasic*, are manifested by my energy. They are in Me, but I am beyond them.

The whole world is deluded by these three *gunas*, and

**due to this delusion, people are unable to know Me,
the imperishable and eternal.**

The cause of our ignorance

Here, Krishna explains the cause of our ignorance. All three *gunas* (*sattva, rajas, tamas*) are created by the Brahman. Whether it is the goodness or the passion to fulfil desires, inertia, or the resistance to change, the Divine manifests all these energies. Let's consider the example of a mobile phone. In that example, these three energies are the operating system of the mobile phone, without which it cannot work.

When there are clouds, we cannot see the sun. In the same way, because of our delusion, we are unable to understand the play of *trigunas*. As long as we are under the influence of these three *gunas*, we cannot perceive the presence of the Divine.

We do not even know that we are slaves of *triguna* energy. Whether we are rich or poor, big or small, learned or illiterate, we are all bound by the illusions of *trigunas*.

Gita 7: 14

**The influence of My *maya* (illusory energy),
consisting of the three *gunas*, is very difficult to
overcome. But those who surrender to Me overcome
it easily.**

What is *maya*?

Maya, meaning 'magic' or 'illusion', is a concept in the

Indian knowledge system. It is the illusion due to which we are not able to see reality. It is a powerful force that creates the cosmic illusion that *prakriti*—the world of natural phenomena—is real. At the individual level, it is the cause of our ignorance— the *ajnana* about our real nature, which we mistake as the ego.

Maya is the material cause of this universe. It is constituted of the three *gunas*, *sattva*, *rajas* and *tamas*. We can overcome this illusion by total surrender to the Divine.

Gita 7: 15

These types of people do not seek Me—miscreants, foolish, contemptible people—whose discrimination has been destroyed by their demonic nature.

What type of people don't surrender?

Krishna says that we can overcome the influence of *maya* through total surrender. This verse tells us what type of people simply cannot surrender to the Divine.

1) Those who are ignorant because *maya* deludes their understanding

2) People of demonical nature who are vile and dejected: Because of this nature, such people lose discrimination, their virtue and the desire to be spiritual.

3) Miscreants who love to cause trouble, break the rules or have criminal intent

4) People who have a feeling of contempt towards others: Such people consider others worthless and despicable.

Gita 7: 16

O Arjuna, four types of pious people worship Me. O Bharatarshabha, they are *arta* (distressed, aggrieved), *jijnasu* (inquisitive), *artharthi* (one in need of money) and *jnani* (wise).

Four types of pious people

After describing people who would not surrender to the Divine, Krishna then talks about people who worship the Divine.

The first type of devotee is the '*aarta*' or the distressed. When such devotees are in trouble and cannot find an answer themselves, they approach Ishvara for help. They would hardly remember Ishvara if they were doing well.

The second type of devotee is the '*jignasu*' or the inquisitive one. Such people have an infinite appetite for knowledge acquisition—economic, scientific, artistic and even spiritual. They worship the deity Saraswati to gain knowledge.

The third type of devotee is the '*artharthi*'. These devotees worship the deity Lakshmi to gain wealth and profit or for material gains. When making losses, they cry for help.

Finally, the fourth type of devotee is the '*jnani*' or the wise one. These devotees seek the Divine for self-realization. They do not want divine intervention for any other purpose. There are no other desires or hidden motives in such a devotee. Krishna says that the wise devotee always strives to connect with him and that such devotees are extremely rare.

Gita 7: 23

But all such fulfilment of desires obtained by these people of modest understanding is temporary. Worshippers of *deva* go to the *deva* (deities). My devotees come to Me.

Don't let your desires drive you.

When these four types of pious people worship the Divine to fulfil their desires, they should understand that such fulfilment is temporary. When desires drive such people, they fail to understand the Brahman because *maya* obscures the Brahman's existence. Due to the influence of *trigunas*, these devotees are consumed by likes and dislikes. Once they begin to understand this, they perform good deeds, overcome the tendency to do *paapa* and become free from *dvandva* (duality of likes and dislikes).

Krishna says that those who worship other deities are people of confused intellect. Their exertion earns only temporary and perishable rewards, like prosperity, wealth, power and position. Only selfishness can fuel the desires for those finite things, letting go of the infinite benefit of true knowledge and devotion.

Gita 7: 27

O Bharata, everyone is engulfed in the likes and dislikes of desires. O Parantapa, everyone has been confused about them since birth.

Don't be driven by likes and dislikes.

We are all born with our own set of *karma* and desires. We chase a particular object because we like it and think we cannot live without it. But when we acquire it, we want to go higher in the value chain. A politician would be happy to be a corporator. Still, once they become one, they want more—state legislature, parliament, ministries, and then ministries of high repute. Ultimately, every such pursuit results in sorrow.

We are driven by the delusion of the pairs of opposites such as pleasure and pain or success and failure, arising from desire and passion. Once we are free from attraction and aversion, we can eliminate the pairs of opposites. Therefore, this subtle but powerful enemy should be fought with discrimination and dispassion.

Gita 7: 28

Those who are always involved in good deeds and have overcome *paapa* (tendency to do immoral acts) are free from the illusion of *dvandva* (duality of likes and dislikes).

Get involved in good deeds.

When we are on the path of self-perfection, we will make vows of silence, fast and study spiritual texts. But we cannot discipline the mind and intellect by doing just that because the mind is not restrained and we have accumulated *karma* from several births.

Just as we cannot grow seeds in the wasteland, we cannot

get spiritual illumination by fulfilling the heart's desires. Therefore, the mind has to be made pure and virtuous, which is possible only by performing good deeds. We need to do good deeds continuously. Some sprinkle of charity, some tiny service to humanity or some inconsequential self-sacrifice for the sake of others would not suffice. We need to do the right thing to set an example for society.

Gita 7: 30

Those who know Me as *adhibhuta* (origin of the world of objects, *prakriti*), *adhideva* (origin of all deities) and *adhiyajna* (origin of all *yajna*—devoted actions), their mind engaged in Me even at the time of death, such people know Me.

Engage in spiritual practice all your life.

When we truly understand, we realize that everything about the elements is all a creation of the Brahman. We retain this wisdom and experience even at the time of death. It is only through a lifetime of spiritual practice that such knowledge is acquired.

We need to remember the Divine even when we are healthy and strong and when the body is energetic and vigorous, not only during distress. Only when good memories of the blissful experience remain fresh in the mind will we remember the Divine even in our last moments. As we don't know the moment of death, spiritual practice should be a continuous component of our lives.

Krishna says: Those people who identify with Me as *adhibhuta* (origin of the manifestation of *prakriti*), *adhideva* (origin of all deities) and *adhiyajna* (origin of all *yajna*), such people are fully aware of Me even at the time of death.

While answering this question, Krishna uses three words: '*adhibhuta*', '*adhideva*', and '*adhiyajnya*'. He says that a *jnani* can understand the Divine as being all three. Like a practised guru, Krishna leads Arjuna to his next question.

Naturally, Arjuna is ready for his next question.

QUESTION 9

WHAT IS MY ULTIMATE GOAL?

In an answer to an earlier question, 'What happens if I lose my path midway?' Krishna explained the theory of reincarnation in detail, talking about having firm faith, the influence of *trigunas* on our actions, the type of people who will not have faith and the nature of the Divine. Given the large number of specialized words used by Krishna to describe the nature of the Divine in the last few verses, Arjuna has an information overload. So, naturally, Arjuna asks:

- What is that which is called the Brahman?
- What is *adhyatma*?
- What is *karma*?
- What is *adhibhuta*?
- What is *adhideva*?
- Who rules *adhiyajna*?
- What is the ultimate goal?

Now we know why the answer to this question is very long—spread over Chapters 8, 9 and part of Chapter 10 of the Gita, covering the themes of *akshar brahma yoga, raj vidya yoga and vibhuti yoga.* Krishna uses these words during his conversation with Arjuna.

The conversation has shifted to a stage where Arjuna has no more questions to outwit Krishna. Now, he wants to use this opportunity to clear many of his doubts about Ishvara, *karma* and so on. He also wants to know more about what happens after death. From the beginning, Krishna has been saying that we don't really die; only the body, *deha*, dies, not the owner of that body, the *dehi*. Arjuna wants to know whether there is a possibility that one doesn't take rebirth, and if so, how it can be done. He also wants to understand why people take birth again and again. This is like asking to close a trail of deliberations to a conclusion.

Gita 8: 1–2

Arjuna asked: O Purushottama, what is that which is called the Brahman, what is *adhyatma*, and what is *karma*? What is *adhibhuta*, and what is *adhideva*?

O Madhusudan, who is it who rules the *adhiyajna* in this body? How would people with self-restraint realize you at the time of death?

Questions about the nature of the Divine

While answering the previous question, Krishna mentioned a few words such as Brahman, *adhibhuta, adhyatma, adhideva* and *adhiyajna*. He also noted that the wise are aware of the Divine even at the time of their death. Now, Arjuna is curious and wants to know more about it. Here, he puts forth seven questions to Krishna, of which six are about these words, and the seventh question is about remembering the Divine at the time of death. Since Krishna used these words, Arjuna wants Krishna to elaborate upon them.

Gita 8: 3

Bhagwan said: *Brahma* is the imperishable Supreme. *Adhyatma* is the essential nature of all living beings. *Karma* is creation, producing the material bodies of living entities.

What are Brahman, *adhyatma* and *karma*?

Krishna explains that the Brahman is the imperishable Supreme.

Adhi means the origin; therefore, we can understand that Krishna is talking about the origin of those forms, essence or quality for all the terms where *adhi* is used. *Adhyatma* (or *atman*) is the same Brahman in every living entity. The *adhyatma* is the inward-perceiving, inward-seeing consciousness lodged with the individuality of the seeker.

Karma refers to all actions done by the Brahman, which cause the birth and death of all beings.

Gita 8: 4

Adhibhuta is of perishable nature, and adhideva is the *purusha* (cosmic consciousness). I alone am the adhiyajna in the body of every individual here.

What are *adhibhuta, adhideva* and *adhiyajna?*

Adhibhuta is the entire perishable universe. It is the universe of objects, or what appears as the material expanse before us.

Adhideva is the origin of all deities who bless all beings. Beyond *adhyatma* and *adhibhuta*, there is *adhideva*. The one infinite Being, or *adhideva*, appears as the two, namely, *purusha* and *prakriti*, or *adhyatma* and *adhibhuta*, the subject and the object. *Adhideva* is the *jivatma*. It enjoys the experiences naturally arising from *prakriti* (physical creation). It is the one that observes through the intellect, the king of sense organs, and it is the tree on which the birds of desires rest after the death of the body.

We may say there is a tripartite of creation over and above the dual concept of creation: *adhibhuta* and *adhyatma*. On the one side, we have the universe, which is *adhibhuta*; on the other side, there is *adhyatma*, the viewer, the beholder of the whole universe, and above these two, we have the connecting link, the transcendental. We may call it the divinity; we may call it *devata*. It is not that there are many *devatas*; all *devatas* are only manifestations of the one *adhidevata* in various forms. There is only one Supreme, and this superintending principal is the *adhidevata*, the essential reality without which no experience can be accounted for.

Adhiyajna is the origin of all the *yajnas*—devoted actions—of individual living beings.

Gita 8: 5

Those who remember Me and think about Me at the time of death also attain my *bhava* (abode); there is no doubt about it.

Remember the Divine all the time.

While dying, most people think of their property, spouse, children or work because such thoughts occupy them for their whole life. Therefore, Krishna emphasizes remembering the Divine at all times, both in life and in death.

Only if we spend our lifetime in spiritual practices can we retain the memory of the Divine at the last moment. If we have to play some role in a drama, we must undergo months of training, memorizing the part. Even to pass an examination, we must prepare for a long time.

Therefore, an intense spiritual practice of a lifetime is essential to attain the Divine at the time of death.

Gita 8: 6

O Kaunteya, whichever *bhava* (form, nature, deity) one remembers at the time of death, one definitely reaches there, always absorbed in that *bhava*.

Constant effort and sincere practice

There are some people who will not realize the *param bhava*. Krishna says that whatever the form, nature or deity we remember at the time of death, that is where we reach because we were absorbed in that *bhava*. So, if we want to reach eternal *brahma*, that is what we must think about without wavering in mind and intellect. Through constant practice, one should be able to balance the *prana* in the middle of the eyebrows while chanting *aum*; this helps at the time of death because this state will come quickly to us. We do not retake birth once we reach *param gati* (eternal bliss). All other destinations till *brahma loka* are transitory in nature.

We are driven by our likes and dislikes, which are framed by our dominant desires. That we will have the same desires playing out in our minds at the time of death is obvious. Therefore, the predominant desires determine the place of rebirth and the type of rebirth. If we want to unite with the Divine, we must remember the Divine all our life, in both good and bad times. Although it may appear difficult, one can succeed through constant effort and sincere practice.

Gita 8: 9–10

The Divine is omniscient, the most ancient one, the controller, subtler than the subtlest, the supporter of all, and the possessor of an inconceivable divine form, illuminated like the sun, removing all darkness of ignorance.

A mind unwavering with devotion through the power of *yoga*, whose *prana* is balanced in the middle of the eyebrows, attains *param purusha* at the time of death.

The eight attributes of the Divine

Krishna describes the different aspects of *paramatma* and the way of meditation. The eight attributes of the Divine are:

- *Kavi:* The poet of poets
- *Puranam:* The Ancient, without beginning
- *Anushasitaram:* Controller of all worlds
- *Anoranīyan:* Smaller than an atom and larger than the largest entity
- *Sarvasya dhata:* The source of sustenance
- *Achintya rupa:* Beyond the senses and incapable of being comprehended by the mind
- *Aditya varna:* His light illumines the sun and everything else.
- *Tamasah parastat:* Beyond the darkness of ignorance

Therefore, we can meditate on any one or all of them, with *prana* balanced in the middle of the eyebrows. Meditating thus takes our mind to the Divine, and as a result, the mind is purified.

Gita 8: 12–13

Having restrained all the gates of the senses with the mind, with emotions kept in check, and *prana* (breathing) situated in the middle of the eyebrows by the practice of *yoga*;

While remembering Me, chanting *aum*, those who depart from this body attain *param gati* (eternal bliss).

Close all the gateways.

We need to close the gateways of the senses and turn the mind inwards to concentrate on the Divine. The storms of sense-attractions may easily extinguish the flame of knowledge if the gateways are open. When we say closing all gateways, it means restraining *all* the senses. The restraints should be complete and perfect. Without sense-restraint, no spiritual practice is possible.

What are such practices? First, one should restrain the organs of perception and action. Then, as an outcome of the regular practice, breathing, that is, *prana*, must be withdrawn and balanced between the eyebrows. Then, with the help of a calm mind, one should meditate on *aum*. With this, the *yogi* would attain the eternal blissful world which is omniscient, eternal, subtler than the subtlest, the sustainer of all, incomprehensible, luminous and beyond ignorance. All dispassionate seekers reach that Brahman alone. The Brahman is the ultimate goal of all *yogis*.

The Vedas tell us about the four stages of self-realization: *prajnanam brahma* (Consciousness is Brahman); *ayam atma brahma* (This Self, *atman*, is Brahman); *tat tvam asi* (You are That); *aham brahmasmi* (I am the Divine).

Gita 8: 22

O Partha, that supreme *purusha* (immortal consciousness) which dwells within all embodied beings and is all-pervading is attainable by steadfast devotion.

Have steadfast devotion.

What we must attain and how we must go about attaining it are explained here. The *purusha*, the immortal consciousness, is the basis—the very foundation, the reality—of all creation. In the same way that cream permeates milk, the Divine permeates the world.

We need to have unswerving devotion to the Divine to attain it. There is no other way. We need to do spiritual practice with intense devotion and one-pointed concentration. Once we understand this, we will attach no value to life's enjoyments, pains and sufferings; we will discover that there is only one reality. Whatever path we follow, we need to have the devotion to surrender ourselves.

Gita 8: 28

Whatever the results of pious work indicated in the Vedas for *yajna, tapa* and *daan,* the *yogi* goes beyond them despite having known them and attains the Supreme abode.

Going beyond good deeds, austerity and charity

So far, Krishna has answered the seven questions Arjuna asked earlier. Once we genuinely comprehend these answers, we may attain the highest state—far beyond any of the rewards springing from doing *yajna* (good deeds), *tapa* (austerity) and *daan* (charity). Every reward arising out of *yajna*, *tapa* and *daan* is in the realm of *maya* (illusion). They have an end; they are not eternal.

Many people do not study the Vedas. Many people cannot perform austerities. Many people cannot offer charities. Is there no way of liberation for them? Krishna says they, too, can attain the Divine by meditating on it and understanding the Brahman.

Gita 9: 1

Bhagwan said: I will now explain to you the most secret *atmajnana* (the knowledge of the Self) and its practical application, knowing which will liberate you from *ashubha* (misfortune).

Eligibility to receive the most secret knowledge

Krishna now discusses a most secret piece of knowledge (*atmajnana*) and its practical applications. The phrase 'most secret' indicates the importance of that knowledge and not the prohibition of its discussion. It means that Krishna is sharing knowledge that ordinary people would not know and beyond which there is nothing else to be known.

Knowledge of the Self or Brahman is generally given to those eligible to receive it, but what is the eligibility? Krishna says that such a person should be free from malice (*asuya*) and be pure of heart. Only a person with a purified mind can understand this knowledge and attain the Brahman.

There are four conditions to be eligible:
- Not indulging in misrepresenting good to be bad
- Praising even the smallest goodness in others
- Not delighting in thinking of the evil in others
- Being free from malice and envy

Gita 9: 2

Atmajnana is pure, supreme, ethical, everlasting and yet very easy to implement. Even so, it is the pinnacle of knowledge and the greatest of secrets.

The pinnacle of knowledge

In the last century, science and technology have advanced to a great extent. Yet, our experience is that all of this knowledge has not brought peace and happiness to humanity; all it may have resulted in is more comfort in our day-to-day lives. Indeed, these advances have fuelled our desires even more.

Worldly knowledge and skills can only deal with material comforts, and such comforts are perishable. The most secret mysteries of life, death and immortality still evade us. Krishna says that this most secret knowledge, which he will impart to Arjuna, would reveal the truth of our existence and the path to liberation. Krishna has classified this as royal knowledge and a royal secret.

This royal knowledge is to be attained by direct experience. Its result is direct and immediate. The practice of this knowledge is effortless; it needs a pure mind distanced from attraction and repulsion.

Gita 9: 3

O Parantapa, those who do not have faith in *dharma* do not reach Me and instead take birth again and again.

Faith and devotion are the keys to success.

Whether we are working for spiritual advancement or worldly gains, faith and devotion to some values and beliefs is the key to success. Our degree of success depends on the intensity of our faith and devotion. If we act with faith and devotion, we usually get what we want.

Our faith and devotion give us enough energy to overcome obstructing forces. The timing of success may not be guaranteed. Still, sooner or later, it is inevitable that we will achieve what we yearned for with faith and single-minded devotion.

The point of vital import here is that *dharma* should be the basis of our ideal or goal. If we do not act according to *dharma*, we will have to take birth again and again. We must be careful about even the tiniest details and minor life dealings. We have to follow utmost care and caution.

Gita 9: 6

As the mighty wind blows everywhere but remains in the sky, so do all living beings always rest in Me.

All beings rest in the Brahman.

Where does the wind originate? It is the vertical and horizontal movement of air in the atmosphere. Global winds form because of pressure differentials and the uneven heating of the Earth's surface by solar radiation.

The ether is an interesting and invisible aspect of reality. The element ether, called *akasha* in Sanskrit, is one of the five ultimate elements and also the subtlest. It is also referred to as space; it is the essence of emptiness.

Krishna gives a beautiful simile to explain how all beings rest in the Brahman. Just as the mighty wind rests in the ether, which has no contact with the wind, all beings rest in the Brahman, which they do not touch. Ether is subtle; the Brahman is subtler. Ether pervades all, and the Brahman pervades all beings.

Gita 9: 12

Rakshasa (people of malicious nature) and *asura* (power-seeking people) are bewildered and deluded by *prakriti* and take shelter in false hope, false *karma* and false *jnana*.

Don't indulge in false hope, false *karma* and false *jnana*.

It is not that everyone in this world would go for spiritual practice and strive for the Divine. Some will work only for selfish gains and use any means to get what they want.

We can broadly say that there are two types of people: those who follow *dharma* and those who have no problems with *adharma*.

People with demonic natures indulge in sense-enjoyment. Their hopes are inflated, and their actions are futile, producing nothing good or permanent. They do not understand the right thing to do, so they have no thought of anything beyond the body. Krishna describes such people as *rakshasic* (malicious) and *asuric* (power-seeking).

The *rakshasa* and the *asura* have immoral desires and use their powers wickedly. They indulge in false hope, false *karma* and false *jnana*.

Gita 9: 15

There are various ways in which people worship *vishvatomukham* (*brahma*). Some worship Me with *jnana* (knowledge), others by *yajna*, and some in unique and distinct forms.

Various ways of worship

People worship the Divine in various ways. Some worship the Divine with *jnana* (knowledge); others identify themselves with the Divine as one reality; yet others distinguish between the Divine and themselves. Finally, some worship the Divine in unique and distinct forms.

Jnana tells us that the Brahman is real and the world is an illusion. The *jiva* is Brahman and not distinct. To act on this knowledge is *jnana yajna* (worship with *jnana*). This approach is summarised as *tat tvam asi* (You are That).

All these aspirants finally attain the deity whom they worship. Whatever the approach, the Divine is still worshipped, which should be done with faith and devotion.

Gita 9: 18

I am the supreme destination; I am the sustainer,
sovereign (self-governing), witness, abode, protector
and friend; I am the creation and dissolution; I am
the repository; I am the seed of this imperishable
creation.

Love the Divine; don't fear it.

The Supreme Being is the supporter of all beings. The
Divine is to be considered our supporter, protector and
friend. Thus, whether we are rich or poor, strong or weak,
we should surrender to the Divine as the supreme controller
of all worlds.

The Brahman is the witness to everything done in the
world. Whatever good or evil is done by us, the Brahman
observes it directly.

The Divine is the abode of the entire world. The Divine
is the refuge and shelter of all beings. The Brahman is the
friend of friends, always present and never disappointing.
The Brahman is the cause, the origin and dissolution of all
beings.

Gita 9: 19

O Arjuna, I give heat. I withhold as well as send forth
rain. I am immortality and death. I am both *sat* and
asat (being and non-being).

The Brahman is both *sat* and *asat.*

The Brahman is the cause of the origin of the world and
all the activities in it. As explained in this verse, in the same

way that heat from the sun and the phenomenon of rain
are interconnected—the sun radiates heat and evaporates
water, which later condenses and is released in the form of
rain—the Brahman and the world are interconnected.

Krishna says that everything in the world, like death and
immortality, being and non-being, are all manifestations of
the Divine.

The words *sat* (being) and *asat* (non-being) are used here
in the sense of the manifested and the unmanifested world.
Sat means that which exists all the time and is unchanging.
The only eternal and unchanging reality is the Brahman.
Asat means that which is impermanent and changing, that
is, the world and the universe, including our body and mind.

Gita 9: 20

**Those with knowledge of *trividya*, who consume
soma rasa, are purified from *paapa* through *yajna*,
and worship to go to *swarga* (heaven). They reach the
realm of Indra and enjoy celestial pleasures.**

The desire to go to heaven

All may not be desirous of liberation. Some people who want
to reach *swarga*, in Indra's kingdom, gain the knowledge
of *trividya* (knowledge of being healthy, wealthy and
wise). They perform *yajnas* and offer *soma rasa* in the
yajna and drink it. Krishna says that such people do enjoy
heavenly pleasures.

English translators who were not exposed to the Indian
knowledge system have spread much misinformation about
soma rasa. It has been called the drink of *devas*. Our

scriptures say that drinking it makes one immortal, with the mind purified of past *karma*. It is akin to *amrita*, or the elixir of life. *Soma*, in Sanskrit, means 'distil', and *rasa* means 'sap' or 'essence' or 'juice'. In the Vedic tradition, *soma* is a plant-based drink offered during rituals. A sacrifice is a spiritual practice; and why would one take an alcoholic drink while performing a spiritual practice?

Gita 9: 21

They enjoy the great pleasures of heaven, and after the fruits of good deeds are exhausted, they return to Earth. Thus, abiding by their *dharma*, they keep desiring and keep returning.

The lure of heavenly pleasures

When some of us seek heaven's pleasures even after learning the Vedas, we will keep returning to Earth. Even if spiritual practices purify us, we may remain attached to sensory pleasures and the desire for heavenly enjoyment. We may have evolved into humans, but we pray for heavenly joys only due to the lure of sense desires. We may get those rewards because of our good *karma*, but these pleasures are temporary.

When we know the three-fold *dharma*—shraddha, *jnana*, *viveka* (faith, knowledge and discrimination)—we do the right thing and accumulate merit. Because of such meritorious deeds, we do get to enjoy heavenly pleasures, but when the effect of these good deeds is over, we have to return to Earth and stay entangled in the cycle of birth and rebirth.

Gita 9: 22

For those who think of no other and worship Me, I care for their day-to-day reasonable and appropriate requirements.

If we do good, we are taken care of.

This verse is one of the most important promises uttered by Krishna. If we have faith in this promise, much scepticism would go away. It is right in the middle of the seven hundred verses of the Gita and is important enough to stand alone. Krishna says that if we worship the Divine with full faith and think of no other desires except to seek liberation, the Divine will protect the devotee and take the responsibility of the devotee's day-to-day reasonable requirements. It says that a devotee need have no fear of the future.

Let us then be true seekers. Krishna promises that the Divine's never-failing hand is always there to protect the aspirant. The difference here is that this type of devotee does not desire enjoyment in heaven or in other worlds.

This is the most remarkable compassion shown by Krishna towards his devotees. Whatever worldly needs there are will be taken care of by Krishna.

Gita 9: 25

Those who are worshippers of *deva* go to *deva*. Those who worship their ancestors go to those ancestors. Those who worship *bhuta* (living beings) go to *bhuta*. Those who worship Me come to Me.

Let there be clarity of goals.

We should be very clear about what we want in life. If we strive hard enough, we will achieve our goal with dedication and devotion.

Krishna says that the object of one's worship will determine the aspirant's goal. We will get nothing other than what we think about intensely. The wise one chooses the goal of liberation from all bondage and works for complete freedom and perfection. Such a wise person understands that there is no use in worshipping this or that *deva* (deity), *pitri* (ancestor) or *bhuta* (a living being), who can only give some perishable objects. Such perishable things would be temporary, and the person would be thrown down to *samsara* once again.

Therefore, we should think clearly about the goal we need to reach. We should not be content with lesser objects that will perpetuate misery and death in our lives. We should aspire for the highest perfection by worshipping the Divine.

Gita 9: 26–27

My devotees, if they offer Me a leaf, a flower, a fruit or some water with a pure heart, I accept it.

O Kaunteya, whatever you do, whatever you eat, whatever you offer, whatever you give away, whatever austerities you perform, do that as an offering to Me.

Every act should be an offering to the Divine.

If we find spiritual practices very difficult, Krishna surprises us here. Krishna explains the effortless nature of worship.

We don't have to make any elaborate sacrifices, practice austerities or give to charitable causes. Krishna says it is enough even if we offer a leaf, a flower, a fruit or even some water to please the Divine. This would even please all the deities, ancestors and living beings. We can get all the rewards we could get by spiritual practices through these simple offerings.

We need to satisfy only two conditions:
1. We should be pure-minded.
2. We should make the offering with devotion.

These conditions are straightforward. One need not be a king or a rich person. Any humble, ignorant person who is pure of mind and full of devotion can attain the Brahman.

Gita 9: 28

When people are free from attachment to good and bad results, they get liberated from the bondage of *karma*. Such renunciate *yogis* are liberated and attain Me.

Don't be attached to good or bad results.

We should not be attached to the outcome, no matter what happens. We should not associate our identity with the results of our actions. We should not forget our vision, values and final goal. Krishna is now talking about the renunciation of the fruits of actions, not the renunciation of actions themselves.

The renunciation here implies an inner sacrifice, effected by surrendering to the Divine all desire and attachment, all self-will and self-action, and all ego-sense. Desire and an attachment to possessions must be cast aside to achieve a life of all-pervading bliss.

There is a tale of King Shibi and the hawk in the Puranas that demonstrates total non-attachment. In this story, King Shibi displays his selflessness and non-attachment to even his own body. In the story, a hawk pursues a dove that seeks refuge in Shibi's kingdom. The dove flies to the king, seeking his protection. The hawk demands that the king surrender the dove. However, Shibi feels his duty is to protect the dove since it came seeking refuge. Instead, he offers his own flesh to the hawk, cutting pieces from his body to match the weight of the dove.

We may not be able to pursue non-attachment to this extent. Even so, the story should inspire us to perform our duties to the best of our abilities. When we do such actions without a sense of doership or desire, they remove the bondage of *karma*.

Gita 9: 29

I am equal to all living beings. No person is especially inimical or very dear to Me. But those who worship Me with devotion dwell in Me, and I dwell in them.

Equality for all

We should neither hate anyone nor give extra favour to others. Similarly, Krishna says that the Divine is neither inimical to anyone nor is anyone very dear to the Divine. We cannot hold the Supreme Being responsible for the good or bad happening to someone.

The Supreme Being has nothing to do with anyone's ups and downs, losses and gains, or pleasures and pains. Each one of us reaps the rewards of our thoughts and actions. As is said, 'One reaps what one sows'. Single-minded devotion leads us to the Supreme Being, who is present in all beings and manifests in the heart of all true devotees.

Gita 9: 30–31

Even when an immoral person worships Me with absolute devotion, that person should be considered equal to a great saintly person.

O Kaunteya, very soon, such a person becomes a *dharmatma* (holy person) and attains eternal bliss. My devotee is never lost.

There is hope even for a wicked person.

Krishna says that even if the wickedest of persons surrenders to the Divine with faith and devotion and strives hard to give up wickedness, such a person would be regarded as being honourable and righteous. Even if a person is the worst type of evil, they will be considered virtuous if they surrenders themselves willingly to the Divine.

The reason is that at long last, the evil person has come to the right decision that the Brahman is the only reality and that they must catch sight of this ultimate truth. Such a person has realized the deceptive nature of the world and has taken final refuge in the Divine. The flame of worship burns up the evil tendencies connected to such a person. Therefore, let no offender be disheartened that the weight of *paapa* is too much to suffer.

Gita 9: 32

O Partha, all those who take refuge in Me will attain eternal bliss even if they are born in *paapayoni* (disadvantaged birth)—a female, a *vaishya* (business people) or a *shudra* (skilled worker).

Everyone can overcome the disadvantage.

Certain people have a disadvantage due to where and how they are born. Krishna mentions three categories of people here: a female, a merchant and a skilled worker. Why are these groups regarded as disadvantaged? It is significant here that those born in a disadvantaged category can attain the Divine if they surrender to the Brahman. All of these people can go beyond the birth and rebirth cycle through faith and devotion.

Krishna is talking about women empowerment thousands of years back. Women face disadvantages across the world, in every society, to a greater or lesser extent. Such disadvantages start at birth and increase at each stage of life. Women endure a lot of pain biologically. They bear the burden of learning and understanding their bodies because there is a lot going on there. Then, there is pregnancy—the pain of carrying a pregnancy to term and the pain of child labour. The bulk of the physical responsibility of nurturing children rests with women.

There are many cultural perspectives against women, and discriminatory customs and practices keep manifesting themselves in one way or another.

Krishna also puts merchants and skilled workers in the category of disadvantaged birth. Merchants must work extended hours to run their business, deal with all kinds of customers and satisfy them. They have a rigorous work schedule and limited social life. They work under high levels of stress and have exposure to security threats.

Skilled workers depend on the demand and supply of their skills, which decides their earning capacity. Their life depends on the prospect of employment by others, no matter how skilled they are. So, Krishna also includes skilled workers in the category of disadvantaged birth.

Gita 9: 33

The same is true for the *brahmana*, the pious person, the devotee, the *rajarshi*. Therefore, having come to this transient and joyless world, just worship Me.

Mere birth cannot take you anywhere.

Krishna says that mere birth does not qualify anyone or provide a passport to self-realization. What is essential is purity and devotion.

A *rajarshi* is a person with power but the attribute of a *jnani*. There is a saying that power corrupts, and absolute power corrupts absolutely. So, there is danger for such a person to deviate from goodness. A birth in a *brahmana* family may provide a conducive environment, but that is not enough. Such a person may get entangled in day-to-day rituals rather than focusing on liberation.

Krishna says that this world and this birth—anywhere—does not give you any advantage or disadvantage. By nature, the body, mind and intellect are attracted to sense-enjoyment wherever we are. The world is transitory and full of misery. There is no real joy in worldly life; the ultimate goal should be self-realization and liberation.

Gita 10: 3

Those who know Me as unborn, without beginning, and the great Ishvara of the world—they are not deluded among mortals and are free from all *paapa*.

Ishvara is unborn and without beginning.

Among all the living beings on earth, human beings embody the highest intelligence. Among mortals, human beings know that Ishvara is unborn and without beginning. All other existences in the world have a beginning and an end. All other beings are born at a particular time and die without fail. The desire for liberation from the cycle of birth and rebirth alone gives a desire to know the Brahman.

Once we strive to be free of delusion, we can be on the path of devotion to the Divine. We understand that all other worldly benefits are transient and unreal. The pursuit of worldly desires leads us to sorrow and death. When delusion is gone, we become free from all *paapa*. When we are free from all *paapa*, we become one with the *paramatma*. The devotion to the infinite glory of Ishvara strengthens our resolve.

Gita 10: 4–5

Discrimination, wisdom, lack of confusion, forgiveness, truthfulness, restraining the senses,

restraining the mind, pleasure, pain, birth, death, fear,
and even fearlessness;

Non-violence, equanimity, contentment, austerity,
charity, honour, dishonour, all these types of *bhava* in
all beings arise from Me alone.

Sixteen good qualities

We are told about sixteen good qualities and four bad
qualities here. Whether good or bad, all of these qualities
originate from the *paramatma*. The good qualities listed here
are discrimination, wisdom, lack of confusion, forgiveness,
truthfulness, restraint of the senses, restraint of the mind,
pleasure, birth, fearlessness, non-violence, equanimity,
contentment, austerity, charity and honour.

The bad qualities mentioned here are pain, fear, dishonour
and death.

The qualities demonstrated by different people result
from their *guna* composition, which influences their
thoughts and actions. Those on the path of spiritual
practices become good and possess all the divine qualities.
Those not on the path of spirituality are attracted to sense-
enjoyment and possess bad qualities.

Gita 10: 6

Seven *maharshis*, four *devarshis*, and fourteen *manu*
were born of My nature from My mind, and from
them came forth all these beings in the world.

Creation is shaped in the mind first.

We have been told that all things are created twice. First, there is a mental creation, and then there is a physical or second creation of all things.

Suppose an architect wants to construct a house. They create or visualize it first in every detail in the mind before starting the construction. The architect always creates an image in their mind until they have a clear picture of what they want to build. These thoughts are then formulated into a blueprint and a construction plan is made. All of these activities are done even before the land is touched—this is the first creation in the mind. The second creation is the actual construction of the house.

In the same way, Krishna tells us that the Divine created this world in the mind and then created all beings. In this verse, Krishna explains the order in which the Divine created people. First, he created the seven *maharshis*, then the four *devarshis* and the fourteen *manus*.

The seven *maharshis* are Marichi, Atri, Angira, Pulah, Kratu, Pulastya and Vashishta. They belong to the line of the first gurus.

The four *devarshis are the* Sanakadi: Sanak, Sanandan, Sanatan and Sanatkumar. They taught the path of withdrawal from worldly life.

The fourteen *manus* are Swayambhu Manu, Svarochisha Manu, Uttama Manu, Tapasa Manu, Raivata Manu, Chakshusha Manu, Vaivasvata Manu, Savarni Manu, Daksha Savarni Manu, Brahma Savarni Manu, Dharma Savarni Manu, Rudra Savarni Manu, Deva Savarni Manu and Indra Savarni Manu. These *manus* taught the path of *dharma*—of righteous conduct of life.

We should be proud that we are descendants of these great sages.

Gita 10: 11

O Partha, solely out of compassion for them, I, dwelling in their hearts, destroy the darkness with the luminous lamp of knowledge.

Use the luminous lamp of knowledge.

Krishna describes the compassion of the Divine for devotees. When the *paramatma* is pleased with the devotion of aspirants, the darkness in their hearts is destroyed with the luminous lamp of knowledge.

We do not get wealth, power and position when the Divine is pleased since these are not eternal. They disappear in time. So, the *paramatma* bestows on the devotees the everlasting gift of liberation.

We are told that when we are on the path of knowledge, *jnana yoga*, we gain the knowledge that we can use as a lamp to dispel the darkness of ignorance.

We know that nothing else but light can dispel darkness. We may struggle with darkness eternally if we don't have light. We may do everything, *japa*, *tapa*, *pranayama* or meditation; yet, ignorance would not be removed. It is the knowledge of the Self which will help.

QUESTION 10

WHICH FORM SHOULD I MEDITATE UPON?

The object of meditation, or *dhyana,* is to meditate on some form or aspect of the Divine. The reason for meditating on the Divine is that He is divine and pure. When our mind is attached to someone or something divine, the result is also divine. On the other hand, if we are concentrating on someone or something in the material world, the result is temporary.

Since the Divine is pure, we, too, can become pure as a result of focusing our minds on it. Various techniques of meditation have been explained in spiritual practices. Some meditate on the breath, a point of light or the third eye, others on the eternal sound of Oṁ, and others on the seven chakras in the body. In such practices, while focusing on the object of meditation, one is also trying to balance the breath and become more aware of it. In other words, on the one hand, we are required to focus the mind on one object (light, third eye, Oṁ, chakra); on the other hand, we are also trying to focus on the breath. The techniques often get complicated, and we don't even know what we are doing.

Krishna has explained various essences, forms and aspects of Ishvara and also demonstrated the cosmic form to Arjuna. So, Arjuna asks: Which of these forms should I meditate upon? Since Krishna says that the Divine permeates all the realms and resides in them, Arjuna wants to know: How may I know you and think of you?

Gita 10: 20

**O Gudakesha, I am to be found in the heart of
all living entities. I am the origin, sustenance and
destination of all beings.**

Jivatma, *atma* and *paramatma*

There is a difference between *atma* and *paramatma*. *Atma*
is the Self. *Paramatma* is the Supreme Self, the Divine Self,
sat (truth) or reality. The difference between *atma* and
paramatma is that the *atma*, or the Self, is present only in
a particular body, whereas the *paramatma* is everywhere.

We have also heard about *jivatma*. What is *jivatma*?
Jivatma is the individual Self, which is a reflection of the
atma within an individual. It is also called the soul. It is a
wave that emerges from the ocean of existence and wanders
from one body to another. After a long process of birth and
rebirth, the *jivatma* returns to the unity of the *atma*, that
is, *paramatma*.

The problem is that the soul that has manifested itself in
a body does not identify with its divine essence but rather
with the physical body, mind and intellect. The aim of all
paths of *yoga* described here is to show the way to this unity.

Gita 10: 21

**Among twelve Adityas, I am Vishnu; among luminous
objects, I am the sun; among the *maruts*, I am
Marichi. I am the moon.**

The glory of Ishvara

Krishna is now talking about various forms and aspects where the Divine is present. Krishna declares that he is Vishnu among the Adityas (son of Aditi), implying that his glory is most manifest in Vishnu. The Adityas, sons of Aditi, are twelve: Vishnu, Aryaman, Indra, Tvashtha, Varuna, Dhata, Bhaga, Parjanya, Vivasvan, Amshuman, Mitra and Pushya. The Adi Parva of the Mahabharata mentions these names.

Among luminous objects, he is the sun. He is also the moon. Among mighty winds, he is Marichi. There are forty-nine types of *maruts* (the wind), seven types of winds in seven groups each. Marichi is the beautiful breeze which makes us feel very pleasant; it means a tender, beautiful breeze, not the cyclonic storm.

Gita 10: 22

Among the Vedas, I am Sama Veda; among the *devas*, I am Vasu; among the *indriyas*, I am the mind; and among living beings, I am *chetana* (consciousness).

The glory of Ishvara

There are four Vedas: Rig Veda, Yajur Veda, Sama Veda and Atharva Veda. Among the four Vedas, the Divine is Sama Veda. The major theme of the Sama Veda is worship and devotion.

There are eight *devas* (deities). Among those *devas*, the Divine is Vasu. Vasu is the elemental aspect of nature—earth, water, fire, air, sky, sun, moon and the Dhruva star.

Most of us are governed by our *indriyas*, or sense organs. These sense organs influence the function of the body, mind and intellect. Among these sense organs, the Divine is the mind. Until the mind is purified, we cannot attain liberation.

The Divine is *chetana* (consciousness) in all living beings.

Gita 10:23

Among the *rudras*, I am Shankara; among the *yaksha* (seekers of wealth) and *rakshasa* (seekers of power), I am Kuber. Among the *vasus*, I am Pavak (fire); among the mountains, I am Meru.

The glory of Ishvara

Rudras are forms of Shiva. They are mentioned in the *Harivamsa*. There are eleven *rudras*: Kapali, Pingal, Bheem, Virupaksha, Vilohit, Shastra, Ajapaad, Ahirbudhnya, Shankara, Chand and Bhav. *Rudra* bestows *jnana*: 'Rut jnanam rati dadati iti Rudrah.' Among the *rudras*, the Divine is Shankara, the original form of Shiva.

Yakshas are semi-celestial beings who are very fond of acquiring and accumulating wealth. *Rakshasas* are beings who seek power. Their leader is Kuber, the deity of wealth and the treasurer of all celestial deities.

There are eight *vasus* (elements)—land, water, fire, air, space, sun, moon and stars. They constitute the gross structure of the universe. Amongst these, fire gives warmth and energy to the rest of the elements. Therefore, among the eight elements, the Divine is fire.

Among all the mountains, the Divine is Meru. Meru is the sacred five-peaked mountain that is considered the centre of all the physical, metaphysical and spiritual universes.

Gita 10: 24

O Partha, among priests, know that I am the chief Brahaspati; among warriors, I am Skanda; and among water reservoirs, I am the ocean.

The glory of Ishvara

A priest performs ritualistic worship and ceremonies in temples and homes. Krishna says that among priests, he is the chief, Brahaspati, the sage who attained oneness with the Supreme Spirit by knowledge and who has been free from worldly pain. Brahaspati is considered their guru by all the *devas*.

Among all the warriors, the Divine is Skanda. Skanda is also called Kartikeya, Murugan or Subhramanya and is worshipped as an ever-youthful man riding a peacock. Skanda is the commander-in-chief of the celestial deities.

Krishna further says that he is nothing less than the mighty ocean amongst bodies of water.

Gita 10: 25

Among *maharshis*, I am Bhrigu; among words, I am *aum*; among *yajnas*, I am *japa yajna* (chanting); among immovable objects, I am the Himalayas.

The glory of Ishvara

Seven *maharshis* are mentioned in the Yajur Veda: Angiras, Atri, Bhrigu, Gautama, Kashyapa, Kutsa and Vashishtha. Krishna says he is Bhrigu. Bhrigu possesses wisdom, glory and devotion. In the Puranas, Bhrigu contested with the trinity of Brahma, Vishnu and Shiva in his grasp of these areas.

Among words, the Divine is *aum*. It is the *anahat nad*, the sound vibration that permeates creation. It is always present at the beginning of Vedic mantras for invoking auspiciousness.

Krishna has described various spiritual practices. The Divine is *japa yajna* (chanting) among *yajnas*, or spiritual practices.

Among immovable objects, the Divine is the Himalayas. The Himalayas are a mountain range in north India that have inspired spiritual reverence and curiosity in many devotees. The atmosphere, environment and solitude are highly conducive to performing spiritual practices.

Gita 10: 26

Among all trees, I am Ashvattha; among *deva rishis*, I am Narada; among the *gandharvas*, I am Chitraratha; among *siddhas*, I am Kapil Muni.

The glory of Ishvara

Among all trees, The Divine is the Ashvattha tree. This tree is also known as the peepal tree or *kalpa vriskha*. It symbolizes the *trimurti*—Vishnu is believed to be the trunk, Brahma its roots and Shiva its branches. The peepal tree, also called the sacred fig tree, has a very calming effect on people who sit under it. The tree expands downward through aerial roots; a full-grown peepal tree is massive and provides cooling shade in a large area.

Among *deva rishis,* the Divine is Narada. Narada is a pure devotee of Vishnu and a master of communication. Narada is the guru of many great people, such as Veda Vyasa, Valmiki, Dhruva and Prahlada. Narada is constantly engaged in singing the glories of the Divine. Narada is also famous for testing devotees of the Divine, and people sometimes misunderstand him as a troublemaker. But his desire to purify famous personalities ultimately results in self-introspection and purification of these people.

Among the *gandharvas,* who are well versed in music and dance, the Divine is Chitraratha. Chitraratha is the chief of the *gandharvas.*

Among *siddhas,* those who have knowledge of *dharma* and have attained spiritual perfection, the Divine is Kapil Muni, the founder of Samkhya. Kapil Muni revealed the Samkhya philosophy system and taught the glories of *bhakti yoga.*

Gita 10: 27

Know that among horses, I am Uchhaishrava—the divine seven-headed horse born during the *samudra manthan*; among elephants, I am Airavata; and among human beings, I am sovereign.

The glory of Ishvara

Krishna says that among horses, the Divine is Uchhaishrava. Uchhaishrava drives the vehicle of the sun. It is the divine seven-headed horse born during the *samudra manthan* (the churning of the ocean by *devas* and *asuras*). The pure-white horse is supposed to be the fastest horse in the universe.

Among elephants, the Divine is Airavata. Airavata was also born during the *samudra manthan*. Airavata is a white elephant and serves as the vehicle mount of Indra. It is also known as *ardha-matang*, or the elephant of the clouds.

Among men, the Divine is the sovereign ruler.

Gita 10: 28

Among weapons, I am Vajra; among cows, I am Kamadhenu; for begetting children, I am Kandarpa; and among serpents, I am Vasuki.

The glory of Ishvara

Among weapons, the Divine is Vajra. Vajra is Indra's weapon, created from the bones donated by Sage Dadhichi after his sacrifice. The Puranas relate the story of the sacrifice offered by the great Sage Dadhichi. Once upon a time, Indra was defeated by an *asura* named Vritrasura. Indra was told that the only weapon that could kill Vritrasura was a thunderbolt made from the bones of Sage Dadhichi. Dadhichi made the ultimate sacrifice of laying down his life so that his bones could be used for making the thunderbolt. The Divine is that thunderbolt.

Among cows, the Divine is Kamadhenu. Kamadhenu

is the mother of all cows, who provides her owner with whatever the owner desires.

The Divine is also Kandarpa. Kandarpa is also known as Kamadeva, the *deva* of sexual desires. Sexual desires are needed for begetting children. Kamadeva is the deity of love, who is responsible for the force of attraction between the opposite sexes.

Among serpents, the Divine is Vasuki. Vasuki has been described as having a gem called Nagamani on its head.

Gita 10: 29

Among *nagas*, I am Ananta (Sheshanaga); among water beings, I am Varuna; among *pitra*, I am Aryama; and among all dispensers of justice, I am Yama.

The glory of Ishvara

Nagas are a powerful, splendid and wonderful race that can assume the physical form of the human, partial human-serpent or the whole serpent. The Divine is Ananta (Sheshanaga) among *nagas*. Ananta is the divine serpent upon which Vishnu rests.

Among all water beings, the Divine is Varuna. Varuna is the *deva* of oceans, water and aquatic animals.

Pitra are ancestors with higher levels of consciousness. The Divine is Aryama among *pitra*. Aryama is one of the twelve Adityas: Vamana, Aryama, Indra, Tvashtha, Varuna, Dhata, Bhaga, Parjanya, Vivasvan, Amshuman, Mitra and Pushya. Aryama is worshipped as the head of the departed ancestors.

Among all dispensers of justice, the Divine is Yama. Yama is the celestial deity of death. Yama dispenses justice for an individual's actions in this life. Yama grants punishment or reward in the next life and does not deviate from his duties.

Gita 10: 30

Among *daityas*, I am Prahlada; I am Kaal among all that controls; among wild animals, I am a lion; and among birds, I am Vainateya.

The glory of Ishvara

Daityas are the clan of *asuras*, children of Diti and the sage Kashyapa. Krishna says that the Divine is Prahlada among *daityas*. Prahlada was the son of the powerful *daitya* king, Hiranyakashipu. However, Prahlada turned out to be one of the greatest devotees of Vishnu.

The Divine is the Kaal (time, the present moment) among all that controls. Time is the great leveller that can wear down the biggest and mightiest in the universe.

Among wild animals, the Divine is a lion. The lion is called the king of the jungle and is amongst the most powerful and majestic animals.

Among birds, the Divine is Vainateya. Vainateya is also called Garuda, a legendary bird or bird-like creature and the vehicle mount, *vahana*, of Vishnu.

Gita 10: 31

I am the wind among purifiers. Among warriors, I am Rama; among fish, I am Makara (shark); and among rivers, I am Jahnavi.

The glory of Ishvara

Wind is the best purifier. It carries away the dirty smells in the air. It helps the fire burn by fuelling it with oxygen. Among purifiers, the Divine is the wind.

Rama is also called *maryada purushottam*, meaning he is the best among people who always remain within the expected boundaries. He was the most powerful warrior on the earth of his time. Yet, he never once exploited his dominant superiority. He utilized his weapons only to do what was right. Krishna says the Divine is Rama among warriors.

Among fish, the Divine is a shark. People are often called sharks when they know how to take advantage of an excellent opportunity. Sharks are observant, curious, fearless, solitary, aggressive, unforgiving and ruthless.

Among rivers, the Divine is Jahnavi, also popularly known as Ganga. The Ganga is a holy river, and many great sages have performed austerities on its banks.

Gita 10: 32

O Arjuna, I am the origin, sustenance and final destination of all creations. Among knowledge, I am spiritual knowledge; in any discourse, I am the logic.

The glory of Ishvara

The Divine is the beginning, middle and end of all living beings. The Divine is all that is created, such as space, air, fire, water and earth. The Divine is the origin (*adi*), sustenance (*madhya*) and final destination (*anta*) of these creations.

The Indian knowledge system describes various types of knowledge (*vidyas*). Some of them are (from Vishnu Puran 3.6.27–28, v29):

- *Vedang* (six types of knowledge): *Shiksha, kalp, vyakaran, nirukti, jyotish, chhanda. Vedang* is called the limbs of the Vedas.
- Vedic knowledge (the four Vedas): Rig Veda, Yajur Veda, Sāma Veda, Atharva Veda
- Fourteen chief *vidyas*: Mimansa, Nyaya, Dharma Shastra, and the Puranas

When we acquire this knowledge, it cultivates the intellect, deepens the understanding and increases awareness of the path of *dharma*.

Additionally, the spiritual practice and the science of spirituality liberate human beings from material bondage. Krishna says the Divine is spiritual knowledge, superior to all the above *vidyas*.

There are four ways in which one can hold a conversation: *samvada* (dialogue), *vada* (discussion), *jalpa* (debate) and *vitanda* (argument).

Samvada (dialogue) is a discussion between two people where one talks and the other listens. The listener can ask questions to clarify doubts. Most Indian scriptures are written in the form of *samvada*.

Vada (discussion) is a discussion between equals to establish the truth or to resolve a conflict. Both parties are convinced they are correct; here, they are willing to listen and accept the opponents' version. There is always some learning that takes place in *vada*.

Jalpa (debate) is a discussion between two persons who are convinced that they are right and their opponent is wrong. The purpose is not to discover or establish the truth but to disprove the other party. The outcome of *jalpa* is a lot of noise.

Vitanda (argument) is a discussion with the sole purpose of defeating the adversary. There is no learning for either party, and their conversation is also not worth listening to.

Logic is the basis for the communication of ideas and the establishment of truths. Krishna says that the Divine is logic in all such discourses.

Gita 10: 33

Among letters, I am the letter 'अ'; among compound words, I am *dvandva*; I am infinite time; and among creators, I am Brahma.

The glory of Ishvara

Among the letters, the Divine is the letter अ. In Sanskrit, all letters are formed by combining a half-letter with अ, simply because अ represents the exhalation of breath, without which no sound is possible. For example, क्+अ=क.

Among compound words, the Divine is *dvandva*. *Dvandva* is a compound of two or more words which, if not compounded, would stand in the same case and be connected by a conjunction. In the Sanskrit language, words are combined to form compound words. The process of making such compound words is called *samasa*. The resulting word is called *samasa pada*, or compound word. There are six kinds of *samasa*: 1) *dvandva*, 2) *bahubrihi*, 3) *karm dharay*, 4) *tatpurush*, 5) *dwigu*, 6) *avyayi bhav*. Amongst these compound words, *dvandva* is the best because the meanings of both source words remain equally prominent in the resulting word. In contrast, in the others, one of the words becomes more prominent, or both words combine to mean a third word.

Krishna says the Divine is infinite time, as there is no beginning or end. Krishna also says that the Divine is the creator of the universe, Brahma.

Gita 10: 34

I am all-devouring death; I am the origin of those things yet to be. In women, I am *kirti* (fame), *shrih* (prosperity) *vak* (fine speech), *smriti* (memory), *medha* (intelligence), *dhriti* (patience) and *kshama* (forgiveness).

The glory of Ishvara

The Divine is all-devouring death. For one who is born, death is certain. All life inevitably ends in death. The final end is called the 'dead end'. The Divine is also the origin of things yet to come.

Here, Krishna mentions certain qualities of women, which are Divine.

These are fame, prosperity, fine speech, memory, intelligence, patience and forgiveness. These are the qualities which make women glorious. The first three qualities are related to external behaviour, and the other four are inner qualities.

These qualities are also the names of the daughters of Prajapati Daksha. Five were considered the best among women—Kirti, Smriti, Medha, Dhriti and Kshama. Shree was the daughter of Bhrigu. Vak was the daughter of Brahma. Therefore, these seven women are the deities of the seven qualities mentioned here.

Gita 10: 35

Among *Sama* hymns, I am *brihatsam*; among *chhanda* (Vedic hymns), I am *Gayatri Mantra*. Among months, I am Margashirsha, and among *ritu* (season), I am *kusumakar* (spring).

The glory of Ishvara

Earlier, Krishna said that among the Vedas, the Divine is Sama Veda. Now he says that the Divine is *brihatsam* among *Sama* hymns, a *sukta* of the *Sama Samhita*.

The Sanskrit language has a system of rhymes and meters for writing poetry. Amongst these, the Gayatri meter is very melodic. Among *chhanda* (Vedic hymns), the Divine is *Gayatri Mantra*.

Among months, the Divine is Margashirsha. Margashirsha is the ninth month in the Hindu calendar, which is believed to be highly auspicious.

Among *ritu* (seasons), the Divine is *kusumakar* (*basant* or spring season). It is the time in India and anywhere in the world when nature is bursting with joy.

Gita 10: 36

I am the risk-taking ability of the gambler; I am the vigour of the strong; I am victory, I am effort; I am the goodness of the virtuous.

The glory of Ishvara

The Divine is the risk-taking ability of the gambler. Everyone cannot take risks like a gambler does. A gambler, too, possesses intellect and ability. But if the gambler misuses these instruments, the Divine is not responsible for their immoral deeds.

The Divine is the vigour of the strong, the victory and the effort required to perform *karma*. The Divine is also the goodness of the virtuous. Instead of boosting our ego for our goodness and strength, we should remember it is the Divine acting through us.

Gita 10: 37

Among the Vrishni, I am Vasudeva; among the Pandavas, I am Dhananjaya; among *munis*, I am Vyasa; and among poets, I am Ushana Kavi.

The glory of Ishvara

Krishna was born in the Vrishni dynasty as the son of Vasudev. There are five Vrishni heroes: Balarama, Vasudeva,

Pradumna, Samba and Aniruddha. The Divine is Vasudeva among them.

The Pandavas were the five sons of Pandu: Yudhishthira, Bhima, Arjuna, Nakula and Sahadeva. Krishna says that among the Pandavas, the Divine is Dhananjaya (another name for Arjuna, the one who conquered wealth).

Among *munis,* people of contemplation, the Divine is Vyasa, the author of the Mahabharata.

Among poets, the Divine is Ushana Kavi. Ushanas belonged to *Kavya gotra*; in Tamil, the oldest poet, Tolkappiyan, is believed to be from this *gotra*.

Gita 10: 38

Amongst means of preventing lawlessness, I am punishment; I am the strategy of the victorious; I am the silence amongst secrets; and I am the wisdom in the wise.

The glory of Ishvara

Punishment is an essential tool for preventing lawlessness. The role of punishment is to deter those in society who might be inclined to perform unlawful actions. Krishna says that the Divine is punishment amongst all measures to deter lawlessness.

We cannot gain victory without a proper strategy. Krishna says that the Divine is the strategy used by the victorious.

A secret is hidden from public knowledge for a particular purpose. The best way to keep something secret is to keep silent. Amongst the methods to keep a secret, silence is Divine.

True wisdom comes with spiritual knowledge. Krishna says that the Divine is the wisdom of the wise.

Gita 11: 3–4

O Parameshwar, you are precisely what you declare yourself to be. Now, I desire to see your divine cosmic form, O Purushottama.

O Prabhu, if you think I am strong enough to view it, kindly reveal that imperishable cosmic form to me.

Desire to see the glories of Ishvara

After having heard Krishna describe the glories of Ishvara, Arjuna now wants to see them with his own eyes.

Arjuna requests: 'O Yogeshwar, I have expressed my wish. If you consider me worthy of it, then by your grace, please reveal your cosmic form to me, and show me your *Yog-aishwarya* (mystic opulence).'

Arjuna is addressing Krishna as Yogeshwara, 'Ishvara of all *yogis*'. Since the object of attainment for all *yogis* is the Supreme Being, Krishna is now addressed as the Ishvara of all *yogis*.

Gita 11: 7–8

O Gudakesha, now see the entire universe with the movable, the immovable, and whatever else you want to see together in one place in My body.

But you will not be able to see this with your eyes. I will give you the divine eyes to see My divine form.

Divine eyes to see the divine form

Krishna had said that everything that is movable and immovable originates and ends in the Divine. But this cosmic form cannot be seen with our physical eyes. Physical eyes are inadequate to see the universal form. Also, the ordinary intellect cannot comprehend it. Therefore, Krishna now grants divine vision with which Arjuna can see the cosmic form.

The granting of spiritual vision is an act of kindness by the Supreme Being. In his mercifulness, Ishvara superimposes divine eyes onto Arjuna's material eyes. He adds his divine mind to Arjuna's material mind. He adds his divine intellect to Arjuna's material intellect. Thus, equipped with divine eyes, mind and intellect, Arjuna can see the divine form.

Gita 11: 16

O Vishweshvar, I see your infinite form in every direction, with many arms, bellies, faces and eyes. I see your universal form with no beginning, middle or end.

The universal form of the Divine

Arjun uses two words to describe what he sees with his divine eyes. *Vishweshvar,* meaning 'Ishvara of the universe' and *vishwarupa,* meaning 'universal form'. He means that the universe is nothing but the manifestation of Ishvara and Ishvara is a manifestation of the universe.

Arjuna is amazed at the vastness of the form he is looking at. He says that no matter what angle he looks from, Arjun cannot discern any end to Divine manifestations. When Arjuna searches for the beginning, he is unable to find it. When Arjuna tries to see its middle, he has no success, and when he searches for the end, he cannot find the limit to the vision manifested before him.

Gita 11: 24

Having seen your form touching the sky, bright in many colours, with mouths wide open and enormous glowing eyes, my heart is trembling with fear. O Vishnu, I am not calm and cannot find courage.

Arjuna is fearful of the cosmic form.

When Arjuna sees the cosmic, eldritch form touching the sky, bright in many colours, with mouths wide open and enormous glowing eyes, he is scared. Arjuna is struck with awe and wonder, his heart is trembling with fear, and all courage is lost. He is not calm anymore.

Arjuna is beset with fear and terror because he had not imagined such a sight of the Divine. Now, he understands what Krishna meant when he said the Divine is omnipotent, omniscient and omnipresent.

Gita 11: 41–42

Considering you as my friend, unaware of your magnificence and also due to my ignorance and affection for you, I inadvertently addressed you as 'O Krishna, O Yadava, O Sakha (friend)',

Whatever disrespect I may have shown you, for the sake of fun, while playing, resting, sitting, eating, when alone or before others—for all that, I beg your forgiveness.

Don't disrespect your loved ones.

Disrespect obviously means a lack of respect. But what is respect? Respect is deep admiration for someone. But the concept of respect includes much more than admiration. When we respect someone, we also honour a person's feelings and needs. Respect also involves considering and conveying importance to that person's desires, goals, thoughts and behaviours. Disrespect is precisely the opposite of this.

Many times, we also disrespect a person out of too much love or too much familiarity. Arjuna considered Krishna his very dear friend. When he realizes that Krishna is the Supreme Divine, he asks for forgiveness for his earlier disrespectful behaviour. Arjun had shared many intimate, memorable moments with Krishna, oblivious of his supreme position.

Gita 11: 45

I am delighted to see what has never been seen before. My mind is fearful and distressed. O Devesh, O Jagannivas, I pray that you show your *deva* form again.

Normal is better.

There are two kinds of devotion. In one type, the devotee thinks about the almighty aspect of the Divine. The dominant sentiment here is one of awe and reverence. In such devotion, a feeling of remoteness and the need to maintain proper conduct always exists.

In the second type, the devotee feels an intimate relationship and bond. The dominant sentiment in such devotion is that of closeness and love. This type of devotion is sweeter than the earlier one.

Arjuna's devotion to Krishna is that of a friend. On seeing the universal form of Krishna, Arjuna experiences tremendous fearfulness and respect. After seeing the cosmic form, he wants to see Krishna in his usual form again.

Gita 11: 48

O Kurupravir, not by the study of the Vedas, nor by performing *yajnas*, nor by charity, nor by performing actions, and not by performing intense *tapa* (austerities) can this form be seen by people in the world, which you have seen.

The kindness of the Divine

Krishna tells Arjuna that what he has seen now is something unusual. There is no amount of self-effort, study of the Vedic texts, performance of rituals, undertaking of austerities, fasting, or acts of charity that could ever be sufficient to see a vision of the cosmic form. This vision was only possible for Arjuna because of the kindness of the Divine towards him.

The logic behind this is elementary. Our eyes are made from matter; hence, all we can see is matter. The Divine is non-material. We need to have divine eyes to see a vision of the divine form.

Then how was Sanjaya, the narrator of the Mahabharata, able to see that cosmic form? The Mahabharata declares that Sanjaya also received the grace of his guru, Ved Vyasa. Therefore, he could see the cosmic form.

Gita 11: 54

O Arjuna, it is possible by single-minded devotion alone to see Me in this form. O Parantapa, only by My divine vision, one can know Me and be in union with Me.

Single-minded devotion is important.

Krishna declares that only by single-minded devotion can one see the Divine, and it is the only way for the Divine to be known and attained. The mind should not be distracted by the desires of sense-enjoyment.

Worldly things and objects generally possess our minds. We offer only a part of our mind to the Divine. When the mind is not distracted by anything else, it acquires divine power and thus attains the Divine.

Three things are mentioned here regarding the union with the Divine: to be known, seen and attained.

We can learn the nature of the Divine by deep study and correct understanding of the scriptures. This approach is the *dwaita* principle.

Next, devotees can see the Divine when they contemplate upon the Divine in a particular form. A devotee can visualize the Divine like a fruit in one's hand. This approach is *visishtadvaita.*

After long spiritual practice, the devotee becomes united with the Divine, like salt in water, raindrops in the ocean or water in milk. Then, there are no longer two entities; the devotee and the Divine become one. This approach is *moksha.*

Gita 11: 55

O Pandava, all those who perform their *karma* for Me, all who are devoted to Me, are free from attachment and are without animosity towards all beings; only such devotees can realize Me.

How can the Divine be realized?

There are five essential qualities needed for the realizing the Divine.

1) *Mat-karma-krit:* All *karma* should be performed for the Divine. This may include *puja, japa,* and *dhyana* as prescribed by the scriptures. It may also be referred to as offering all our work to the Divine.

2) *Mat-paramah:* We should believe that our first priority is liberation. Many of us spend day and night in the pursuit of worldly enjoyment. These enjoyments are perishable. They cannot lead us to freedom and perfection.

3) *Mad-bhaktah:* We should have single-minded devotion. We should realize that the Divine alone, and nothing else, is worthy of devotion.

4) *Sang-avarjitah: Sanga* means attachment. We should not be attached to our *karma* or the results of the *karma*.

5) *Nirvairah-sarvabhuteshu:* We should develop affection for all beings and aversion to none. We should realize that all beings are different forms of the Divine.

This verse of Chapter 11 of the Gita is of incredible importance. It is the very essence of the Gita. It contains, in a nutshell, all the different paths of spiritual practices.

QUESTION 11

WHO IS A BETTER DEVOTEE?

Krishna has shown multiple forms and aspects of Ishvara to Arjuna to worship and meditate on. So, there is a question in Arjuna's mind: Which *yogi* is better—one who worships with form or the one who worships the formless Brahman?

Krishna answers the question diplomatically. He says: 'Those who worship Me with their minds focused on Me with unwavering faith are the very best, in My opinion.' It is not a question of better but following the path with regular practice.

Krishna summarizes various types of devoted actions and spiritual practices here. One may do *sagun bhakti* or *nirgun bhakti*. *Nirgun bhakti* is more difficult than *sagun bhakti*. Those who remember the Divine with single-minded devotion—*dhyana yoga*—also attain the Divine. By performing our *karma* with single-minded devotion, we can attain the Divine, too. One can attain the Divine by renouncing the result of *karma* by acquiring *jnana*.

Thus, Krishna explains the range of practices, specifically *karma*, *dhyana* and *jnana yoga*. Krishna answers the question now by saying that *jnana* (knowledge) is better than *yajna*, *dhyana* (meditation) is better than *jnana*, and renunciation of the results of *karma* is better than *dhyana*. Such renunciation (of the results of *karma*) leads to eternal bliss.

At the end of the verse, Krishna concludes that devotees who follow *dharma* (cosmic law underlying right behaviour and social order) with total faith in the Divine are very dear to him.

Gita 12: 1

Arjuna said: Who do you consider a better *yogi*—one who worships you in a particular form or one who worships you in an impersonal form?

Who is a better devotee?

Some of us worship the deity, for example, Ganesha or Lakshmi, which is worshipping the Divine in a personified form. Others don't worship the Divine in a particular form. Arjuna's question is simple and clear. Who is superior— those who worship the Divine form (*sagun bhakti*) or meditate on the formless, attributeless Brahman (*nirgun bhakti*)?

Krishna has already described the eternal reality of *atma*, and later, explained the *nirgun* aspect as imperishable Brahman. After seeing the cosmic form of Krishna, it is very natural for Arjuna to question Krishna about the superiority of either of the two.

Arjuna's question is the question on behalf of all of us— which is the better method of worship—*sagun* or *nirgun*?

Gita 12: 2

Bhagwan said: Those who worship Me with their minds totally focused on Me with unwavering faith are the very best in My opinion.

Single-minded devotion is important.

Krishna says that whichever method is used, what is important is the single-minded, unwavering devotion to the Divine. He declares that whoever worships the Divine with absolute faith and single-minded devotion is the best of *yogis*. There are three aspects mentioned here:

- Worshipping the Divine
- The mind focused on the Divine
- Unwavering faith

Whether it is *sagun* or *nirgun bhakti* is immaterial. Whether the devotee is a *yogi*, a *sanyasi* or an ordinary person doesn't matter either.

Gita 12: 3–4

Those who worship the formless, the indefinable, the unmanifest, which is all-pervading, unthinkable, unchanging, eternal and immovable;

Such persons, by restraining their senses and being even-minded in all places, by being engaged in the welfare of all beings, also attain Me.

Worship the formless with a calm mind.

The Divine is one, regardless of whether we worship the Divine in a particular form or the formless Divine. Therefore, the goal of both types of worship is the same. Here, Krishna is talking about formless worship.

When worshipping the formless Divine, we should be aware of the attributes of the Brahman: indefinable, unmanifest, all-pervading, unthinkable, unchanging, eternal and immovable.

What are the attributes of the aspirant? The aspirant must:

1. Possess self-restraint of the senses
2. Be even-minded in all places
3. Be engaged in the welfare of all

Gita 12: 5

For those who have their minds attached to the unmanifested, the struggle is greater because the unmanifested goal is more difficult to attain than the manifest one.

It is difficult to focus the mind on the formless.

Krishna says that most people have difficulty worshipping the formless. They will struggle to focus on the unmanifest because there is no reference point. Krishna mentions that *nirgun bhakti* is a difficult path as devotees must continuously restrain all the senses, be even-minded under all circumstances and engage in the welfare of all creatures. So, there is an implicit comment that worshipping the personified deity is relatively easier than worshipping the impersonal form.

Many people complain that their spiritual practices are not making any difference. It is simply because their minds are not purified. When the mind is not pure, worshipping the formless will be a continuous struggle. The mind will keep running towards sense-enjoyment. We should understand that *nirgun bhakti* is easier when we are on the path of *jnana yoga* with renunciation of the *karma* and the results of the *karma*.

Gita 12: 9

O Dhananjaya, if you are unable to fix your mind on Me, you can still reach Me with constant practice.

Constant practice is the key.

We cannot focus our minds if we don't practice constantly and regularly. Earlier, too, when Arjuna said that it is difficult to restrain the mind, Krishna said that one can restrain the mind by constant practice. We should understand that the mind is the real cause of our struggle.

Krishna has used the word *abhyasayogena*, that is, constant practice. This is common in all the *yogas—karma*, *bhakti*, *dhyana* and *jnana*. Without practice, no *yoga* can develop and lead the person to liberation.

Gita 12: 10

If you are unable to practice constantly, then perform all your *karma* with devotion. Thus, by performing *karma* with devotion, you shall achieve the stage of perfection.

Perform *karma* with devotion.

We make resolutions at the beginning of every new year. We know how much we adhere to such resolutions. The problem is that there are so many attractions and distractions that we forget those resolutions. The same thing is true for our resolution to do regular spiritual practice. Krishna understands our dilemma and says that if you cannot do regular practice, perform your *karma* with devotion.

Whatever we do—good actions, charitable deeds, helping others—should be done with devotion and offered to the Divine without any desire for personal reward. This is called *nishkama karma*.

Some good actions are *japa*, prayer, *kirtan*, worship, fasting and keeping silent. By such actions, the mind is purified.

Gita 12: 11–12

If you are unable to do even this, in that case, act with self-restraint and renounce the results of all *karma*.

ate, *dhyana* (meditation) is better than *jnana*, and renunciation of the results of *karma* is better than *dhyana*. Such renunciation (of the results of *karma*) leads to eternal bliss (perfection).

Jnana (knowledge) is better than practice, *dhyana* (meditation) is better than *jnana*, and renunciation of the results of *karma* is better than *dhyana*. Such renunciation (of the results of *karma*) leads to eternal bliss (perfection).

Renounce the results of *karma*.

So far, Krishna has given two alternatives: practice regularly and perform your *karma* with devotion. Now, he says if someone cannot follow these two alternatives, that person may simply renounce the results of all *karma*. Such renunciation, too, will result in eternal bliss.

Thus, Krishna explains the range of practices, specifically *karma yoga, dhyana yoga* and *jnana yoga*. Krishna answers the question now by saying that *jnana* (knowledge) is better than practice, *dhyana* (meditation) is better than *jnana*, and renunciation of the results of *karma* is better than *dhyana*. Such renunciation (of the results of *karma*) leads to eternal bliss.

In Krishna's view, this is the easiest way. We are engaged in various actions every day. While performing these actions, let us just remember the Divine and surrender the results of those actions to the Divine. This option is doable by everyone.

When we do this, we always remember the Divine. Just by surrendering all the results of our *karma* to the Divine, all *paapa* is destroyed, the mind becomes pure and liberation is attained.

Gita 12: 13–14

One who does not hate anyone, who is friendly and compassionate, who is free from attachment and is free from ego, who is unaffected by pain and pleasure and is forgiving;

who is ever content, steady in meditation, self-restrained with determination and devoted to Me is dear to Me.

Who is dear to the Divine?

Now, Krishna narrates the qualities of devotees. When a devotee has these qualities, such a person becomes dear to the Divine. There are twenty-seven qualities mentioned in verses 13 to 19.

- Friendly and compassionate
- Free from attachment
- Free from ego
- Unaffected by pain and pleasure
- Ever content

- Steady in meditation
- Self-restrained with determination
- Devoted to the Divine

Gita 12: 15

One who is neither agitated by people nor agitates people, who is not affected by joy, sorrow, anxiety and fear is dear to Me.

Some more qualities of devotees

- Not agitated by people
- Do not agitate people
- Not affected by joy, sorrow, anxiety or fear

Gita 12: 16

One who is free from desires, is pious, dedicated, indifferent to loss and gain and free from selfishness in all undertakings; such a devotee is dear to Me.

Some more qualities of devotees

- Free from desires
- Pious
- Dedicated
- Indifferent to loss and gain
- Free from selfishness in all undertakings

Gita 12: 17

One who neither celebrates nor despairs, who neither grieves nor desires, who has renounced both good and bad results (of *karma*), such a devotee is dear to Me.

Some more qualities of devotees

- Neither celebrate nor despair
- Neither grieve nor desire
- Have renounced both good and bad results (of *karma*)

Gita 12: 18–19

One who is impartial to friends and enemies and is not affected by praise or insult, who is the same in heat and cold, joy and sorrow and free from attachments;

One who is equal in censure and praise, quiet and content with whatever happens, without attachment to one's home, and who is of steady mind, such a devotee is dear to Me.

Some more qualities of devotees

- Impartial to friends and enemies
- Not affected by praise or insult
- Remain the same in heat and cold, joy and sorrow
- Free from attachments
- Equal in censure and praise
- Quiet and content with whatever happens
- Without attachment to their homes
- Remain of steady mind

Gita 12: 20

Those who follow the nectar of *dharma* (the right thing to do) as declared above with absolute faith in Me as the supreme goal, such devotees are very dear to Me.

Who is very dear to the Divine?

After mentioning the twenty-seven qualities of devotees that make them dear to the Divine, Krishna talks about the actions that make a devotee very dear to the Divine. Krishna says that those who follow the practices mentioned earlier with total devotion and faith, with liberation as the final goal, are very dear to the Divine.

No one might succeed on the first attempt, but a true devotee keeps on trying. They continue with their practices. If that is not possible, they perform their *karma* with devotion. If that is also not possible, they renounce the results of their *karma*. What is needed is faith and single-minded devotion, whatever the path. Such devotees are very dear to the Divine.

QUESTION 12

WHAT IS TRUE KNOWLEDGE?

As we understand, knowledge is an awareness of facts. It may also refer to familiarity with objects or situations. When we have knowledge of facts, which is also called propositional knowledge, we move away from opinion or guesswork by virtue of justification.

All of us know some things and don't know other things. When we don't know something, we don't know the things we are wrong about in that context.

We have been told that knowledge is attainable and that knowledge must be infallible and about real things. True knowledge must possess these qualities.

The Gita enquires into the consciousness and perceptivity of our experience. Krishna tells us to rely more on our immediate, direct knowledge. Our true knowledge is based on our own experience, which comprises concepts, labels, ideas, images, and so on.

Arjuna now wants to know what is true knowledge and the object and purpose of knowledge.

Gita 13: 1

**Arjuna said: O Keshava, I wish to understand
what *prakriti* and *purusha* are and what
kshetra and *kshetrajna* are. I also wish to know what
is *jnana* (knowledge), and what is the goal of this
knowledge?**

What is knowledge?

Arjuna now questions Krishna about the disposition
of *prakriti* (Mother Nature) and *purusha* (cosmic
consciousness). There has been a detailed discussion on
karma, *dhyana* and *bhakti yoga*. Now, there is a detailed
discussion on *jnana yoga*, including the question: what is
jnana?

Arjuna now wants to dive deep into the subject of *jnana
yoga*. The path of *jnana yoga*, or the path of knowledge,
involves scriptural study by devotees who want to know more
about the subject. Arjuna wants to know: what is *jnana*—
knowledge—and what is the goal of this knowledge? He also
wants to know what is *kshetra, kshetrajna, jnana, jneyam,
purusha and prakriti*? He also wants to know the purpose
of acquiring this knowledge.

Gita 13: 2

**Bhagwan said: O Kaunteya, this body is called
kshetra—the field of activities, and the one who has
knowledge of this body is called *kshetrajna*—the
knower of the field.**

The body is the field of activities.

Kshetra means field. The field is necessary for growing agricultural produce. In the same way, the body is essential for all activities, whether physical, mental or spiritual. We perform spiritual practices like *tapas* and meditation with the body. Therefore, the body, the *kshetra*, is the field for spiritual growth.

Without any consciousness, the body is inert. The body cannot know itself. There is a consciousness within the body known as *kshetrajna*—the knower of the field. This consciousness witnesses all the actions of the body, its sense organs, the mind and the intellect. This consciousness is changeless, pure, deathless. *Kshetrajna*, the knower of the field, is certainly different from *kshetra*, the field. So, the knower of the body is distinct from the body.

Gita 13: 3

O Bharata, you should know that I am the *kshetrajna*, knower of the body, in all the *kshetras* (bodies), and the knowledge of *kshetra* and *kshetrajna* is true knowledge.

What is true knowledge?

The answer to this question is *tat tvam asi* (You are That). The *jivatma* in the body is none other than *paramatma*. The *jivatma* is the *kshetrajna*—the knower of the field and the witness to all that is happening. So, the *jivatma*, who is the knower of the body, is *paramatma* itself.

Therefore, there is only one knower of the body, who

is present in everybody as the witness. The Divine is the knower in all the bodies. The *jivatma* is only a fictional entity with no real existence, except in *paramatma*.

Krishna says that this knowledge of *kshetra* and *kshetrajna* is true knowledge. This knowledge gives us the greatest strength and courage. Knowing that 'the Divine is part of me' can give us joy and bliss.

Gita 13: 6–7

The *kshetra*—body—is composed of the five great elements, the *avyakta* — the ego, the intellect, the unmanifest *prakriti*, the eleven senses and the five sense objects.

This *kshetra* and its various features can be explained by the aggregate of its desires—envy, pleasure, pain, intelligence and willpower.

What is *kshetra* made of?

Krishna says that the body is made of twenty-four elements:
- Five gross elements—earth, water, air, fire and ether
- Five subtle elements—sight, smell, taste, sound and touch
- Five knowledge-acquiring senses—eyes, nose, tongue, ears and skin
- Five working senses—hands, legs, mouth, rectum and genitals
- The ego
- The mind
- The intellect
- The unmanifest prakriti (*mulaprakriti*)

This *kshetra*—the body—and its various features can be explained by the aggregate of its desires. These desires are envy, pleasure, pain, intelligence and willpower.

Kshetra does not simply mean the physical body alone. All that is perceived by the body is also *kshetra*. Also, the modifications due to desires created by the senses, mind, intellect and ego are also part of the *kshetra*.

Gita 13: 8–12

Humility, freedom from hypocricy, non-violence, forgiveness, simplicity, respect for gurus, cleanliness of body and mind, steadfastness, balance, self-restraint towards the objects of the senses;

Dispassion towards sense-objects, absence of ego, reflecting on the imperfection of birth, death, old age and disease;

Non-attachment, absence of constant craving for children, spouse, home and so on; even-mindedness to all desirable and undesirable events;

Relentless and undivided devotion towards Me; an inclination for solitude and aversion for mass gatherings;

The constant pursuit of spiritual knowledge and absolute truth: All these I declare to be knowledge. What is contrary to it is ignorance.

What is knowledge?

In Verses 8–12, Krishna tells Arjuna about both knowledge and the object of knowledge. The knowledge that helps build the moral and spiritual qualities needed for self-realization is defined as knowledge (*jnana*) here. We cannot attain the Divine if we don't know about these qualities:

- Humility
- Freedom from hypocricy
- Non-violence
- Forgiveness
- Simplicity
- Respect for gurus
- Cleanliness of body and mind
- Steadfastness
- Balance
- Self-restraint towards the objects of the senses
- Dispassion towards sense-objects
- Absence of ego
- Reflecting on imperfection of birth, death, old age and disease
- Non-attachment
- Absence of constant craving for children, spouse, home and so on
- Even-mindedness to all desirable and undesirable events
- Relentless and undivided devotion towards Me
- An inclination for solitude and aversion for mass gatherings
- Constant pursuit of spiritual knowledge and absolute truth

Krishna says that the lack of this knowledge is ignorance.

Gita 13: 13

I will declare to you about the object of knowledge, knowing which one attains immortality. The eternal supreme Brahman is neither *asat* nor *sat*.

What is the object of knowledge?

In the next six verses, Krishna explains the object of knowledge—the supreme Brahman. The earlier five verses, 8–12, dealt with knowledge and its qualities. That is not good enough. We need to know what the object of this knowledge is. Will this knowledge show the way? Krishna answers these questions now.

We are taught about ethical principles and a moral code of conduct in all professional courses. But that is not enough. In the Gita, Krishna takes Arjuna to the highest rung of spiritual knowledge. If we know about the Brahman, which is both being and non-being, we can attain immortality.

Gita 13: 14

That—*kshetrajna*—exists everywhere in the world, with hands and feet everywhere, eyes, heads and mouths everywhere and ears everywhere.

The Divine is present everywhere.

The Brahman pervades the entire universe with hands, feet, eyes, head and mouth everywhere. The Brahman is present in all living and non-living beings. All we have to do is witness and experience *paramatma* everywhere. Because *paramatma* pervades all, it is our duty to follow *dharma* in our life and conduct.

Whatever we think or do is known to *paramatma*. So, whatever we think and do should be pure and good. This is the *sagun* aspect of the Brahman, the all-pervasive cosmic consciousness. It is the basis and foundation of the manifested and unmanifested universe.

Gita 13: 15

That (*kshetrajna*—the knower of the body) is the original source of all sense organs and *gunas* but is without all *indriyas*. That supports all without attachment. That is simultaneously the master of the *gunas* but transcends all *gunas*.

The Divine is beyond the *trigunas*

The Brahman is the creator of all beings and, therefore, the source of all sense organs in the body. The Brahman is also the creator of *gunas*, the mental tendencies and energy because of which we act in this world. The Brahman is the creator of all sense organs but does not have sense organs.

The Brahman supports all beings and non-beings without any attachment and without any favours. Though the Brahman is the master of all *gunas*—*sattva*, *rajas* and *tamas*—it is beyond the influence of the three *gunas*.

Gita 13: 16

That (*kshetrajna*—the knower of the body)
exists within and outside of all beings and also
in all movable and non-movable beings. That is
incomprehensible because of its subtleness. That exists
far away, yet is near.

The Divine is within and outside of all of us.

The Brahman does not walk, yet walks. The Brahman is far away, but is also near. It exists inside everything, but is also outside everything.

Krishna earlier said that to know the Divine is true knowledge. But here, he says that the Supreme Being is beyond our understanding. Even if it seems contradictory, this means that the Divine is not knowable by our senses, mind and intellect. The body, mind and intellect are created from material energy, so they cannot comprehend the Divine. However, if the Divine bestows kindness upon someone, like Arjuna, that person can know the Divine.

Gita 13: 17

That (*kshetrajna*—the knower of the body) exists
undivided in all beings, yet is separate from them.
That is the creator, sustainer and destroyer of all
beings.

The Divine is the creator and destroyer.

The Divine exists undivided in all of us. Time, *karma* and the composition of *gunas*, which separates the natures of

all individuals and all non-living things, are the creation of
the Divine. There is nothing in this world where the Divine
does not exist.

So, it may appear that the Divine is divided amongst all
of us, but since it is all that exists in us, it remains undivided
as well. For example, when we look at our room, the space
within it may seem divided by the objects it contains, yet all
objects are within it. The room is one; it is not divided by
the things within it.

Another example is that of the ocean. The ocean creates
so many waves, but all those waves exist within the ocean.
The waves appear and disappear.

Gita 13: 18

**That (*kshetrajna*) is the light in all luminous
objects and is said to transcend all *tamas*. That is
the knowledge, the knowable and the purpose of
knowledge. That is situated in the heart of everyone.**

The Divine is the knowledge, its object and its purpose.

The Divine is situated in the heart of all of us. Krishna
gives an example to make things clearer. Various objects
illuminate, such as the sun, moon, stars and fire. The light
in all these illuminating objects is the Divine. Without the
presence of the Divine, they would not have any power
to illuminate.

The Divine has been given three names: *Ved-kṛit* (One
who manifested the Vedas), *Ved-vit* (One who knows the
Vedas), and *Ved-vedya* (One who is to be known through

the Vedas). Therefore, Krishna says that Brahman is the true knowledge, the object of knowledge and the purpose of knowledge.

Gita 13: 24

Those who thoroughly understand the play of *guna*, *prakriti* and *purusha* are not born again, whatever their present living conditions.

Understand the play of *guna*.

When we acquire this knowledge and understand the object and purpose of this knowledge, we will understand the play of the three *gunas*. The wise person can distinctly see the difference between *prakriti* and *purusha*.

Once we understand the play of the *gunas* within us, we know that we are driven by *gunas* of *prakriti*—*sattva*, *rajas* and *tamas*. Then, we don't take refuge in *prakriti*, that is, bondage and the cycle of birth and rebirth, but in *purusha*, the blissful and blessed Divine. We get liberated.

Gita 14: 5

O Mahabaho, *prakriti* is the origin of *sattva*, *rajas* and *tamas gunas*, which bind the *deha* (body) to the imperishable *dehi*.

The *gunas* bind us to the body.

We have been told that the three *gunas*—*sattva*, *rajas* and *tamas*—are born of *prakriti*. These *gunas* are the energies and mental tendencies with which we act in this world. The body is the field for these three *gunas*.

Dehi, the *kshetrajna*, is devoid of these qualities. The *dehi* transcends them. However, most of us forget this relation and associate ourselves with the *gunas*, identify with them and bind ourselves to the body.

Due to this, the *jivatma* becomes a personified being subject to all the troubles of life and death. This is called *avidya*—ignorance. We have to go beyond the play of these *gunas* and rise to the higher awareness which will make us free and perfect.

Gita 14: 6

Amongst these, *sattva guna* is the purest, illuminating, healthy, full of well-being, and most desirable. O Anagha (Arjuna), it binds one by creating attachment to happiness and knowledge.

What is *sattva guna*?

Sattva guna is the purest of all the three *gunas*. *Sattva guna* is luminous and dispels the darkness of ignorance. When *sattva guna* is in action, the individual's food habits and lifestyle are healthy and promote overall well-being. Therefore, *sattva guna* is the most desirable of all *gunas*.

But there are issues associated with *sattva guna*. It becomes an obstacle because it creates an attachment to knowledge and happiness. *Sattva guna* binds the *jivatma* by attachment to happiness and knowledge. When we are happy, we attribute this to the experience of the senses and the mind. Similarly, when we say that we have knowledge about a subject, we attribute it to our intellect. This association with the senses, the body, the mind and the intellect binds us to birth and rebirth.

Gita 14: 7

Know that the *rajas guna* is the essence of passion arising from attachment to desires. O Kaunteya, it binds the *dehi* by creating an attachment to result-oriented *karma*.

What is *rajas guna*?

Rajas guna is the essence of passion in thoughts and actions. When we have desires for things we don't have, we work passionately to possess them. We have *trishna*—the passion for objects we do not possess. We have attachments to the things we possess. *Rajas guna* causes both passion and attachment. Under the influence of *rajas guna*, we act with passion to gain objects of sense-enjoyment, wealth, fame, power and position.

Rajas guna is the emotional energy which drives this world. Our mad rush in the world is the influence of *rajas guna*. Due to passion and attachment, we see that countries fight for territories and people fight to defeat their enemies.

Rajas guna binds us by attachment to the results of our *karma*.

Gita 14: 8

Know that *tamas guna* is born of ignorance and is the
cause of delusion in all living beings. O Bharata, it
binds one by *pramada* (negligence), *alasya* (indolence)
and *nidra* (sleep).

What is *tamas guna*?

Tamas guna is born of ignorance. Earlier, Krishna defined
knowledge and said that the lack of knowledge is ignorance.
Knowledge helps in building the moral and spiritual
qualities needed for self-realization. When we don't have
this knowledge, we are deluded, and we continue to strive
only for sense-enjoyment and for the results of our *karma*.
Due to a lack of knowledge, we resist all changes, whether
good or bad.

Under the influence of *tamas guna*, even the wise are
sometimes blind to the realities of a situation. They become
lethargic and enjoy sleeping for longer than needed. Most
of the time, we get influenced by *tamas guna*, and we sleep,
remain idle, neglect our duty and shirk responsibilities.

Gita 14: 10

O Bharata, sometimes *sattva guna* prevails over *rajas*
and *tamas*; sometimes, *rajas guna* overcomes *sattva*
and *tamas*; and sometimes, *tamas guna* dominates
sattva and *rajas*.

Different *gunas* dominate at different times.

Krishna says that at any given time, one *guna* dominates

the others. Sometimes, *sattva guna* dominates; at other times, *rajas* or *tamas guna* may dominate. When *sattva guna* dominates, it prevails over the other two *gunas*. So, when *rajas guna* dominates, the other two are overpowered; when *tamas guna* is dominating, the other two *gunas* are subdued.

Therefore, we have to be aware of the *guna* which is dominating. It is easy to be aware of this, as we know which type of behaviour has taken over our body, mind and intellect.

Gita 14: 11

When all the gates of the body function with the enlightenment of *jnana*, then it may be known that *sattva* is dominant.

Know when *sattva guna* is dominant.

How do we know that *sattva guna* is dominating? Krishna says that when all the gates of the body function with the wisdom of *jnana* (knowledge), we will know that *sattva guna* is dominating.

Which are the gates of the body? These are:
- Two eyes
- Two ears
- One nose
- One tongue
- Skin
- The urinary tract
- The excretion opening

Our body functions with these nine gates. They work under the influence of our senses. They create the desires for food, taste, smell, touch and beauty. When we are under *sattva's* influence, we are not driven by these sense organs.

Gita 14: 12

O Bharatarshabha, *lobh* (greed), *pravritti* (passion), *arambhah* (initiative), *spriha* (aspiration) and *ashamah* (restlessness of activities) arise when *rajas guna* is dominant.

Know when *rajas guna* is dominant.

We know that *rajas guna* is the essence of passion arising from attachment to desires. When *rajas guna* dominates, we engage in several activities to fulfil our desires.

We take the initiative because of the constant yearning for the results of our *karma*. We work with passion to get the desired results. We want more of what we like and enjoy, and hence, we become greedy. We have many aspirations to be something in life or become famous. We become restless. In a passion to get results, we may overlook the ethical and moral aspects of our actions.

The figure below presents the three *gunas*—*sattva*, *rajas* and *tamas*—and their combinations in the form of a Venn diagram.

Figure 1: Diagram representing the play of *triguna* and their combinations

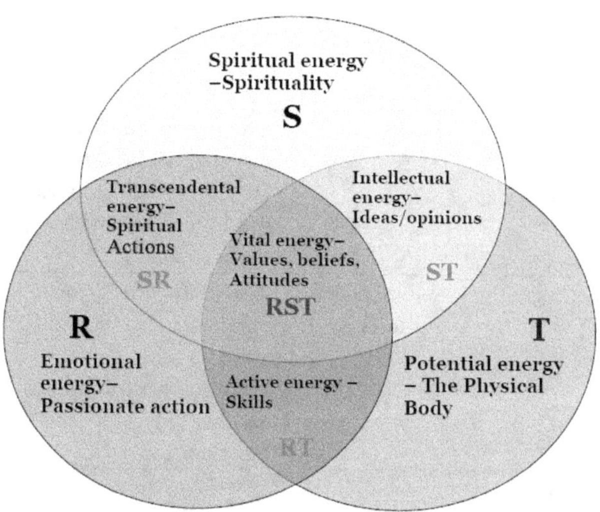

Table 1: Three *gunas*, their combinations and their influences

ENERGY	ATTRIBUTE	INFLUENCE
Sattva: Spiritual energy (S)	Spirituality	It influences us towards goodness, truth, purity, knowledge through reason and understanding.
Rajas: Emotional energy (R)	Passionate action	It provides emotional energy for action to realize a cause, pursue an interest or fulfil a purpose in life.
Tamas: Potential energy (T)	Inertia	It represents the physical body and its power of resistance to changes in the present state.
Transcendental energy (RS)	Spiritual emotions	Spiritual emotion is a state of experiencing the Divine within ourselves and others.

ENERGY	ATTRIBUTE	INFLUENCE
Intellectual energy (RT)	Ideas/opinions	It influences our capacity for imagination, recognition and appreciation. It is also responsible for processing feelings and emotions.
Active energy (ST)	Skills	This energy builds our essential skills (communication etc.), work skills (domain-specific) and life skills (interpersonal).
Vital energy (RST)	Values, beliefs, attitudes	Also called *prana*, this influences our values, beliefs and attitudes. It shapes our actions towards ourselves, one another, the planet and the universe.

Gita 14: 13

O Kurunandana, *aprakashah* (lack of knowledge), *apravritti* (inertia), *pramada* (negligence) and *moha* (illusion) develop when *tamas guna* is dominant.

Know when *tamas guna* is dominant.

We know that *tamas guna* is born of ignorance. When we don't have knowledge, it deludes us, and we continue to search for sense-enjoyment.

When we don't have knowledge, we interpret everything based on what is good for us and what suits our purpose. We neglect to do the right thing because we are not aware of the right thing to do.

We easily give up when we are feeling lazy. Even when we know that we must get up and start working, we keep wasting time.

Gita 14: 16

The result of *sattvic karma* is *nirmal* (pure), the result of *rajasic karma* comes with *dukham* (pain), while *tamasic karma* results in *ajnana* (ignorance).

Results of *sattva*, *rajas* and *tamas karma*

When *sattva guna* is dominating, we do the right thing. We work with our senses restrained and with a calm mind. We are not looking for the result, and we are not attached to the result. Whatever the outcome, we are neither happy nor sad in such a situation. Therefore, Krishna says that the result of *sattvic karma* is pure.

Under the influence of *rajas guna*, we aspire for favourable results from our actions. We are worried about failure. If we succeed, we will feel happy, but if we don't succeed, we may face uncertainty about our future. This is the mindset when we are under the influence of *rajas guna*. Therefore, Krishna says that the result of *rajasic karma* is pain.

Under the influence of *tamas guna*, we believe in the status quo. We resist changes because we are worried about the outcome. When *tamas guna* is dominating, we want to avoid work. This is due to ignorance. *Tamas guna* fuels further ignorance.

Gita 14: 19

When a person knows that there is no cause of action other than the *gunas*, and knows what is beyond these *gunas*, that person attains My Divine nature.

There is no cause of actions other than the *gunas.*

Krishna says that whatever actions we do, the cause is *guna.* The *triguna* composition in us influences our senses, body, mind, intellect and ego. There is no other agent.

Let us look at this knowledge with the example of a mobile phone. The body of the mobile phone is like our body. Just as the mobile is dead if there is no charge, we are dead if there is no consciousness—*dehi*—in our body. All mobile phones operate according to some operating system, whether Android or Apple. The *gunas* are the operating system of our body, mind and intellect. If the operating system crashes, the mobile phone is of no use. All the applications we download on our phones are like our desires and attachments. We have to rise above these desires and attachments.

Gita 14: 20

When living beings rise above these *gunas* influencing their bodies, they become free from birth, death, old age and miseries and attain immortality.

Rise above the *gunas.*

We have to rise above the three *gunas, sattva* included, if we are to liberate ourselves from the cycle of birth and rebirth. Even though *sattva* is pure, it attaches us to happiness and knowledge.

These *gunas* are not our enemies; these are the energies under whose influence we work. But if we are driven by goodness, results or indolence, we still remain bound to this world of birth, death, old age and miseries. For each of us, many births have already come and gone. Many more will come unless we understand the play of the *gunas* and go beyond them.

QUESTION 13

HOW DO WE GO BEYOND THE *TRIGUNAS*?

The three *gunas* are at war with each other in our minds. When one *guna* achieves victory, it temporarily defeats the others. Knowing this, we would now like to know which *guna* within us dominates more than others. This is not an easy question to answer because we have to analyze ourselves and not anyone else. We need to look within. We need to understand what thoughts, feelings and emotions we should watch out for to trace them back to a specific *guna*. If we conduct this analysis for a while, we will know which *guna* predominates in us.

Once we can rise beyond identifying with the three *gunas*, we will see *prakriti* the way Ishvara sees *prakriti*, as a detached observer. Thus, when we realize our identity with Ishvara, we will attain the state of liberation, of self-realization.

So, Arjuna asks: 'How do we go beyond the *trigunas*?'

When a person understands that all the drama of life is only a performance of the three *gunas*, and only the three *gunas* do anything anywhere; when a person also realizes that there is something above the three *gunas*, the person can rise above the play of the *gunas*.

Krishna explains this in Chapter 14 of the Gita.

Gita 14: 21

Arjuna said: O Prabhu, what are the characteristics of those who have gone beyond the three *gunas*? How do they conduct themselves? How do they go beyond these *trigunas*?

How do we go beyond *trigunas*?

Krishna has told Arjuna that we are all influenced by these three *gunas* and remain bound to our actions under their influence. We remain attached to happiness, knowledge, the result of our actions or to sense-enjoyment due to *gunas*. If we aspire for liberation, we must rise above these *gunas*.

The concept of *gunas* is useful because it helps us to understand why we feel the way we do about certain experiences in life. For example, if we are feeling sad or depressed for no apparent reason, it may be due to the effects of *tamas guna*. On the other hand, if we are unable to sleep at night despite being tired, then this could be due to our overactive mind under the influence of *rajas guna*.

All three *gunas* are necessary for life to be real. We cannot judge these *gunas* as good or bad. We need to simply acknowledge their existence and be aware of them. They are present in all aspects of our lives, including thoughts, emotions and actions. So, if we want to remain unaffected by our desires and the play of these *gunas*, we need to rise above them or go beyond them.

Therefore, Arjuna wants to know how we can go beyond the influence of the *gunas*. He wants to know about the character and conduct of a person who has risen above the *gunas*. Arjuna wants to know how to become a calm and wise person.

Krishna's response to Arjuna's question is very illuminating. If we aspire for liberation, we should study, understand and practice the knowledge given here.

Gita 14: 22–25

Bhagwan said: O Pandava, such people do not hate knowledge, activity or ignorance when they are present, neither desire them when they are absent.

They remain unconcerned and are not agitated by the *gunas*. They understand that it is the *gunas* that are acting. Thus, they remain calm and are not disturbed by them.

They remain the same in pleasure and pain. They treat alike a lump of earth, a stone and a piece of gold. They remain the same towards what they like and don't like. They are firm, and they remain the same in praise or censure.

They remain the same in honour and dishonour. They are equally disposed towards friends and foes. They have given up the fruits of all their initiatives. Such people are said to be beyond the *gunas*.

Gunatita **is the one who has gone beyond the** *gunas***.**

What happens when you rise above the influence of these three *gunas*? Earlier, Krishna said that the person who rises above the *gunas* is unmoved by the forces of energies of the three *gunas* (Gita 14: 20).

Sattva may indeed bring happiness, *rajas* may bring results to our actions, and *tamas* may bring sense-enjoyment. But the person who has gone beyond *triguna* does not react to these feelings. Such a person also does not long for them when they are absent. It does not matter whether the *gunas* function or cease to function. We should understand that these emotions should not control us, whether it is the knowledge of *sattva*, the activity of *rajas* or the enjoyment of *tamas*.

A person who has risen above the *gunas* has immovable firmness and equal-mindedness. Such a person may be called *gunatita*.

The difference between the *gunatita* and the rest of us is apparent in their reactions to small things, such as little disappointments, worries and anxieties. We are thrown off-balance and become restless, discontented and dispirited by hardships. The *gunatita* is imperturbable and undaunted in such situations.

Gunatita has equal-mindedness. *Gunatita* remains the same towards friends and enemies, pleasure and pain, honour and dishonour, censure and praise, stone or gold.

Gita 14: 26

Those who serve Me with unswerving devotion and have gone beyond the *gunas* are ready to be *brahma bhuyaya* (self-realized).

Gunatita is a self-realized person.

The Divine, by its nature, is beyond the three *gunas*. How do we go beyond *triguna*? If we can go beyond *triguna*, we become one with the Brahman. First, we have to be aware of our *triguna* composition. A great deal of enquiry, self-control and meditation is necessary for this. Along with this, we need to have single-minded devotion. This devotion (*bhakti*) helps the devotee to transcend the *gunas.*

Single-minded devotion is needed for any spiritual practice. Even when Krishna talks about true knowledge, he talks about the need for devotion. Whether we practice *karma yoga*, *jnana yoga* or *dhyana yoga*, we need to cultivate devotion. Here, Krishna answers Arjuna's question, '*Katham chai tam stringunan ativartate*'—'How can a person go beyond those three *gunas*?' Krishna says that by firm devotion, we can acquire knowledge that will take us beyond the *gunas.*

Gita 15: 1

Bhagwan said: They speak of an eternal Ashvattha (peepal) tree with branches going downwards and roots going upwards, whose leaves are like *chhandas* (hymns, mantras). Those who are the knowers of the Vedas know this.

The Ashvattha tree

Krishna compares the world to an Ashvattha tree. This tree is unlike any other tree that we see around us. Most trees have roots below and branches above. But this Ashvattha tree, compared to the *samsara* (the world of beings and non-beings), has roots above and branches below.

Krishna says that the Brahman originates the *avyakta* (imperceptible), and from them arise the whole universe along with all beings. So, the Divine is the highest source (above), and below, we find the universe and its beings. So, this tree is said to have its roots above (in *paramatma*) and its branches below. *Paramatma* is the root and the universe is the branches of this tree of *samsara*.

Gita 15: 2

The branches of the tree and twigs, representing sense-objects, spread upwards and downwards, nourished by the *gunas*. The roots of the tree extend everywhere from the branches, binding people of the world to *karma*.

Gunas nourish the Ashvattha tree.

We live in a world of millions of people with all kinds of desires and passions. The world has grown strong and has deeply established its roots in the universe.

Krishna explains how the world is similar to the Ashvattha tree. The branches of the tree extend both upwards and downwards. In the same way, human beings, based on their *karma*, move up and down in their life. A bud is a young part of the plant. Flower buds bloom into flowers, whereas growth buds develop into young branches. These growth buds are the places where the tree grows. Krishna says that, like these buds, if we act under the influence of the *gunas*, we will be nourishing our desires by these *gunas*. Like water and fertiliser nourish a tree, the three *gunas* nourish this eternal tree of material existence.

These desires are unending and ever increasing, similar to the roots in the ground and aerial roots. As a result, we get further entangled in this world of material consciousness.

Gita 15: 3–4

Its form is not perceived here as such, neither its end, origin nor foundation. This firmly rooted Ashvattha tree has to be cut by the strong axe of non-attachment.

After that, one should search for the ultimate goal from where there is no return and seek refuge in the ancient and primal *purusha*, which is the source of this creation.

Cut this Ashvattha tree by non-attachment.

As we grow, our desires and aspirations keep increasing. There is no limit to these desires. There is no beginning and no end. They are insatiable. We are deeply attached to what we have. We are deeply attached to this *samsara*. Krishna says that the only way to move forward is to fell this Ashvattha tree with the strong axe of non-attachment. We have to overcome the attachment to our sense-enjoyment.

Once we cut the tree by practising non-attachment, we can work to liberate ourselves from this world. We need to take refuge in *purusha*—the immortal consciousness, which is the source of this creation.

Gita 15: 5

The wise can reach the imperishable abode free from pride and delusion, victorious over the weakness of attachment, dwelling constantly on the Divine, free from the desire to enjoy the senses.

Free yourself from pride and delusion.

A wise person becomes free from pride and delusion by overcoming the weakness of attachment. The wise person is free from the desire to enjoy the senses. Once one overcomes these hurdles, one can focus the mind on the Divine and reach the destination.

The qualities of a wise person are described here:
1. Free from pride (*ahamkara*) and delusion
2. Overcoming the weakness of attachment to the world of senses
3. Dwelling constantly on the Divine
4. Free from the desire to enjoy the senses

Gita 15: 10

Deluded people do not see it (Ishvara) as they enjoy sense-objects under the *gunas'* influence, nor do they see it when it leaves. But those with the vision of knowledge can see it.

Why don't we feel Ishvara within us?

Krishna says that because of our ignorance (lack of true knowledge), we are unaware of our own divine identity and believe that the physical body is the real identity. Only when we acquire spiritual knowledge do we understand that the *dehi* (*atma*, soul) gives life to the body. Without the *dehi*, the body is lifeless. We should understand that Ishvara is within us in the form of *dehi*, the soul.

The situation is similar to that of a person who has purchased a mobile phone for the first time and has to figure out how it works. We have to go through some training to operate it. The mobile phone cannot work without being charged and then switched on. The same thing is true for us. The *dehi* is the power which makes the body alive.

Gita 15: 20

O Anagha (Arjuna), thus, this very confidential *shastra* (scripture) has been imparted by me. O Bharata, knowing this, people will become wise and accomplish all their duties.

This knowledge will make you wise.

Krishna says that the true knowledge about the *kshetra* (the body) and the *kshetrajna* (the knower of the body) is the greatest and most important knowledge. Why are these superlatives used to describe this knowledge? Because knowing this, a person understands how to live a life full of meaning and purpose. The person becomes:

- Wise, having self-knowledge; and
- Capable of attaining freedom and liberation from the cycle of birth and rebirth.

All other existing knowledge in the world does not enable and empower us to reach the highest state of perfection and freedom. All other knowledge may confer merit and temporary comfort in life, but liberation is still not attained.

Gita 16: 1–3

Bhagwan said: Fearlessness, purification of one's conscience, remaining firm in *jnana yoga*, charities, restraining the senses, *yajna* (devoted action), self-study of *shastras, tapa* (austerity), simplicity;

Non-violence, truthfulness, absence of anger, renunciation, peacefulness, absence of crookedness, compassion towards all living beings, absence of greed, gentleness, modesty, absence of fickleness;

Vigour, forgiveness, fortitude, cleanliness, bearing enmity towards none, absence of pride; O Bharat, these are the virtues of those who are born with *daivi* (divine) nature.

Virtuous qualities of good people

Once we perform spiritual practices, we become wise and calm. We develop good qualities, which may also be called divine qualities. Here, Krishna summarizes these divine qualities:

1. Fearlessness	6. Worship of God
2. Purity	7. Austerity
3. Scriptural study	8. Straightforwardness
4. Charity	9. Non-violence
5. Control of the senses	10. Truthfulness

11. Renunciation   15. Gentleness
12. Calmness and patience   16. Modesty
13. Absence of slander   17. Steadfastness
14. Absence of greed   18. Strength

Gita 16: 4

Pride, arrogance, self-importance, anger, cruelty and ignorance—O Partha, these are the qualities of those who are born with *asuri* (ignorant) nature.

Bad qualities of ignorant people

As the wise develop good and virtuous qualities because of their right actions, those who are ignorant develop qualities which are harmful to them and to others. We develop these qualities because of the influence of the *gunas* and lack of restraint towards sense-enjoyment:

1. Self-importance   12. Delusion
2. Arrogance   13. False values
3. Pretension   14. Worry
4. Anger   15. Attachment
5. Cruelty   16. Greed
6. Ignorance   17. Egoism
7. Impurity   18. Slander
8. Absence of discipline
9. Absence of truthfulness
10. Absence of faith in God
11. Endless desire for sense-pleasure

Gita 16: 7–8

People with *asuri* nature don't know what *pravritti* (proper action) or *nivritti* (avoidable action) are. Also, there is neither purity, good conduct, nor truth.

They say: 'The world is devoid of truthfulness, without morality and without Ishvara. It is brought about by what else but the mutual union of the male and female for sense-gratification.'

The nature of ignorant people

Those who are ignorant of true knowledge do not know the right thing to do. They cannot differentiate between proper action and avoidable action. They do not hesitate to act in immoral ways.

Two words, *pravritti* and *nivritti*, are used here. *Pravritti* means 'what should be done', and *nivritti* means 'what should not be done'—the do's and don'ts of life. The wise person knows both, but the ignorant person, driven by desires and attachment, does not care about these do's and don'ts. They think the world is simply the result of the mutual union of the male and female for sense-gratification.

Those who are ignorant can only see what they want to see. That is the truth they believe in. Adi Shankaracharya mentions a story in his *bhasya* on Verse 5.18.1 of the Chhandogya Upanishad. A group of blind men hear that an elephant has been brought to the village. None of them are aware of its shape and form. Out of curiosity, they say, 'Let us inspect and know it by touch'. The first person touches the trunk and says, 'This being is like a thick snake'. Another person reaches its ear; to him, it seems like a kind of fan. Another person who holds the leg of the elephant says, 'The elephant is like a tree trunk'. The blind man who touches its side says, 'The elephant is a wall'. Another who feels its tail describes it as a rope. The last grabs its tusk and says that the elephant is hard, smooth and like a spear.

Gita 16: 9–10

Holding on to this view, people with deprived character and limited intellect perform fierce actions and undermine the welfare of the world.

Such people have insatiable desires and are endowed with pride, the feeling of superiority and arrogance. Thus, illusioned, they work in this world with tainted motives and beliefs in false ideologies.

Ignorant people undermine the welfare of the world.

Such ignorant people remain firm on their sensual enjoyment and do not believe in the possibility of karmic reactions. They take part in self-serving and even cruel deeds without any regrets. If they occupy positions of power, they impose their ignorant views upon others. They do not hesitate to further their selfish goals, even if it destroys the world. We have read many such examples in our history books.

Such people have insatiable desires. They are full of duplicity and imagine themselves to be what they are not. They embrace wrong notions. They are proud and believe that nobody is more rational than them.

Plato was born around 428 B.C.E. He was a disciple of

Socrates and the teacher of Aristotle. Plato believed that evil is a consequence of ignorance. He expressed this view in his early dialogue, the *Protagoras.* In a conversation that appears in this book, he says: 'No one willingly pursues evil, or at least what he takes to be evil; furthermore, faced with the choice of two evils, no one will choose the greater if he can choose the lesser.... Evil is a matter of 'miseducation', and this can be corrected by better education.'

Gita 16: 11–12

They have endless worries which end only with death. They are fully convinced that the gratification of desires is the only goal.

Trapped with hundreds of hopes, they are driven by desires and anger. They strive to accumulate wealth by any means to seek sense-enjoyment.

Ignorant people are driven by desire and anger.

There is no end to the desires, needs and enjoyments of such ignorant people. This pursuit of sense-enjoyment can end only with such a person's death.

We should know that desires do not end with death. Such a person is caught in the endless cycle of birth and rebirth.

Being ignorant, they believe there is nothing more than sensual enjoyment in the world. The concepts of *dharma* and *moksha* are alien to them. They believe there is nothing beyond the body and the senses and conclude that only bodily pleasures are to be pursued in the world.

They have no rest or peace of mind. They need wealth to

fulfil their desires, and they will do anything to earn money. When their desires are not met, they get angry and lose the power of discrimination.

Paramhansa Yogananda used to tell a story about a man who had a bad temper. He would hit anyone in front of him whenever he got angry, including his boss. So, he lost one job after another. He asked Yogananda for help. Yogananda told him, 'The next time you are angry, count to one hundred before you act.' He tried it but came back and said, 'I get angrier when I do that. While I am counting, I am blind with rage for having to wait so long.'

Gita 16: 13–16

'I have gained this today and will fulfil this aspiration too. I have this much wealth today and will earn more in the future.'

'I have defeated this enemy today, and I will defeat other enemies too. I am Ishvara. I am the enjoyer. I am *siddha* (perfect), powerful and happy.'

'I am rich and surrounded by aristocratic relatives. There is no one like me. I shall sacrifice, give to charity and rejoice.'

In this way, they are deluded by *ajnana* (lack of knowledge). Bewildered by such fantasies, entangled in the web of illusions and addicted to the gratification of desires, they fall into a filthy hell.

Ignorant people live in a fool's paradise.

Ignorant people always live in a fool's paradise. What do they think? Krishna gives enough examples. They think:

- 'I have gained this today and will fulfil other aspirations too.'
- 'I have this much wealth today and will earn more in the future.'
- 'I have defeated this enemy today, and I will defeat other enemies too.'
- 'I am Ishvara. I am the enjoyer. I am perfect, powerful and happy.'
- 'I am rich and surrounded by aristocratic relatives.'
- 'There is no one like me.'
- 'I shall sacrifice, I shall give to charity, I shall rejoice.'

Krishna says that such misconceptions are the result of a lack of true knowledge. Ignorant people live in a world of fantasies driven by desires and sense-enjoyment. Krishna says that if there is a hell, they will definitely go there.

Gita 16: 17–18

Self-conceited, obstinate and endowed with wealth, pride and arrogance, they only perform good deeds with pride for the sake of doing so and without following proper norms.

These envious people, full of ego, power, superiority, desires and anger, hate Me in their own bodies and that of others.

Ignorant people are full of pride, arrogance and hatred.

There are two signs of arrogance: glorifying oneself and humiliating others. These are also the first signs of ignorance. Such ignorant people consider themselves knowledgeable, intelligent, great and outstanding and deride other people, try to expose their defects and embarrass them. They hate good people. They hate the Divine because they cannot believe anyone to be greater or higher than themselves.

They are full of power, ego, wealth, pride and prosperity. Even when they perform charitable acts, they tend to glorify their own name. They do not give to the deserving. They just follow their own rules. Let's take the example of Napoleon.

Napoleon, the French military leader, lost the war with Russia in 1812 because of his pride and arrogance. Napoleon was ignorant of the harsh Russian winter. The invasion ended with the retreat of Napoleon's army after his troops suffered greatly from the bitter cold. The events which were acted out on the plains of Russia during the war were the stuff of a Greek tragedy. Napoleon ignored the significance of the winter because of his ego and overconfidence.

Gita 16: 21–22

There are three gateways to hell: *kama* (desires), *krodha* (anger) and *lobha* (greed). Therefore, one should abandon these three.

O Kaunteya, those people who are free from these three gates of darkness, who practice what is good for oneself, reach eternal bliss.

Three gates to hell: desire, anger and greed

Krishna says there are three gates to hell: *kama*, *krodha*, and *lobha*, that is, desire, anger and greed. If we are controlled by these three, we are assured of entry into the lower worlds. These three gates can be avoided by dispassion, love and detachment. Desire is to be surmounted by dispassion, anger by love, and greed by detachment.

There is still hope for the wise ones who have become conscious of these three vices. A terrible future awaits even wise people if they do not overcome these vices. If they strive for purity by restraining their senses, they will be able to avoid the gateway to hell.

Ravana was a devotee of Shiva and also a great scholar. There was no need for him to abduct Sita, the wife of Rama. In his anger, he kidnapped Sita to take revenge for his sister, Shurpanakha, being defaced. In the process, he lost everything, including his brother, son and army. Finally, he lost his life.

Therefore, we should strive to acquire true knowledge and go beyond the influences of *triguna*.

Gita 16: 23–24

Those who act on the impulse of desires, casting aside the rules and regulations of *shastras* (scriptures), attain neither perfection, pleasure nor eternal bliss.

Therefore, let the *shastras* be your benchmark in determining *karya* (ethical actions) and *akarya* (unethical actions).

Be aware of ethical and unethical actions.

Ethical actions are those that follow social norms, and such actions are acceptable to society. Unethical actions are those that are against social norms or are considered unacceptable by society.

Impulsive behaviour driven by desires does not lead to perfection, pleasure or eternal bliss. Some people tend to ignore rules and regulations to fulfil aspirations. Such people act in their own way and try to give a rationale for their actions. Everyone understands that it is only a mask to cover up their own behaviour. They do not follow the advice of the scriptures because of ignorance and desire for sensual pleasures.

If we summarize the answer given by Krishna, we will note that he has dealt with the following issues:

1. How does one know that a person has transcended the three *gunas*?
2. How does such a person conduct themselves in the world?
3. How does a person actually transcend the three *gunas*?
4. What are the qualities we develop if we rise above the three *gunas*?
5. What happens to ignorant people?

Finally, Krishna summarizes three main causes of a person's downfall: desire, anger and greed. He says that we always need to watch out for these three in our daily lives. He calls them gateways to hell because they lead to the path of destruction rather than the path of liberation.

When we have successfully conquered desire, anger and greed, we attain the supreme goal of self-realization, of oneness with Ishvara. Whenever in doubt, we should refer to our scriptures for guidance.

QUESTION 14

WHAT IS THE NATURE OF FAITH?

We all repose our faith somewhere or the other. Where we decide to place our faith shapes the direction of our life.

In early Western societies, there was a view that 'religion is faith' and 'science is knowledge'. Whether one is a material scientist, a social scientist or a spiritual master, one cannot avoid the leap of faith required in the acceptance of knowledge. In Abrahamic religions, religious faith has a very different meaning than in the Indian knowledge system. These religions believe that you must have faith in God, and if you don't have faith in Him, then God will punish you.

'For it is by grace you have been saved, through faith—and this not from yourselves, it is the gift of God—not by works, so that no one can boast' (Ephesians 2:8–9).

In the Bhagavad Gita, faith has been explained in various places. Krishna says, 'The ignorant, the faithless and sceptical people suffer a downfall. There is no happiness for such sceptical people in this world or in any other.' (Gita 4: 40)

'The ignorant' is one who has not received knowledge properly or is ill-disposed to obtaining knowledge.

'The faithless' is one who does not develop any faith or confidence in this knowledge and, therefore, does not strive for self-realization.

'The cynic' is one who is full of scepticism in regard to the knowledge imparted to them. Even though they have been taught and the concepts explained to them, they simply refuse to reflect or practice.

Gita 17: 1

Arjuna said: O Krishna, those who disregard the *shastras* but still perform actions endowed with faith, what is their faith according to *sattva, rajas* or *tamas* (goodness, passion or inertia)?

The nature of faith when you don't follow the rules

Earlier, Krishna has talked about the behaviour of people with true knowledge (Gita 13: 3) and those who are ignorant of knowledge. Those who have knowledge develop divine qualities (16: 1–3), and those who are ignorant develop flawed qualities (16: 4). People with such flawed qualities disregard the teachings of the scriptures and follow the impulses of the body and the mind. Such people do not attain perfection, happiness or freedom from the cycle of life and death.

Krishna further said that one should follow ethical actions based on the rules and regulations given in the scriptures. In those days, there was no Constitution or written laws to follow. Society used to follow the teachings of the scriptures.

Arjuna wants to know the nature of the faith of those who do not follow the scriptures. He also wants to know the types of faith based on the influence of *gunas*.

Gita 17: 2–3

Bhagwan said: There are three types of faith in all human beings based on their innate nature. They are characterized by *sattva, rajas* and *tamas gunas*. Listen about them.

O Bharat, the faith of each person is in accordance with the nature of one's disposition. All people have faith, and whatever is the nature of their faith, that is what they are.

Faith is an inseparable feature.

We all have faith in someone or something. It is an inseparable feature of the human personality. Someone may have faith in the logical ability of their intellect, the sensitivities of their senses or the philosophies they believe in. As an example, someone may say, 'I don't believe in the Brahman because I cannot see him.' From this, we understand that this person does not have faith in the Brahman but has faith in their own eyes.

We also meet people who say they believe in science, not religion. But based on new discoveries, scientific theories also change. So, can we say that this belief in science is false? Scientists also need to have faith in their discoveries.

According to Hindu Dharma, our true nature is based on our experiences in past births. We could have done a lot of good in earlier lives, or feelings of greed and power could have driven us. Based on those actions in our previous life, our faith in this birth could be *sattvic, rajasic* or *tamasic.*

Gita 17: 4

Sattvic people worship the deities. Rajasic people worship to seek wealth and absolute power. Tamasic people worship *preta* and *bhutgana*—ancestors and spirits of dead people.

Faith based on the *guna*

People with the dominance of sattva guna worship deities to acquire good qualities associated with such deities. This could be due to the lack of knowledge of the Divine or due to traditions in the family.

People with the dominance of *rajasic guna* are drawn to power and wealth. They are driven by passion and desire and seek pleasure, sensual enjoyment or revenge. Therefore, they worship those who represent wealth and power.

People with the dominance of *tamasic guna* worship ancestors and the spirits of dead people. Ancestor worship is still practised in different forms around the world today, for example, in India, Africa, Korea and Japan, even in some so-called modern societies. Some people believe that the souls of the dead may return to the living and influence their lives. Some believe that they can communicate with the dead. Some of the beliefs are related to death and the afterlife, the possibility of communication between the living and the dead and influencing the destiny of those who have died.

Gita 17: 8

Sattvic **people like food that is juicy, succulent, nourishing, pleasing to the heart and promotes longevity, strength, health, pleasure and happiness.**

Sattvic **food is juicy and nourishing.**

Now, Krishna focuses on the food we eat. Our body is the product of the food we consume and assimilate. The food we eat creates and modifies plasma, blood, muscle, fat, bone,

bone marrow, nerves and reproductive tissues. It is food that makes the body and the mind. The mind functions under the influence of the type of nutrients supplied, just as the quality of fuel affects the performance of a car.

According to Ayurveda, a *sattvic* diet includes light and healthy foods. *Sattvic* foods are supposed to increase energy, happiness, calmness and mental clarity. That means eating food that is nutritious, fresh and tasty. *Sattvic* food is fresh, full of vital life force and energy, nutritious, pure and easy to digest. Some examples are nuts, soaked and sprouted lentils, fresh fruits, fresh milk, butter, ghee, herbs and spices.

Sattvic foods are ripe, raw, delicately cooked and freshly prepared. This diet is full of nutrient-rich foods and low in processed and fried foods. The Chhandogya Upaniṣhad (7.26.2) says, '*ahara shuddhau sattva shuddhih*'—'People with pure minds prefer pure *sattvic* food'.

Gita 17: 9

Rajasic people like food that is pungent, sour, salty, very hot, spicy, dried out and burning (full of chillies), which results in agitation, despair and ill health.

Rajasic food is hot and spicy.

When food is cooked with too many chillies, sugar and salt, it becomes *rajasic*. There is excessiveness to everything. We can add the word 'very' to all the ingredients. Krishna says that *rajasic* food is very bitter, very sour, very salty, very hot, very pungent, very dry and full of chillies.

Consuming such food may lead to ill health, agitation and despair. Passionate people enjoy such food. Some people may relish hot and sour food, but it produces grievous discomfort, pain and disease in the end.

Gita 17: 10

Tamasic people like overcooked or undercooked food, having little or no flavour, or food that is putrid, preserved, unused and mixed together.

Preserved food is *tamasic*.

Tamasic food is overcooked or undercooked with spices. *Tamasic* food has little or no flavour and is putrid, preserved, unused and mixed together. If we look at the food stores of today, we will find foods that are *tamasic*.

Tamasic food includes preserved food, under- or overripe fruits, processed and canned foods. These foods draw more energy for digestion, causing a feeling of sluggishness and inertia.

Gita 17: 11–13

That *yajna* (offering) is of the nature of *sattva*, which is offered according to the scriptural rules, without expectation of reward or because it ought to be done.

O Bharatshreshtha, that *yajna* which is done for the sake of its results and to seek out self-importance, know it to be *rajasic*.

That *yajna* which is done without following rules and

regulations, without distribution of food, without mantras, without paying remuneration and without faith, that (*yajna*) is declared as *tamasic*.

Three types of *yajna*

The word '*yajna*' is difficult to translate into English. Many people have translated it as 'sacrifice'. *Yajna* comes from the root '*yaj*', which means 'to worship'. There are multiple synonyms of the word *yajna* with different meanings. It is also called *karma*, or action, or the act of sacrifice, offering, or worshipping. Here, it can be understood as any action done with the sense of offering oneself or total surrender.

Sattvic yajna is done according to spiritual texts and without expectation of rewards. It is done as a duty.

Rajasic yajna is done for the sake of results and also to increase one's importance.

Tamasic yajna is done without following any rules. Food is cooked for self-consumption and is not shared. Those who are assisting are not paid any remuneration. It is done only as a ritual and without proper mantras.

Gita 17: 14

Reverence for holy beings, self-realized persons, the guru and the wise; cleanliness, simplicity, self-restraint of senses and non-violence—these are declared as *tapa* (austerity) of the body.

Guidelines for healthy and simple living

Austerity is associated with self-denial. It could be associated with fasting or other austere practices.

Krishna explains two types of austerities for the body: the first is worshipping or revering holy beings, self-realized persons, gurus and the wise; the second is related to outlook—purity, simplicity, restraining of senses and non-violence.

The purification of the body is done with these two actions. Reverence for holy beings, self-realized persons, gurus and wise people would instil humility towards people who have knowledge and have made progress in their spiritual journey. We can learn a lot from them with this respect and reverence towards them.

Austerity of the body is also related to cleanliness and simple living. *Tapas* also includes restraining the senses and controlling physical anger with non-violence.

Gita 17: 15

Speech that does not cause agitation, which is truthful, for the good of others, and is used for gaining knowledge is declared *tapa* of speech.

Tips for good communication

Austerity of speech is related to our communication style. Many times, we speak where there is no need to speak. At other times, we speak too much without thinking. Krishna here explains the art of good communication—most relevant for the modern era of Facebook, Instagram and Twitter. Many people have suffered because of the intemperate language they used.

One's ability to communicate clearly and effectively with employees, within teams and across the organization is one of the foundations of success. In today's complex and rapidly evolving environment, effective communication is more important and challenging than ever. The ability to communicate might be a person's most critical skill.

Krishna says austerity of communication has four aspects:

- Communication should not excite, trouble or cause distress to others. It should be gentle and peaceful.
- Communication should be truthful.
- Communication should be used for the good of others.
- Communication should be used for gaining knowledge. Many times, we use our speech for useless debates and discussions just to prove our point. This should be avoided.

When we use our speech in these four ways, it will help us in dealing with people with a calm mind.

Gita 17: 16

The serenity of mind, joyfulness, silence, self-control and purity of purpose is called the *tapa* (austerity) of mind.

Maintain serenity of the mind.

The mind should be clear, calm and light. This is possible if the mind is serene. Single-minded devotion and true knowledge lead to serenity. It implies internal purity. We should also have purity of purpose. We should not try to manipulate the situation and others' feelings for selfish gains.

The mind should be full of joy. There should be no scope for anger, hatred, lust, fear and greed. This is possible if we have restrained our mind from attachment to sensual enjoyment.

We should be able to remain silent. There should be no scope for unnecessary communication and gossip. We can maintain silence by not reacting to external sounds and through the stillness of the mind.

Peace of mind is an inner feeling independent of the external environment. We should train our minds to remain calm, no matter what is happening around us. We should not allow the outside world and negative thoughts to influence the state of our mind.

When our mind is peaceful, we don't indulge in overthinking, and there is no restlessness. We experience a kind of inner freedom. It is a joyous feeling.

Gita 17: 17–19

When all three types of *tapas* are performed with full faith and devotion, without expecting any rewards, such *tapas* are declared as *sattvic*.

When all three types of *tapas* are performed with pride to gain respect, prestige and praise, they are called *rajasic*. Their results are uncertain and momentary.

When all three types of *tapas* are practised with irrational beliefs by torturing oneself or for the purpose of harming others, then such *tapas* are called *tamasic*.

What are *sattvic, rajasic* and *tamasic tapas?*

Sattvic tapa requires three things: full faith, single-minded devotion and no desire for rewards. These three conditions apply to all three types of *tapa*, that of the body, speech and mind. Austerity loses its sanctity if material rewards are sought from its performance.

Rajasic tapa is spiritual posturing only. It does not yield the benefit of *tapa* because the performer does it for show and fame. Such austerity is impulsive and for a short duration only. This austerity remains an act of self-fulfilment.

In the name of austerity, some people torture their bodies. This is against the scriptures. One should not do too much fasting or adhere overly long to a vow of silence or other vows. They may turn out to be harmful and injurious to health. Such austerity is *tamasic.*

These three verses are a kind of warning to people who perform spiritual practices or austerities for self-advancement. The points to note are:

1. There should not be any foolish notions about austerity practices.
2. In the name of austerity, one should not torture the body and cause injury to oneself.
3. No austerity should be done for just name and fame.

Gita 17: 20–22

Charity given to a worthy person simply because 'this ought to be given', without consideration of anything in return, at the proper time and place, is stated to be *sattvic.*

Charity given hesitantly, expecting reciprocation, or looking for some benefit, is said to be *rajasic*.

Charity given with disrespect and insult to undeserving persons at the wrong place and time is declared to be *tamasic*.

Different types of charitable acts

Most of us have heard about seven types of *daans*:

1. *Bhoomi Daan*—giving self-acquired land
2. *Gau Daan*—donating a cow
3. *Kanya Daan*—a ritual during Hindu marriage
4. *Tula Daan*—giving something equal to one's weight
5. *Vidya Daan*—teaching someone for free
6. *Aahaar Daan*—donating food
7. *Arth Daan*—donating money

Sattvic charity is offered as a sacred duty and not for gaining honour or name in the world. It is given to deserving people at the right time and place. It is offered without expecting any benefit. *Sattvic* charity is done out of compassion and with the feeling of oneness of all beings.

Rajasic charity is just a social celebration and no more. It is given with some reservations and conditions. It is a kind of transaction where the person doing the charitable act expects some return from this act.

Tamasic charity is done grudgingly. The person who does the charitable act is reluctant and uneasy, feeling that they are losing money or something valuable. There is no concern about whether the person receiving the donation deserves it or needs it.

Gita 17: 23–26

Aum, tat, sat has been declared as the three-fold representation of Brahma. The same Brahma is the creator of the Vedas and *yajna.*

Therefore, Brahma's devotees always begin their *yajna, tapa* and *daan* by chanting *aum* according to scriptural regulation.

The seekers of *moksha* (liberation) perform various acts of *yajna, tapa* and *daan* without expecting results by chanting *tat.*

The word *sat* is used to express harmony and goodness. O Partha, the term *sat* is also used for auspicious *karma.*

The purpose of chanting *aum, tat, sat*

'*Aum, tat, sat*' represents a threefold name for the Supreme consciousness, the Brahman, the creator of this universe. When we chant *aum tat sat*, it is believed to awaken the higher consciousness to connect the Self with the Brahman.

Aum tat sat can be translated as 'the Supreme reality', 'absolute truth', or 'all that is'.

Krishna says that all sacred and pious work should begin with the sound of *aum*. The sound of *tat* reminds us to renounce any reward for the act we are engaged in. The sound of *sat* reminds us of what is good and true. It is believed that if there are any oversights and inaccuracies in the practice of *yajna, japa* or *dhyana*, they are rectified by the utterance of these three names of Brahman, *aum tat sat.*

The mantra *aum tat sat* points to the true knowledge of

all the scriptures—'*Brahma satyam jagan mithya*', that is, 'the Brahman is real; the universe is unreal'.

Gita 17: 28

O Partha, all *yajna*, *tapa* and *daan* performed without faith are called *asat*, and they are useful neither here nor hereafter.

Faith is the key to success.

Returning to Arjuna's question, Krishna says that faith (*shraddha*) is the key to success in both worldly and spiritual life. We cannot achieve anything, even small matters of day-to-day life, without faith.

The need for unwavering faith is greater in spiritual practices. Whether we are performing *yajna*, *daan*, or *tapa*, it becomes useless if there is no faith. It is no more *sat*; it becomes *asat*—something not done at all. Such acts, done without faith, bring no good either here or hereafter.

Therefore, as seekers, we must do our spiritual practices with faith and realize the Divine. Practices done with faith will help to understand the Self. Therefore, we should hold on to faith as support. Faith is very important for us. As food is necessary to sustain our body, our faith is necessary to nourish our souls.

HOW IS *SANYASA* DIFFERENT FROM *TYAGA*?

This is the last question asked by Arjuna: I wish to know the essence of *sanyasa* (life of renunciation). How it is different from *tyaga* (relinquishing the fruits of action)?

Krishna first defines what is *sanyasa* and *tyaga*. He then defines a *tyagi* and a *sanyasi*.

Using this opportunity, Krishna tells Arjuna about the importance of doing one's own *karma* (*svadharma*) and explains that no profession or work is inferior to any other. Krishna stresses that it is better to do one's own natural *karma* than to do another's *karma*.

Krishna further discusses the motive behind any *karma*. He says that there are three motivations to fruitive *karma*: *jnana* (the knowledge), *jneyam* (the object of knowledge) and *parijnanata* (the knower). There are three essentials factors for *karma*: *karanam* (the cause), *karma* (the act itself) and *karteti* (the doer).

When a person is not a *sanyasi* and still wants to strive towards self-realization, Krishna sums the highest and most secret knowledge again. He says that a *yogi* can attain

Brahma with a refined intellect combined with firmness of willpower and restrained senses.

Finally, Krishna lists the advantages of doing *karma* with devotion and total surrender. He says that those who perform their *karma* with total surrender to the Divine attain the eternal, imperishable abode.

Gita 18: 1

Arjuna said: O Mahabaho, I wish to know the essence of the life of *sanyasa*. O Hrishikesh, how is it different from *tyaga* (relinquishing the fruits of action), O Keshinishudan?

Sanyasa versus *tyaga*

Several times during the conversation, Krishna used the words *sanyasa* (life of renunciation) and *tyaga* (relinquishment of fruits of actions), for example, in Verses 3: 30, 4: 20, 4: 41, 9: 28, 12: 6, 12: 11, 12: 12, 12: 16, 14: 25. So far, these two terms were not explained.

Hence, Arjuna's question: How is renunciation different from relinquishing the fruits of action?

Gita 18: 2

Bhagwan said: Learned people know that *sanyasa* is giving up *karma* motivated by desires, whereas wise people declare that renouncing the fruits of all *karma* is *tyaga*.

What are *sanyasa* and *tyaga*?

Sanyasa is giving up *karma* motivated by desires. A *sanyasi* does not abandon *niyat karma* (regular/obligatory *karma*), as it is not proper to do so. Further, inappropriate *karma* can be given up, but *karma* involving *yajna*, *tapa* and *daan* should never be abandoned. A *sanyasi* is not affected by the three types of results of *karma*: unfavourable, favourable and mixed. These results do not accrue to a *sanyasi*.

What is *tyaga*? Tyaga is renouncing the fruits of all *karmas*.

A *tyagi* does not abandon *karma* involving *yajna*, *tapa* and *daan* because they know that *yajna*, *tapa* and *daan* clear impurities. A *tyagi* performs these *karmas* without attachment and without expectation of results.

There are three types of *tyaga*. A *tyagi* who gives up *niyat karma* (regular/obligatory *karma*) due to illusion is described as *tamasic*. *Tyaga* is *rajasic* when one does not perform *karma* for fear of physical difficulty or because it is painful. Such *tyaga* does not even give the benefits of *tyaga*. *Sattvic tyaga* is when *niyat karmas* (regular/obligatory *karmas*) are performed without attachment to their results. Also, a *sattvic tyagi* does not hate unfavourable *karma* and is not attached to favourable *karma*.

Those who do not renounce (*atyagi*, not a *sanyasi*) the results of their *karma* are affected by three types of results—unfavourable, favourable and mixed—even after death.

Gita 18: 3–5

Some *manishinah* (philosophers) say that inappropriate *karma* should be given up, but others declare that *karma* involving *yajna*, *tapa* and *daan* should never be abandoned.

O Bharatasattam, hear from me the conclusive opinion about *tyaga*. O Purushavyaghra, three types of *tyaga* have been described.

Great philosophers declare that *karma* involving *yajna*, *tapa* and *daan* should never be abandoned;

they should always be performed because *yajna, tapa* and *daan* get rid of impurities.

Don't give up the performance of good *karma*.

Karma literally means 'action' or 'doing'. The Indian knowledge system explains three types of *karma—karma, akarma* and *vikarma*.

Karma means movement in the outside world, and cessation of any such movement amounts to *akarma* (inaction). Karma has also been classified into several categories. There are two main classifications: *niyatam*, or prescribed actions, and *nishiddha*, or forbidden actions (*vikarma*). Prescribed actions are those that are enjoined in the scriptures. In today's context, we may interpret them as one's duties.

Niyat karmas include performing one's *svadharma*, attending to one's parents and family and working for the all-round development of one's nation. Forbidden actions include killing another being, stealing, cheating and so on.

Some people say that inappropriate *karma* should be given up. At the same time, some people say that devoted and proper actions involving offerings, austerity and charity should never be given up.

So, Krishna pronounces a final decision on this debate:

1. *Na tyajyam:* Acts of *yajna, tapa* and *daan* should not be abandoned.

2. *Karyam eva tat:* Acts of *yajna, tapa* and *daan* should be performed.

Krishna emphasizes his conclusion by expressing it in negative and positive forms. Sometimes, we are told that these acts of *yajna*, *tapa* and *daan* should also be abandoned because even good acts create bondage and lead to the cycle of birth and rebirth. Krishna is very clear: These acts should never be abandoned, but they should be performed without desire for the fruits of actions.

Gita 18: 7–9

Abandonment of regular and obligatory *karma* is not proper. Giving up of such *karma* because of illusion is described as *tamasic*.

***Tyaga* is *rajasic* when one does not perform *karma* for fear of physical trouble and because it is painful. Such *tyaga* does not even give the benefits of *tyaga*.**

O Arjuna, 'This *karma* ought to be done'; when regular and obligatory *karma* is performed without attachment to the results, such *tyaga* is viewed as *sattvic*.

Tamasic, rajasic and *sattvic tyaga*

After explaining what types of actions should never be abandoned, Krishna now classifies *tyaga* according to the *gunas*. We should never abandon the right thing which we need to do. It is unavoidable. But people with the dominance of *tamasic guna* even renounce obligatory actions and duties.

When people renounce *karma* because of fear of bodily trouble and avoid actions because they are painful, such *tyaga* is defined as *rajasic tyaga*. Such people do not benefit from renunciation because performing one's obligatory duties without expecting results is the most magnificent of all types of *tyaga*.

When *sattvic guna* dominates, people perform their duties with the thought that it ought to be done. They abandon attachment to the action and to the fruits of action. Such relinquishment of fruits of actions always leads us to a full and joyful life. Such *tyaga* helps us in overcoming the ego and egocentric desires.

Gita 18: 12

There are three types of results of *karma*: unfavourable, favourable and mixed. They accrue to those who are attached to the personal reward even after death but never (accrue) for a *sanyasi*.

Three types of results of actions

One can get three types of results by performing *karmas*: *ishtam*, or favourable results, *anishtam*, or unfavourable results, and *mishram*, or mixed results, which are neither favourable nor unfavourable. These results remain with the performer of *karma* even after death. However, this applies only when the actions are performed with a desire for personal gains.

A *sanyasi* who has renounced all selfish actions and relinquished the results of all *karma* is not bound by these results.

When a *sanyasi* has renounced such desire for the fruits of actions and action is done only as a duty, then no such results accrue to a *sanyasi* from such actions.

Gita 18: 13–14

O Mahabaho, learn from me the five components
declared in Samkhya for achieving success in all
karmas at the end of their performance.

These five factors are *adhisthan* (the place), *karta* (the
doer), *karanam* (a cause), *cheshta* (necessary efforts)
and *daivam* (providence).

Five components to achieve success

Krishna explains the teachings of Samkhya, where five
factors necessary for achieving success in all *karma* are
described. These five factors are:

1. *Adhishthan*—an establishment, the place of work
2. *Karta*—the doer, the one who wields the instruments of
   action
3. *Karanam*—the cause, purpose or reason, the desire
   which propels us to act
4. *Cheshta*—requisite efforts, which are undertaken by the
   five bodily instruments (*karmendriyas*), the five senses
   (*jnanendriyas*), the mind and intellect. Each of these has
   different and distinct functional capacities and is called
   cheshta.
5. *Daivam*—providence, the unseen forces of past actions
   performed already and coming to fruition now.

Gita 18: 15–16

These are the five factors for any type of *karma*
performed by people—by this body, speech or mind—
whether right or wrong.

Even after this, if someone thinks because of an untrained intellect that 'I am the doer', they do not understand at all.

We cannot claim individual success.

The five factors mentioned earlier are needed to perform any action and achieve success in any endeavour. Whatever the action, whether it is done by the body, speech or mind, these five factors are needed to do it. The three kinds of actions are *kayik* (actions performed by the body), *vachik* (actions performed by speech), and *manasik* (actions performed by the mind). A person may be called ignorant if they think they are the only claimant for the success of an action.

Whether we do virtuous or immoral acts, these five factors are responsible. But because of the ego, we think that we are the doers of our actions. When we are successful, we proudly say, 'I achieved this' or 'I accomplished that'. We make these statements because in our ignorance, we think we are the doers. Such people don't understanding anything about the functioning of this world.

Gita 18: 17

Those who think 'I am not the doer' and whose intellect is emotionally unattached, even when they slay a living being, they neither slay nor are bound to this world, even after death.

Perform your duty as a 'warrior'.

A warrior is a person who shows great vigour and courage.

A warrior is willing to lay down their life for the sake of their country. Here, Krishna is telling Arjuna that he should fight this war without any emotional attachment to the results of the war. In this war of Mahabharata, warriors will fight, and they will kill and get killed. Krishna says that if they fight with the sense of duty and the feeling that 'I am not the doer', they will neither be accused of killing others nor be bound by the cycle of birth and rebirth.

We get bound to this world because of the sense of 'I, me and myself' and take personal credit for all our actions. Our attachment to worldly objects and the sense of success or failure also cause bondage. Our actions do not bind us when this false sense of self is gone. It certainly does not mean we go out on a rash driving adventure on city roads without any sense of attachment and claim that 'I am not the doer'. Such rash driving is not a lawful act, and we will be punished for this act.

Gita 18: 18

There are three motivations for fruitful *karma*: *jnana* (the knowledge), *jneyam* (the object of knowledge) and *parijnanata* (the knower). There are three elements of *karma*: *karanam* (the cause), *karma* (the act itself) and *karteti* (the doer).

Motives and elements of action

Krishna discusses three motives—the expectation of results—behind any *karma*. These are:

1. *Jnana* (knowledge)

2. *Jneyam* (the object of knowledge)
3. *Parijnanata* (the knower)

Knowledge is a primary motivator for action. It provides the knower insight into the object of knowledge. These three are the motivation for all actions. For example, knowledge of the wages to be paid by the employer motivates employees to work; knowledge of the good performance of a company motivates an investor to invest; knowledge of the prospect of winning a gold medal in sports motivates a sportsperson to excel. Also, knowledge about the prospect of a good employment opportunity motivates a student to study hard. In all these examples, there exists knowledge, the object of knowledge and the knower.

There are three essential elements of *karma*. This is the triad of action.
1. *Karanam* (the cause)
2. *Karma* (the act itself)
3. *Karteti* (the doer)

This triad constitutes the content of any action. The doer performs the action because of the cause of action. In the coming verses, Krishna explains one of three motivations and two of the three elements—*jnana*, *karma* and *karta*—based on the *gunas*.

Gita 18: 20–22

That knowledge is *sattvic*, which sees unity in diversity and harmony in all separate lives, that is, it is inclusive and comprehensive.

That knowledge is *rajasic*, which recognizes that various objects and entities are different from one another.

That knowledge is *tamasic*, which considers one idea or part of it to be complete in itself, that is, each object or being exists by itself and is perfect by itself. The knowledge acquired is specific, experiential and difficult to teach by texts.

Three types of *jnana* (knowledge)

Jnana means knowledge or wisdom. Knowledge here refers to the knowledge of *kshetra* (the body, mind and intellect) and *kshetrajna* (*dehi*, the supreme consciousness), rather than worldly knowledge (*vijnana*) obtained through learning or experience. *Jnana* is an inward experience or awareness which frees one from worldly burdens. A *yogi* who gains knowledge moves through the following steps:

- *Viveka* (Discrimination)—The ability to distinguish reality from deception
- *Vairagya* (Renunciation of the results of action)—The ability to detach from the dualities, for example, pain and pleasure, of the world.
- *Shatsampat* (six virtues)—Developing six virtues of the mind, namely, *shama* (calmness), *dama* (restraining the senses), *uparati* (no worldly distractions), *titiksha* (endurance), *shraddha* (faith) and *samadhana* (balance)
- *Mumukshutva* (Longing for knowledge to the point that all desires fade)

According to the *gunas*, knowledge is of three types:

- *Sattvic* knowledge sees unity in diversity and harmony in separate lives. It is inclusive and comprehensive.
- *Rajasic* knowledge recognizes that various objects and entities are different from one another.
- *Tamasic* knowledge considers one idea or part to be complete in itself, that is, each object or being exists by itself and is perfect by itself. The knowledge so acquired is specific, experiential (no dry philosophical speculation) and tough to teach through texts only.

There is a story about *tamasic* knowledge. A person started believing that he was dead. He stopped going to work, arguing that he was dead. He used it to his advantage with his wife. Whenever she asked him to do any work, he would say, 'How can a dead man do anything?' Finally, his wife got fed up and took him to a doctor. The doctor, too, was perplexed about this man. The doctor then had an idea. He asked, 'Does a dead body bleed?' The man replied, 'No.' So, the doctor pricked him with a pin. Lo and behold! There was blood. The doctor said, 'You are bleeding, so you are alive.' The man looked at the blood and said, 'Oh, I have learnt a new thing today—even dead men bleed!'

Gita 18: 23–25

That *karma* is *sattvic*, which is essential for society, free from attachment, without love or hatred, and which is done without desire for rewards.

That *karma* is *rajasic*, which is prompted by desires
and aspirations, accomplished with self-esteem and
performed with lots of effort.

That *karma* is *tamasic*, which is done due to
attachment to a vocation, ignoring possible loss or
injuries and going beyond one's real capacity.

Three types of *karma* based on *trigunas*

Here, *karma* refers to *niyat karma*.

Sattvic karma is essential for society, free from attachment,
without love or hatred and is done without the desire
for rewards.

Rajasic karma is prompted by desires and aspirations,
accomplished with self-esteem and performed with lots
of effort.

Tamasic karma is done due to attachment to a vocation,
ignoring possible loss or injuries and going beyond one's
real capacity.

Gita 18: 26–28

That *karta* is *sattvic*, who is free from attachment,
non-egoistic, full of perseverance and enthusiasm, and
is unaffected by success or failure.

That *karta* is *rajasic*, who is passionate, result-
oriented, greedy, competitive, ruthless and influenced
by the outcomes of joy and sorrow.

That *karta* is *tamasic*, who is unpredictable,
materialistic, persistent, misleading, audacious,
laidback, procrastinating and sceptical.

Three types of *karta* (the doer)

Jiva is a part of Ishvara in us, which is also the agent of action (*karta*) and the enjoyer of pleasure and pain (*bhokta*). Though the *jiva* is a *karta*, its actions are ultimately caused by Ishvara as the dweller in all beings. Because we don't understand the play of *guna*, we say, 'I am the doer'.

Krishna here reiterates that thinking 'I am the doer' is wrong. One who thinks 'I am not the doer' and whose intellect is not emotionally involved in action, attains *moksha* (liberation).

Sattvic karta is free from attachment, is non-egoistic, full of perseverance and enthusiasm and unaffected by success or failure.

Rajasic karta is passionate, result-oriented, greedy, competitive, ruthless and influenced by the dispositions of joy and sorrow.

Tamasic karta is unpredictable, materialistic, persistent, misleading, audacious, laidback, procrastinating and sceptical.

Gita 18: 30–32

The intellect is *sattvic*, O Partha, when it understands what is proper and improper action, what should be done and what should not be done, what is to be feared and what is not to be feared, what is binding and what is liberating.

The intellect is *rajasic*, O Partha, when it fails to differentiate between right and wrong, between what should be done and what should not be done.

The intellect is *tamasic*, O Partha, when it is full of
doubt about right and wrong and sees everything
with an opposing view and opinion.

Three types of intellect

Krishna also explains the nature of *buddhi* (intellect) based
on the *gunas*.

The intellect is *sattvic* when it understands what is proper
and improper action, what should be done and what should
not be done, what is to be feared and what is not to be
feared, what is binding and what is liberating.

The intellect is *rajasic* when it fails to differentiate
between right and wrong, btween what should be done and
what should not be done.

The intellect is *tamasic* when it is full of doubt about
right and wrong and sees everything with a contradictory
view and opinion.

Gita 18: 33–35

Willpower is *sattvic*, O Partha, when it holds steady
the body, mind, intellect and the vital force (*prana*)
because of the regular practice of *yoga*.

O Arjuna, when willpower holds on to duty, desire
and wealth out of attachment and expectation of
results, that willpower is *rajasic*.

The willpower is *tamasic*, O Partha, when it is given
up unwisely because of hope, fear, grief, despair and
pride.

Three types of *dhriti* (willpower or resolve)

We need firm resolve or strong willpower to perform our actions. Some people fight without fear, some roam freely in dark and dangerous forests, some climb mountain peaks, and some train very hard to go to space. These are some examples of resolve and willpower. Krishna explains three types of resolve.

Willpower is *sattvic* when it holds steady the body, mind, intellect and the vital force (*prana*) because of the regular practice of *yoga*.

When willpower holds on to duty, desire and wealth out of attachment and expectation of results, that willpower is rajasic.

Willpower is *tamasic* when it is surrendered unintelligently out of hope, fear, grief, despair or pride.

Gita 18: 36–39

Now hear from me, O Bharatasharbha, the three types of pleasure which one enjoys from force of habit and to get away from misery.

That pleasure is *sattvic*, which may be unpleasant initially but is everlasting in the end. This pleasure is born out of self-realization.

The pleasure is *rajasic* when it is very enjoyable initially because of the gratification of the senses but finally results in pain.

The pleasure is *tamasic* when it is due to sleep, inactivity or recklessness. The pleasure is illusory throughout.

Three types of *sukh* (pleasure)

We want results most of the time when we perform *karma*. We seek pleasure out of habit or to get away from misery. When we perform our *karma* with the expectation of results, we derive pleasure, even if temporary. There are three types of pleasure, according to *triguna*:

That pleasure is *sattvic,* which may be unpleasant initially but is everlasting in the end. This pleasure is born out of self-realization.

The pleasure is *rajasic* when it is very enjoyable in the beginning because the senses are gratified, but it finally results in pain.

The pleasure is *tamasic* when it is due to sleep, inactivity or recklessness. The pleasure is illusory throughout.

Gita 18: 41–44

O Parantapa, the *karmas* of the knowledge-oriented, power-oriented, wealth-oriented and skill-oriented people are clearly set apart according to the *gunas* backed by their own nature.

The occupation of a knowledge-oriented person involves equality, self-discipline, simplicity, transparency, compassion, uprightness, knowledge with a logical approach, and devotion.

The occupation of a power-oriented person involves courage, intensity, determination, resourcefulness, a competitive spirit, generosity and devotion.

The occupation of a wealth-oriented person involves production and trade. In contrast, the skill-oriented person works for others most of the time.

Four types of occupations

After explaining various factors related to *karma*, Krishna now describes four types of occupations based on our *karma* orientations. However, these four types of professions are not free from the influence of the three *gunas*. The duties of the knowledge-oriented (*brahmins*), power-oriented (*kshatriyas*), wealth-oriented (*vaishyas*), and skill-oriented (*shudras*) people are clearly divided according to *gunas*.

The occupation of a knowledge-oriented person has elements of humility, self-discipline, simplicity, transparency, compassion and knowledge with a logical approach and devotion.

The occupation of a power-oriented person will have elements of courage, intensity, determination, resourcefulness, competitive spirit, generosity and devotion.

A wealth-oriented person will be involved in agriculture, business, industry, production and trade.

A skill-oriented person will have excellent skills in some areas and will use those skills for employment or livelihood.

Gita 18: 45–46

People can attain perfection by working in accordance with their occupations, based on their *gunas*. Now, let us discuss how one can become perfect by following one's own *karmas*.

People can attain perfection in their occupations by performing their *karma* and working devotedly for *tat* (That who is pervading all).

Attaining perfection in one's occupation

How can one attain perfection in one's occupation? Krishna says that by working in accordance with their natural occupation, based on their *gunas*, people can attain perfection. One can become perfect by following one's *karmas* and working devotedly for *tat* (That who is pervading all).

What about those who don't like what they are doing? Krishna stresses that it is better to do one's own natural *karma*, even if imperfectly, than to do another's karma perfectly. By doing one's *karma*, a person does not incur any wrong. One should not abandon one's own *karma*, even if one sees shortcomings in it. As fire is hidden by smoke, similarly, all activities have some hidden unpleasant component.

Since most of us are compelled by our nature to engage in our respective duties, the best way for us is to continue our work in a spirit of surrendering to the Divine.

There are three messages for us, whether we are on the path of *karma*, *bhakti* or *jnana*.

- Path of action (*karma*): *Karma yoga* works for the betterment of people, without any expectation. Sometimes, people think it is very hard to follow *karma yoga* because it is difficult to overcome the desire for fame, money, power and so on. It becomes easier to follow this path if one surrenders the result to the Divine.
- Path of devotion (*bhakti*): It is the path of attaining union with the Divine through the path of devotion

or total surrender. This path leads one to experience and understand surrender. Strongly emotional people inclined more towards the heart than the intellect should follow the path of *bhakti yoga*.

- Path of true knowledge (*jnana*): It is the path of union with the Divine following the path of knowledge. One who is very inquisitive, has lots of questions and is willing to strive to get answers to these questions should follow the path of knowledge. Such people are more inclined towards the intellect than the heart. Scholars and thinkers can attain more progress on their spiritual journey by following the path of *jnana yoga*.

Therefore, if one becomes aware of the composition of one's *guna* and understands one's true nature, one can follow the path accordingly, attain perfection in one's profession and attain the Divine.

Gita 18: 47–48

It is better to do one's own vocation defectively than to do another's vocation very well. By working in one's vocation, a person does not suffer harm.

One should not abandon one's own vocation, even if one sees shortcomings, O Kaunteya. As fire is hidden by smoke, similarly, all activities have some hidden unpleasant element.

Take pride in your work.

Generally, being proud of yourself is a negative quality. But Krishna says that being proud of your work is not a negative trait. When we take pride in our work, we give our absolute best consistently. But if we are driven by a desire to outshine everyone else, then this pride is nothing but self-importance.

At the same time, we should not be ashamed of our work. We should not give up our work because of the feeling that it is inferior to others' work. We should not feel bad about our work because we feel that it is difficult to perform and there are possibilities of making mistakes.

Many times, we are fascinated by other people's work. We find it glamorous and exciting. We may feel that we can do that work better than what we are doing, just as Arjuna thinks it is better to be a *jnani* than a warrior.

Krishna says that we should not fall into this trap. We should neither get attached to our work nor feel aversion towards it. There are hidden unpleasant moments in every type of work, as fire is hidden by smoke.

Gita 18: 51–53

With a refined intellect and firmness of willpower, giving up sound and other sense-objects, beyond love and hate;

Remaining aloof, eating lightly, speech, body and mind under perfect control, engaged in meditation, always remaining detached;

Free from ego, arrogance of power, desire, anger, possessions without proprietorship, and remaining peaceful, such a person is fit to attain Brahma.

Who is fit to attain self-realization?

When a person is on a spiritual path and wants to strive for self-realization, Krishna sums up key points the person needs to focus on. He says that a person who is fit to attain the Divine with self-realization can use some of the following qualities:

- Refine your intellect: Train your intellect to observe and control your desire for sense gratification.
- Use your willpower to give up sense-objects: You can increase your resolve through your willpower to not indulge in sense-enjoyment.
- Go beyond love and hate: Love and hate are two prime emotions that we feel. We need to rise above them.
- Remain aloof: The cause of restlessness is our own greedy nature. That is why we should remain aloof from greed and acquisitiveness.
- Eat lightly: It is very important to remain healthy.
- Have control over your speech, body and mind: Always think, speak and act according to the dictates of your conscience and the call of the higher good.
- Practice meditation: Meditation is the most effective way to spiritualize your consciousness.
- Remain detached: We cannot enjoy a life of true happiness without detachment. A person who remains detached from within is happy.
- Be free from ego, arrogance of power, desire and anger: These are the primary obstacles on the path of liberation.
- Possess things without feelings of proprietorship: The idea is to be away from attachment to the objects or pleasures in the world. We need to treat these objects only as a means for higher use.

Remain peaceful: One of the most critical conditions for long-lasting happiness is the ability to remain inwardly calm, no matter what happens.

Gita 18: 54–55

Having attained Brahma, such a blissful person who neither grieves nor desires and remains equal to all living beings becomes My best devotee.

My devotees know the truth of who and what I am. Knowing the truth about Me, they enter *tat* (spiritual kingdom) afterwards.

What happens when one is self-realized?

Krishna says such a blissful person becomes the best devotee. Such a person has true knowledge and knows there is nothing to seek or grieve for. They treat everyone equally. They do not see any distinction between elite and ordinary people. They have the same outlook on angels, humans, animals and creeping and crawling beings. In summary, such a person:

- Does not grieve;
- Has no desires; and
- Remains equal to all living beings.

Such devotees know the truth of who and what the Divine is. Knowing the truth about the Divine, they enter *tat* (spiritual kingdom) afterwards.

Gita 18: 56–58

Those who perform all *karma* with total surrender unto Me attain the eternal, imperishable abode by My grace.

My devotees renounce all *karmas* to Me by intellect, by employing *buddhi yoga* (*jnana yoga*) with a mind always focused on Me.

By focusing your mind on Me, you will overcome all obstacles by My grace, but if you do not listen to Me due to your ego, you will perish.

Perform all *karma* with total surrender.

Krishna describes the advantages of doing *karma* with devotion and total surrender. He says those who perform all *karma* with total surrender to the Divine attain the eternal, imperishable abode. He says, 'My devotees renounce all *karmas* by mentally surrendering unto Me, by employing *buddhi yoga* (*jnana yoga*) with a mind always focused on Me.'

Therefore, devotion and knowledge sustain and strengthen each other. When we know the Divine, we also become the perfect devotee. A perfect devotee also becomes the sage of supreme wisdom.

The great sage Shankaracharya propounded the truth that there is only One, not two. So, there is neither a devotee nor one to be devoted to. Once we surrender totally, we become one with the Divine. The choice is left to us. If we surrender, we will be happy and overcome all difficulties. If we don't, we will suffer eternal bondage.

Gita 18: 59

If, because of ego, you think, 'I will not fight', your thinking is wrong because your own nature will compel you (to fight).

Our true nature will compel us to follow *svadharma*.

Krishna warns Arjuna, 'By focusing your mind on Me, you will overcome all obstacles by My grace, but if you do not listen to me because of your ego, you will perish. If, because of your ego, you think, 'I will not fight', your thinking is wrong, because your own nature will compel you (to fight).'

Krishna repeats the importance of *svadharma*—occupation based on our true nature. If, due to misconception, we do not wish to follow our natural vocation, we will be forced to do it. *Svadharma* is that action which is in accordance with your skills, nature (*svabhava*) and duty (*karma*).

Svadharma consists of two words—*sva* and *dharma*. *Sva* means 'own', and *dharma* refers to *dharma* related to an individual's attributes, not the cosmic *dharma*. There's a term in Japanese called 'Ikigai', which means 'reason for being'. This resonates very strongly with *svadharma*.

The question is: Can we follow *svadharma* in today's world? We must work for a living and choose a profession based on survival or expediency rather than ability or interest. How can modern people follow *svadharma*?

We know that if you love what you do and do what you love, life becomes a joy. If we want to lead a life of bliss, we will have to make an effort to move towards a profession more in tune with our *svadharma*.

Gita 18: 61

O Arjuna, Ishvara resides in the hearts of all living beings. All these beings keep moving in life by My *maya* (the *prakriti*) as if they are travelling in a *yantra* (moving machine).

Life moves like a *yantra*, a moving machine.

Ishvara resides in the hearts of all living beings. Due to the influence of the *gunas*, we perform our tasks in automatic mode. Krishna uses the word *yantra* or moving machine. This also brings to our attention that in that era, *yantras* did exist.

We should not be under the impression that the Divine is far away or that we can do anything that Ishvara would not notice. There is some bad news here. Krishna repeats that the Divine exists within us and resides in the hearts of all living beings.

We are all subject to the power of m*aya* or illusion. Sant Kabir says, '*Maya* is the biggest con I know of'. *Maya* is the illusion or the manifestation we all see, hear, smell and experience with all our senses. Still, it is not an easy subject to understand. Many wise people have tried to explain *maya* but have not succeeded. Even for those who understood it, it was not easy to explain it to others. Sant Kabir says further, '*Maya* roams around with the trap of *triguna* and speaks the sweetest words'. Krishna compares *maya* to a *yantra* which we have boarded and are going wherever it takes us.

So, the only way to take care of *maya* is to remove the trap of *triguna*, that is, understand the play of *triguna* and learn to go beyond it. Only with *jnana* (true knowledge) can we overcome *maya* to get rid of our pride and egoism and achieve eternal bliss.

Gita 18: 63–64

Thus, I have revealed the wisdom, which is more secret than all secrets. Reflect on it fully, and then do as you wish.

Hear again from me the most secret and final statement. I am telling it to you since you are very dear to Me.

Do as you wish.

Krishna now tells Arjuna that he has told Arjuna everything. Krishna says: 'Now reflect over it fully and do as you wish.'

Even after saying, 'Do as you wish', Krishna says that because Arjuna is very dear to him, he would repeat the secret of life again. He says:

'Absorb your mind in Me, be my devotee, worship Me, offer your obeisance to Me, and you will certainly come to Me. I promise to you truly, as you are dear to Me. Abandon all *dharma* (regular activities), surrender to Me alone, and I will liberate you from all *paapa* (immoral actions). Don't grieve.'

Gita 18: 66

Abandon all regular activities and surrender to Me alone; I will liberate you from all *paapa* (immoral actions). Don't grieve.

The final promise and advice

Krishna has gone into great detail to explain to Arjuna the difference between 'renunciation' and 'renunciation of the fruits of action'. In the process, he covered the concept of *karma*, *karta*, motivation to act and four types of occupations based on our true nature. He told Arjuna that we should not abandon our *karma* on the pretext of renunciation. We should perform our *karma* even if we don't like some part of it. This is because every occupation and vocation has some hidden unpleasantness.

This is his final promise and advice:

- Abandon all duties; just surrender to the Divine. Total surrender is the direct path to attaining ultimate liberation. When we perform our duties, we get *punya* (merit), but surrendering to the Divine confers liberation.

- Surrender to the Divine only. We may worship other deities with total surrender, but the result will still bind the devotee to this world.

- Krishna says: 'I will liberate you from all *paapa*.' In the scriptures, various methods have been prescribed to overcome some types of *paapa*. However, if one surrenders to the Divine, all *paapa* will be taken care of because the union is complete.

- Finally, Krishna says, 'Don't grieve'. This is the last piece of advice to all the devotees and faithful disciples. The most certain thing in life is that we will pass away one day. Even so, the fear of death is the biggest fear in life. So, when something is inevitable, why grieve over it?

There is a story in the Mahabharata. During their exile in the forest, the Pandavas were thirsty one day and saw a lake in the distance. Yudhishthira asked Bhima to go and fetch water. When Bhima reached the lake, a *yaksha* appeared and said, 'I will only let you take the water if you first answer my questions.' Bhima paid no heed and proceeded to take water. The *yaksha* pulled him into the lake. The same fate was in store for the other three brothers, Arjuna, Nakula and Sahadeva. When nobody returned, Yudhishthira got worried and approached the lake. Once again, the *yaksha* said, 'Answer my questions if you want to drink water from the lake, or I will pull you in, just as I have done to your four brothers.' Yudhishthira agreed to answer the questions. The *yaksha* asked sixty questions, each of which Yudhishthira answered. One of these questions was: *'Kim ashcharyam?'* 'What is the most surprising thing in this world?'

Yudhishthira replied, 'At every moment, people are dying. Those who are alive witness this phenomenon; yet, they do not think they will also have to die one day. What can be more astonishing than this?'

Therefore, Krishna says, 'Don't grieve. Surrender to Me and fight.'

EPILOGUE

Why should one read the Bhagavad Gita?

In India, almost everyone has heard about the Bhagavad Gita. Some have read it thoroughly and tried to practise the teachings of Krishna in their daily lives. Some have devoted their lives to propagating the message of the Gita. Some find it very difficult to read and understand.

People believe that the Gita gives us a direction for our lives. It provides us with the knowledge to know ourselves. It teaches us how to handle a crisis and how to overcome it. The Gita tells us how to put our knowledge to practical use.

In the Gita, Krishna tries to satisfy Arjuna by answering his questions and resolving his doubts. The Gita does not mandate any specific path. While it describes various paths like *jnana yoga*, *karma yoga*, *dhyana yoga* and *bhakti yoga*, it tells us that whichever path we follow, we should do so with faith and single-minded devotion.

In the final verses of the Gita, Krishna tells us that though the knowledge given here is true, everyone may not be ready to receive it. After listening to Krishna attentively, Arjuna acknowledges his words and chooses to fight the battle he was avoiding in the beginning.

Sanjaya says that by the grace of the Divine, he was able to hear this conversation. He says that anyone who follows the teachings of the Gita will earn prosperity, be victorious and follow the path of morality.

Gita 18: 67

Do not share this knowledge with those who do not perform any austerity, never with those who are not devotees; not with those who don't want to listen, nor with those who display malice towards Me.

Who is not fit to receive this knowledge?

Krishna says that this knowledge should not be shared with certain people. He says:
- Don't share this knowledge with those who do not perform any austerity.
- Never share it with those who are not devotees.
- Never share it with those who do not want to listen.
- Never share it with those who display malice towards the Divine.

This is true for sharing all types of knowledge, not only for the Gita. One must be devoted to attaining knowledge and following the rules for gaining that knowledge in any discipline. There is no use in teaching someone who does not want to listen or has malice towards the teacher.

Gita 18: 68–69

One, who with supreme devotion in Me, teaches this profound knowledge to my devotees, performs the highest act of devotion. Such a person will certainly come to Me, without doubt.

No one among all mankind is more dear to Me. Nor will there be another one who will be more dear to Me on earth.

Teaching this knowledge is the highest act of devotion.

Krishna declares that those who teach this knowledge perform a supreme act of devotion and are doing the greatest service to humanity. Such a person definitely attains liberation.

The knowledge in the Gita encompasses the deepest secret of life. It provides the key to liberating us from the cycle of birth and rebirth. It is vital to acquire this knowledge, but offering it to others is an infinitely greater effort.

Krishna says that those who teach the Gita are the dearest to him.

Gita 18: 70–72

And the one who will study our spiritual dialogue, I believe that such a person is worshipping me through *jnana yajna.*

Even those who hear this with complete faith and without malice will be liberated and will attain the blissful world attained by doing *punya karma* (pious activities).

O Partha, have you heard this with full attention of mind? O Dhananjaya, has your *jnana-sammoha* (delusion due to knowledge) been destroyed?

We should remain attentive during a dialogue.

Krishna equals the reading of the Gita to a *jnana yajna,* the scriptural study and regular contemplation of the deeper meanings of the teachings. A *jnana yajna* triggers interest in the true knowledge of the Gita in a seeker. Such a seeker offers ignorance and negative tendencies in the fire of knowledge.

However, this reading has to be done with total faith and devotion and without malice. Sometimes, people read the scriptures only to nitpick and find faults in the teachings. They read the scriptures with malice to prove their knowledge is better than that of others. Nowadays, we find many such people misinterpreting the teachings of the Gita. They assign meanings to the words in a modern context, whereas those words were used in a different context in that era.

Krishna finally asks Arjuna: 'Have you heard this with full concentration of mind? Has your *jnana-sammoha* (delusion due to knowledge) been destroyed?'

We know that people have tiny attention spans. Even during conversation, many times, our minds tend to stray. Krishna wants to ensure that Arjuna has heard and understood the entire dialogue.

Gita 18: 73

Arjun Said: O Achyuta, my illusion (*moha*) is destroyed by your grace. I know where I am. I am now free from doubts and shall do as you instructed.

No more doubts remaining!

Arjuna responds that he has listened to Krishna with full attention, and his delusion is destroyed. When Arjuna first went to the no man's land in the middle of the battlefield, he had had an anxiety attack. He had lost the faculty of reasoning. He had forgotten where he was and had just wanted to run away from the problem at hand.

But after listening to Krishna, he accepts that his delusion is destroyed. He understands the gravity of the situation and realizes where he is.

These are the core teachings of the Gita:

Keep the mind under control.

- A mind under control is like a friend. A mind not under control is like an enemy (6: 5, 6).
- Practice moderation (6: 16).
- Avoid lust, greed, anger, arrogance, jealousy and delusion (2: 62, 63).

Perform your duty diligently.

- Remain the same during pleasure, pain, gain, loss, success, failure, fame, infamy and so on (2: 14, 2: 38).
- Perform your duty (6: 1).
- Take pride in your own vocation (18: 47).
- Perform all actions as offerings to the Divine (18: 46).

Engage in the welfare of all.

- Do not harm any living being (17: 14).
- See the Divine as the ultimate inner recipient (5: 29, 15: 14).

Thus, the Gita defines a goal that is down to earth and rational. It gives a simple philosophy about God and humanity. It provides a logical, clear and humanistic way to live a life founded in the Divine and relevant to humanity.

Arjuna represents those of us who are struggling with day-to-day challenges. If we try to understand and imbibe the wisdom given in this discourse, we can act with faith and devotion.

Gita 18: 78

It is my conviction that wherever there is Yogeshwar Krishna and the Archer Partha, there will be *shri* (prosperity), *vijaya* (victory), *bhuti* (happiness) and *niti* (ethical action).

How do we achieve prosperity, victory and happiness?

We all want prosperity, victory and happiness. This is the last verse of the Gita. All the most precious rewards of life—victory, peace and prosperity—come to the person who feels the presence of Krishna and Arjuna in their heart.

Sanjaya concludes that wherever there is Krishna, the Ishvara of *yoga*, and Arjuna, the warrior, there will be:

- Prosperity
- Victory

- Happiness
- Ethical action

Krishna and Arjuna represent *jnana* (true knowledge) and *karma* (action). Krishna represents the actionless Divine, and Arjuna represents action driven by true knowledge.

The Bhagavad Gita tells us about the glory of Ishvara and how we are connected to each other. We will find the joy within only when we understand our true Self and begin our spiritual journey. The Gita reminds us that we are here to play our part and tap into our *svadharma*, the path of right action. Reading the Bhagavad Gita introduces us to the true nature of life and helps us be free from false notions and beliefs.

I have been reading the Bhagavad Gita since my younger days, and it has been critical in allowing me to understand and discover my potential. After all, I have had my own fears about success in my profession and leading a happy family life. Many times, I have realized that my mind is full of unwanted, unnecessary thoughts. I have found that reading the Bhagavad Gita relaxes my mind and reduces unnecessary fears in life. The Bhagavad Gita has helped me—and indeed, continues to help me—balance my mind and think in a proper way when trying to understand how I should live, and make decisions that will improve my life and the lives of those around me.

Visit our Website

Scan QR Code

9 789348 098382